TO ALL THE NATIONS
LUTHERAN HERMENEUTICS AND
THE GOSPEL OF MATTHEW

LWF Studies 2015/2

THE
LUTHERAN
WORLD
FEDERATION

To All the Nations

Lutheran Hermeneutics and the Gospel of Matthew

Edited by
Kenneth Mtata and Craig Koester

LWF Studies 2015/2

Bibliographic information published by the German National Library

The Deutsche Nationalbibliothek lists this publication in the Deutsche Nationalbibliografie; detailed bibliographic data are available on the internet at dnd.dnd.de

Printed in Germany · H 7981

This book was printed on FSC-certified paper

Cover: The Saint John's Bible. In 1998, Saint John's Abbey and University commissioned renowned calligrapher Donald Jackson to produce a hand-written, hand-illuminated Bible. Photo © LWF

Editorial assistance: Department for Theology and Public Witness
Layout: Department for Theology and Public Witness
Design: LWF-Office for Communication Services
Printing and Binding: Druckhaus Köthen GmbH & Co. KG

Published by Evangelische Verlangsanstalt GmbH, Leipzig, Germany, under the auspices of
The Lutheran World Federation
150, rte de Ferney, PO Box 2100
CH-1211 Geneva 2, Switzerland

ISBN 978-3-374-04233-3
www.eva-leipzig.de

Contents

Preface 7
  Martin Junge

Introduction to Matthew and Lutheran Hermeneutics

Introduction 11
  Craig Koester and Kenneth Mtata

Contemporary Approaches to Matthew: A "Lutheran" Critique 15
  Eve-Marie Becker

Reading Matthew in Light of a (Recovered) Hermeneutic of Law and Gospel 27
  Mark Allan Powell

Matthew's Gospel for the Reformation: "The Messiah ... Sent and Manifested" 45
  Timothy Wengert

Text, Context and Tradition: Implications for Reading Matthew 59
  Roger Marcel Wanke

Sermon on the Mount

How Do We Deal with a Challenging Text? 75
  Bernd Oberdorfer

Matthew and the Hermeneutics of Love 89
  Oda Wischmeyer

Perfection of Christian Life in the Face of Anger and Retaliation. Martin Luther's
Interpretation of the Sermon on the Mount 99
  Hans-Peter Grosshans

On Loving your Enemy

The Secret Link between Faith and Love: Luther on the Beatitudes (Mt 5:43–48) 117
  Vítor Westhelle

Theology of the Cross, Liberation and Discipleship

A Theology of the Cross and the Passion in Matthew: An Indian Dalit Perspective.... 135
Joseph Prabhakar Dayam

The Flight to Egypt: A Migrant Reading–Implications for a Lutheran Understanding of Salvation.. 153
Monica Jyotsna Melanchthon

Matthew, Judaism and Lutheran Tradition

Matthew's Pharisees: Seven Woes and Seven Warnings 171
Laurence Edwards

Preaching Reconciliation: From "Law and Gospel"
to "Justice and Mercy" in Matthew 185
Esther Menn

List of Contributors 197

Preface

Martin Junge

The Gospel of Matthew begins with the "account of the genealogy of Jesus the Messiah, the son of David, the son of Abraham" (Mt 1:1) and ends with the instruction to go to "all nations" (Mt 28:19) with the good news of the Messiah. This universal view is symbolized by Abraham and Sarah, leaving their own people to encounter people they did not know. This captures well what gospel means in Matthew.

Matthew not only includes the recognized and highly regarded patriarchs of Israel but also some "strange" women, namely Tamar, Rahab, Ruth and Bathsheba, in Jesus' family tree.

Theoretically, the stories of these women should have disqualified them as matriarchs of Jesus: Tamar was the victim of rape (Gen 38); Rahab a Canaanite harlot (Josh 2–6); Ruth a foreigner who accompanied her mother-in-law after they had both been widowed; and Bathsheba "the wife of Uriah" (2 Sam 11:3), the victim of a king, who abused his power and forced himself on her, and who, as a result, bore a son, Solomon.

The Gospel of Matthew places the birth of Jesus in an ambivalent context: a place of familiarity and strangeness. Jesus is presented as one who walks with both "insiders" and "outsiders." The message of the gospel in Matthew builds bridges between the nations and Israel.

Such apparent internal contradiction in Matthew merits serious study in community as has been happening within the LWF hermeneutics program since its inception in 2011.

First, bringing together Lutherans from all parts of the globe provides the opportunity to do more than simply to confirm the readers' diverse contextual experiences. Matthew shows us that by attentively reading together we encounter the good news that God has broken boundaries between people who were estranged from each other. Even those with less heroic or attractive histories are invited to hear the good news that Jesus brings.

Second, studying Matthew through this lens of ambivalence allows us to encounter the good news in the strangest of places. Good news comes from God but God chooses to appear there where we sometimes do not expect to find God. Hermeneutics therefore sharpens our eyes and ears to see and hear what God is doing.

Third, on the one hand, a hermeneutic informed by the Gospel of Matthew is comforting because certain features are familiar to us, while, on the other, it is uncomfortable since some features are strange to us. A critical, communal and attentive reading of the Gospel of Matthew allows us to recognize the good news, even in the most ordinary words and stories of God's action in the world.

In light of the 500th anniversary of the Reformation, which recalls the rediscovery of grace, we embrace this hermeneutic of an open invitation to the banquet (Mt 22:1-14) informed by the Gospel of Matthew. We encourage the churches of the Reformation to rediscover the grace that invites all in the story of Jesus' genealogy. When Jesus calls us to go and make disciples or learners "of all nations" (Mt 28:19), he opens up a possibility for us to go beyond that which is familiar to us, to build bridges from the known to the unknown. As we accept this invitation, this promise also becomes a reality for us: "I am with you always, to the end of the age" (Mt 28:20). I commend this book to you for study at home, in the churches, seminaries and universities. God is with you to the end of the ages.

Introduction to Matthew and Lutheran Hermeneutics

Introduction

Craig Koester and Kenneth Mtata

> Do not think that I have come to abolish the law or the prophets; I have come not
> to abolish but to fulfill (Mt 5:17).

Matthew's Gospel has always had a central place in the life of the church. This is the gospel that gives us the Sermon on the Mount and the version of the Lord's Prayer that is most commonly used in Christian worship. It contains the story of the magi visiting the infant Jesus, which figures prominently in the celebration of Christmas and Epiphany. Matthew's version of the passion narrative has inspired such musical compositions as Johann Sebastian Bach's Saint Matthew Passion, which continues to be performed each year during Holy Week.

Yet, Matthew's Gospel has also had a peculiar relationship to Lutheranism. In Luther's Preface to the New Testament of 1522, he commented that John's Gospel, Paul's letters, and 1 Peter far surpassed Matthew and the other gospels in their importance for the church's proclamation. Among Lutheran interpreters of the Bible, a common hermeneutic has involved the contrast between law and gospel. Those categories were drawn from Paul's letters, and the practice of contrasting them has contributed to negative perceptions about the law. Yet, Matthew has a much more positive perspective on the law, emphasizing that Jesus came not to abolish it but to fulfill it.

In 2014, Lutheran scholars from around the world met at the Lutheran School of Theology in Chicago, to consider Matthew's Gospel from perspectives that are informed by the Lutheran tradition and the contexts of the church globally. This was the third in a series of hermeneutics consultations organized by the Lutheran World Federation in anticipation of the 500th anniversary of the Reformation in 2017. Like the previous consultations that focused on the Gospel of John and the Psalms, this one included scholars from LWF member churches, Jewish scholars, ecumenical partners and related institutions. The essays in this volume were initially presented at the consultation in Chicago.

The first part considers the way in which interpretive frameworks inform how we read the biblical text. Current scholarship on Matthew's Gospel has often focused on historical questions, including theories about the way in which the Gospel preserves and adapts traditions about the life and message of Jesus, and how it relates to first-century social contexts. The most common view among scholars is that Matthew developed Mark's basic narrative, which means that Matthew is seen as secondary and less significant. Yet, contributors to this volume ask whether attention to the theological aspect of Matthew might help us to reclaim the value of this Gospel.

Matthew's attitude toward the Jewish Law or Torah is different from that of Paul, and these essays point out that the distinctiveness of Matthew's perspective needs to be recognized. They also call for greater clarity about how the Lutheran categories of law and gospel are to function. Some interpreters have used those categories to divide up biblical books according to content, but for Luther and Melanchthon they had to do with the way in which texts function in proclamation. Law and gospel have to do with the effect of the preached word on the listener, and whether the message indicts the listener or brings assurance and comfort. The same biblical passage can function as either law or gospel, depending on its effect. Returning to this dynamic understanding of law and gospel holds promise for contemporary preaching.

The second part focuses on the Sermon on the Mount, which is one of the best known and yet most disputed parts of Matthew's Gospel. This is where Jesus says that those who are angry with someone will be subject to divine judgment (Mt 5:21-22). He says that people are to love their enemies (Mt 5:44) and to "turn the other cheek" when someone strikes them and not resist those who are evil (Mt 5:39). Yet, many interpreters recognize that acting thus would soon lead to a breakdown in civil society, because those with power would oppress those who are more vulnerable.

The Sermon on the Mount also presents distinctive challenges for Lutheran interpreters. Whereas some might want to emphasize justification by faith alone, these chapters give specific directives concerning the living of life, and such directives seem more like law than gospel. Accordingly, a common pattern for Lutheran interpreters has been to treat the demands in the Sermon on the Mount as a means of revealing human shortcomings, so that people become aware of their need for the gospel.

It is surprising that Luther's own interpretations of these chapters in Matthew assume that the directives are intended to shape the living of life. Since the Sermon on the Mount begins with the Beatitudes, which proclaim that people are "blessed," Luther reads the entire passage under the assumption that it offers good news rather than law to the listeners. Yet, he takes the ethical dimension seriously. On the one hand, he does not want to restrict its rigorous character to a select group of people, like those who retreat from secular life by going to a monastery. On the other, he does not take it as a straightforward design for civil society, as some of the radical reformers did. Instead, he considers the idea of love for the enemy in light of the need for people in positions of authority to order society for the sake of its members. The essays included here explore these dimensions and their implications for contemporary readers.

Part three considers aspects of Matthew's Gospel in light of contemporary theological understandings of liberation and the strong emphasis on a theology of the cross in the Lutheran tradition. Each essay works with a keen sense of the reality of suffering as it is experienced in different social contexts. Matthew's Gospel tells of Mary, Joseph and the child Jesus moving to Egypt in order to seek refuge from persecution (Mt 2:13–18). Given the current movements of migrants, who now seek places of safety outside their homelands, the story in Matthew can contribute to a theologically informed response, which highlights Christ's identification with those who are vulnerable and displaced. Similarly, the final chapters of Matthew recount the crucifixion, in which Christ undergoes suffering and marginalization. The Lutheran emphasis on the theology of the cross points to the way in which Christ identifies with those who suffer, and that makes it possible for people to identify with Christ. The challenge noted in this volume is to construe the message of Jesus' suffering in a manner that does not end with the acceptance of oppression but includes the prospect of change.

The fourth part turns to the difficult question of the relationship of Matthew's Gospel and the Lutheran tradition to Judaism. Matthew's account of Jesus' trial depicts the Jewish leaders declaring that Jesus' blood should be on them and on their children (Mt 27:25). That passage contributed to the idea that Jews are the killers of Christ, which fueled Christian anti-Semitism. The negative attitude toward "law" in Lutheran theology and Luther's own pointedly anti-Jewish statements have been associated with tragic consequences in violence against Jews.

The essays in this section take the troubled history of relationships between Jews and Christians—especially Lutherans—as an occasion for dialogue that can lead to a better understanding of one another and of our own traditions. Joint reflection on Matthew's Gospel is a factor in that it includes a positive appreciation of Jewish law and tradition. At the same time, attention to Jewish tradition calls for a more nuanced view of the

Pharisees than is apparent in Matthew's narrative. It involves recognizing that Jesus' disputes with his opponents, as depicted by Matthew, reflect differences between members of the Jewish community, who share a common tradition while differing over its interpretation. The process is a dynamic one that can lead to new insights and relationships among Jews and Christians today.

Together, these essays are an invitation to consider Matthew's Gospel in ways that are theologically engaged and attentive to contemporary social contexts. The contributors come from various parts of the globe and their perspectives are informed by the situations in which they live and work as well as by a theological tradition rooted in the Reformation. In the sixteenth century, the Lutheran movement was shaped in major ways by the interpretation of Scripture. These essays show some of the ways in which engagement with Scripture continues to be a central and enlivening aspect of Lutheran communities today.

Contemporary Approaches to Matthew: A "Lutheran" Critique

Eve-Marie Becker

The rise of the status quo

In synoptic studies, the Gospel of Matthew frequently appears to be of secondary importance only. Matthew tells us something about the early reception of Mark rather than revealing to us how the concept of early Christian gospel writing originated. This perspective on Matthew is the result of around 200 years of research during which the assumption of the so-called Markan priority has been generated: Mark is regarded as the earliest gospel and was later used as a source, or *Vorlage*, by such gospel writers as Matthew and Luke. As Mark's successor, Matthew preserved and only slightly revised the Markan gospel outline.

The hypothesis that Mark was the first gospel to be written has a history of its own. Karl Lachmann among others posits that it is motivated by what we could call the scholarly optimism of philologically reconstructing Christianity's literary origins. In nineteenth-century Protestant theology, this hypothesis constituted a significant paradigm shift from how, from patristic times onwards, interpreters such as Jerome, Augustine and John Chrysostom[1] up to Luther and even Gotthold Ephraim Lessing have read and understood the Gospel of Matthew: According to its position in the New Testament canon as the first and, probably, most original gospel writ-

---

[1] Cf. Peter Widdicombe, "The Patristic Reception of the Gospel of Matthew. The Commentary of Jerome and the Sermons of John Chrysostom," in Eve-Marie Becker and Anders Runesson (eds), *Mark and Matthew II, Comparative Readings: Reception History, Cultural Hermeneutics, and Theology*, WUNT 304 (Tübingen: Mohr Siebeck, 2013), 105–19.

ing and, last but not least, because of its direct historical affiliation to a disciple figure[2] it was thought most authentically to lead its readers back to the actual beginnings of the gospel proclamation, originally in Hebrew.[3]

After such a long reception history of privileging Matthew, the nineteenth-century's prioritizing of Mark has persistently challenged gospel exegesis. Redefining the "historical order" of the gospels has qualitative implications: Matthew is only number two then. This scholarly view had and continues to have an impact on exegetical work,[4] mainly with regard to preparing scholars for approaching Matthew in terms of redaction criticism: Matthew only rearranges the outline of Mark's Gospel. In the late nineteenth and twentieth centuries, the premise of the Markan priority has been further developed and modified. Still, in contemporary scholarly debates it widely reflects a major consensus among exegetes: it mostly appears as the so-called two-source hypothesis. We assume that Matthew is built on expanding Mark and incorporating a second source, the source Q:[5] The Gospel of Matthew obviously contains a vast amount of sayings (Q; QMt) that are transmitted independently of Mark. As is the case in crucial parts of the Sermon on the Mount (Mt 5-7), the sayings material can refer back to the historical Jesus and thus is of elementary meaning for reconstructing the historical Jesus figure and its message.

Currently, both types of research quests—Matthew's reception of Mark and Matthew's value as a special source to the historical Jesus—widely define scholarly work. They even function as a rationale for Matthean exegesis, whenever contemporary studies either (a) try to identify Matthew's literary and/or socio-religious profile, or (b) take Matthew in its special transmission of Jesus sayings as a historical document for first-century Judaism.

Profiling Matthew in literary,
socio-religious and theological terms

Based on Graham N. Stanton's earlier survey, which was rooted in redaction criticism,[6] David C. Sim points out that in Matthean studies the "defining

---

[2] Cf. Eusebius, Historia ecclesiastica 3:39.5.

[3] Ibid., 3:24.6; 5:8.2f., cf. also Irenaeus, Adversus haereses 3:1.1.

[4] Cf. J. Andrew Doole, *What was Mark for Matthew? An Examination of Matthew's Relationship and Attitude to his Primary Source*, WUNT 2.344 (Tübingen: Mohr Siebeck, 2013).

[5] It is claimed that Matthew has made use of a third type of source: the so-called special material ("M") which is unique, i.e., it is not shared by Luke. Cf. e.g., Ulrich Luz, "Art. Matthäusevangelium," in RGG⁴ 5 (2002), 916–20, here 918; Ulrich Luz, *Das Evangelium nach Matthäus. 1. Teilband Mt 1-7*, EKK I/1 (Neukirchen-Vluyn: Neukirchener Verlagshaus, ⁵2002), 47–52.

[6] Cf. Graham N. Stanton, "The Origin and Purpose of Matthew's Gospel: Matthean Scholarship from 1945–1980," in *ANRW* 2.25.3 (1985), 1890–1951; cf. David C. Sim,

issue for the past two decades has been the social setting of the Gospel and its underlying community."[7] Sim emphasizes how the debate is actually about "whether this Christian community was still within Judaism or had separated from it, both physically and ideologically."[8] Accordingly, the questions to be discussed are, Where did the Gospel of Matthew "stand in relation to the broader Jewish community? Where did it stand in relation to the variety of viewpoints in the emergent Christian movement? How did it relate to the Gentile world and the issue of Gentile converts? What was the attitude towards Rome, and how were these views expressed in the Gospel narrative?"[9]

In his survey of more recent research, Sim evaluates Matthew's relation to Judaism and the Gentile world and from there reflects on its standing in earliest Christianity.[10] A variety of scholars make the case for an intra muros conflict (e.g., David Sim, Warren Carter, Boris Repschinski and Anders Runesson) according to which "the Matthean community was engaged in an internal Jewish conflict," while another, meanwhile possibly minor group of scholars, tend to support Stanton's extra muros position (e.g., Roland Deines, Ulrich Luz).[11] As we can see here, the Gospel of Matthew is closely related to Judaism—more precisely, it is possibly even of Pharisaic provenience.[12] Sim guesses that especially the "question of Matthew's position within the very broad first century Christian movement will significantly increase in importance."[13] He claims that "Matthew's Christian Jewish theology was to a large extent opposed to some fundamental aspects of the Pauline Gospel"—he calls it: Matthew's "anti-Paulinism."[14] This appraisal is similar to how especially Gerd Theißen reads the speech parts in Matthew as hidden polemics against Paul (cf. e.g., Mt 5:19).[15]

"Matthew. The Current State of Research," in Eve-Marie Becker and Anders Runesson (eds), *Mark and Matthew I, Comparative Readings: Understanding the Earliest Gospels in their First-Century Settings*, WUNT 271 (Tübingen: Mohr Siebeck, 2011), 33–51, here 48.

[7] Ibid., 35f.

[8] Ibid., 36.

[9] Ibid., 36.

[10] Cf. on this Warrant Carter, "Matthew: Empire, Synagogues, and Horizontal Violence," in Becker and Runesson, op. cit. (note 6), 285–308.

[11] Cf. the references in Sim, op. cit. (note 6), quote 38.

[12] Anders Runesson, "Rethinking Early Jewish–Christian Relations: Matthean Community History as Pharisaic Intragroup Conflict," in *JBL 127* (2008), 95-132; Anders Runesson, "Building Matthean Communities. The Politics of Textualization," in Becker and Runesson, op. cit. (note 6), 379–408.

[13] Sim, op. cit. (note 6), 51.

[14] Ibid., 45.

[15] Cf. Gerd Theißen, "Kritik an Paulus im Matthäusevangelium? Von der Kunst verdeckter Polemik im Urchristentum," in Oda Wischmeyer and Lorenzo Scornaienchi (eds), *Polemik in der frühchristlichen Literatur. Texte und Kontexte*, BZNW 170 (Berlin/

When contextualizing Matthew within the Christian movement of the first century, questions regarding the literary genre and the specifics of Matthean theology appear on the scene: Some scholars see Matthew in close relation to ancient biography (e.g., David E. Aune);[16] others—by proceeding from the narrative pragmatics of conflict language—define the Matthean Gospel as an "inclusive story" (e.g., Ulrich Luz).[17] When it comes to a theological profiling of Matthew, three types of accentuations are assessed: first, Matthew provides a shift in his portrayal of the Jesus figure (especially Christology, Mt 1:23; the empowered teacher, Mt 5–7), secondly, a more elaborate concept of discipleship and community (e.g., Mt 18; 28:16–20), and thirdly a comprehensive reflection on ethics (e.g., Mt 5–7).[18]

It is by no means accidental that the Sermon on the Mount is at the center of interpretation: As it is an example par excellence for the Matthean composition technique, it is pivotal for Matthean theology and ethics and thus inspires political readings[19] as much as liberation theology. However, hermeneutical interests largely depend on exegetical premises: while a theological inspired reading of Matthew appraises his dealing with the two sources, Mark and Q, current contributions to feminist criticism tend to focus on text passages which are unique for Matthew ("M"), such as the genealogy in Matthew 1.[20] Migration or immigration studies can easily join in (cf. Mt 2:13–23). Such a scientific aim can be of value: while since patristic times gospel exegesis has tended to harmonize the different gospel stories,[21] modern readings—informed by historical-critical exegesis—are more ambitious in uncovering specific sources

---

New York: Walter de Gruyter, 2011), 465–90. In a general sense, Sim analyzes Matthew's polemics against scribes and Pharisees, false Christians, Gentiles and the Roman Empire. David C. Sim, "Polemical Strategies in the Gospel of Matthew," in ibid., 491–515. On polemics, cf. also Lorenzo Scornaienchi, "The Controversy Dialogues and the Polemic in Mark and Matthew," in Becker and Runesson, op. cit. (note 6), 309–21.
[16] David E. Aune, "Genre Theory and the Genre-Function of Mark and Matthew," in Becker and Runesson, op. cit. (note 6), 145–75.
[17] Luz, "Art. Matthäusevangelium," op. cit. (note 5), 917f. Luz, "Das Evangelium nach Matthäus," op. cit. (note 5), 46f. The history of Jesus (Jesusgeschichte) "stellt ihnen, die in ihrer eigenen Geschichte und in der matthäischen Jesusgeschichte die Feindschaft von Israels Führern und die Trennung von Israel (vgl. 24,1f) erlebt haben, vor Augen, daß der Konflikt in und mit Israel der weg ist, den Gott selbst Jesus geführt hat. *Die von Matthäus erzählte Jesusgeschichte... stabilisiert die christliche Identität der Gemeinde*" (47).
[18] Luz, "Art. Matthäusevangelium," op. cit. (note 5), 919f.
[19] Luz, *Das Evangelium nach Matthäus*, op. cit. (note 5), 288f.
[20] J. Capel Anderson, "Mark and Matthew in Feminist Perspective: Reading Matthew's Genealogy," in Becker and Runesson, op. cit. (note 1), 271–88.
[21] Cf. e.g., how Eusebius (e.g., Historia ecclesiastica 1:7.1ff.) intends to harmonize the Lukan and the Matthean version of the genealogy.

and materials in Matthew in order to mark differences between various gospel accounts possibly caused by religious or theological conflicts.

MATTHEW AND THE TRANSMISSION OF JESUS TRADITIONS

Somewhat in continuity with patristic exegesis according to which Matthew was an apostle who preached in Hebrew (Eusebius), current studies treat Matthew as a source that can most authentically provide access to the (original) teachings of the historical Jesus in their Jewish setting(s). Here, studies in the history of motifs and traditions that are especially collected within the sayings material (Q) and its Matthean adaption (QMt) are crucial. Once scholars see Matthew in close relation to Judaism—or even in an intra muros position—attempts are made to correlate Matthew to a group of (early Christian) writings that share the literary interest of transmitting Jesus traditions close to their Jewish origins. Hereby, the Gospel of Matthew as well as the Letter of James and the Didache, the teachings of the twelve apostles, are read as texts that possibly belong to the same Jewish–Christian milieu and contribute to similar ideological and religious discourses.[22]

Since, in accordance with the so-called "third quest" and its succeeding scholarly debate, historical Jesus research has highlighted Jesus' Jewishness, the Gospel of Matthew has continuously been moved into the sphere of first-century Judaism. This applies to the method of tradition history as much as redaction criticism: either the Matthean Gospel as a whole leads us back to the origins of the Jesus traditions or even to the historical Jesus or Matthew, as a literary author, is seen as significantly contributing to the formation of Jewish-Christian literature which adheres more explicitly to its Jewish roots. Both types of research quests impact the interpretation of the Sermon on the Mount. In a final step we will reflect on these paradigms in light of a Lutheran hermeneutical critique.

THE SERMON ON THE MOUNT AS A CASE STUDY

Together with the missionary commission (Mt 28:16–20), the Sermon on the Mount functions formally and materially as a hermeneutical key. In the formal sense, Matthew 5–7 reflects Matthew's composition technique since here the author extensively combines the Markan narrative outline with Q and "M" material as much as redactional interests. In a material sense, Jesus continu-

---

[22] Cf., e.g.: Huub van de Sandt and Jürgen Zangenberg (eds), *Matthew, James and Didache: Three Related Documents in their Jewish and Christian Settings* (Atlanta: Society of Biblical Literature, 2008); David Sim and Boris Repschinski (eds), *Matthew and His Christian Contemporaries* (London: T & T Clark International, 2008).

ously appears as a teacher and interpreter of the Torah in Matthew so that Jesus' final commissioning (Mt 28:20, *didáskontes*) de facto leads back to his previous teachings and sermons, such as chapters 5ff. (cf. Mt 5:2, *edídasken*).

We cannot have a look at Matthew 5–7 in its totality here, nor can we reflect in detail on the disposition of the Sermon on the Mount where the "Lord's Prayer" (Mt 6:5–13) has, without a doubt, a central position.[23] I will rather focus on Matthew 5:17–20 where Jesus' role as a lawgiver according to the Jewish tradition becomes most explicit.

> v. 17 Do not think that I have come to abolish the law or the prophets; I have come not to abolish but to fulfill.
>
> v.18 For truly I tell you, until heaven and earth pass away, not one letter, not one stroke of a letter, will pass from the law until all is accomplished.
>
> v.19 Therefore, whoever breaks one of the least of these commandments, and teaches others to do the same, will be called least in the kingdom of heaven; but whoever does them and teaches them will be called great in the kingdom of heaven.
>
> v. 20 For I tell you, unless your righteousness exceeds that of the scribes and Pharisees, you will never enter the kingdom of heaven.

In his careful exegesis of the text, Ulrich Luz presents a most complex analysis by distinguishing between tradition and redaction.[24] He largely sees verse 17 as a redactional element, possibly based on a traditional saying (cf. Mt 10:34); he relates verse 18a either back to Q or to a special Jewish-Christian tradition; and he defines verse 18b as a redactional addition; also verse 19 is identified as a mixture of tradition—deriving eventually from "strict Jewish-Christian Torah observant circles" or QMt—and Matthean redaction. Verse 20, on the contrary, is seen as a purely redactional addition.[25] Regardless of whether especially verses 18 and 19 can be traced back to tradition or have to be identified as Matthean redaction—both verses raise the question of how to interpret Matthew's ideas about the continuing validity of Jewish law. Accordingly, Luz concedes that especially verses 18f. are a *crux interpretum*. Since Luz himself sees Matthew as a substantial redactor at work here, he concludes his interpretation by stating that Matthew, in fact, means what is written: Jesus says, that the Torah and the prophets should be observed according to his own example.[26]

---

[23] Cf. Ulrich Luz, "Art. Bergpredigt I. Neues Testament," in *RGG⁴* 1 (1998), 1309–11, here 1310.

[24] Luz, *Das Evangelium nach Matthäus*, op. cit. (note 5).

[25] Ibid., 307f. (quote): "streng judenchristlich-gesetzestreue(n) Kreise(n)."

[26] Ibid., 321: ("[Matthäus meint] das, was da steht, wirklich...: Die Torah und die Propheten sollen nach der Meinung und gemäß dem Vorbild Jesu erfüllt, d.h. ganz, ohne jeden Abstrich, gehalten werden... ."

What do we do with such a result of exegetical work? Will we finally reject Matthew 5:17-20 as an obsolete relic of the Jewish beginnings of Christianity? Luz points in that direction, claiming that for those who belong to this pagan Christian church the Jewish Christian program of Matthew 5:17-20 belongs to the past.[27] Or, will we take Matthew 5:17-20 as evidence of how at least parts of the early Christian movement do not actually leave Jewish settings but rather continue first-century Judaism? For Luz, the so-called *Wirkungsgeschichte*, reception history and reception theory, of this text provides a helpful tool for its interpretation.[28] Likewise, this may apply to Lutheran hermeneutics. By looking at how Luther reads Matthew 5:17-20, we will, however, get a sense of how ambiguous textual interpretation can be: while Luther affirms that textual passage in his dispute with the Anabaptists, he tends to reject it by warning that it could lead to a "nomistic interpretation" of Christ.

A Lutheran critique of current Matthean exegesis

For Luther, the Gospel of Matthew obviously did not belong to the group of writings which he thought of as elementary for the teaching of the gospel. In his "Preface to the New Testament (1522)," he instead mentions that

> John's Gospel and St. Paul's epistles, especially that to the Romans, and St. Peter's first epistle are the true kernel and marrow of all the books. They ought properly to be the foremost books, and it would be advisable for every Christian to read them first and most, and by daily reading to make them as much his own as his daily bread.[29]

---

[27] Ibid., 323 (quote): "... für uns, die wir eben dieser heidenchristlichen Großkirche angehören, (gehört) das judenchristliche Programm von Mt 5,17-20 der Vergangenheit" an.

[28] Ibid., 310-13; 320-24. To the history of interpretation, cf. also Hans Dieter Betz, *The Sermon on the Mount: A Commentary on the Sermon on the Mount, including the Sermon on the Plain (Matthew 5:3-7: 27 and Luke 6:20-49)*, Hermeneia (Philadelphia: Fortress Press, 1995); Betz has even argued for overcoming source criticism by—instead—explaining the composition of the Sermon on the Mount by its "literary genre and function," 70.

[29] "der rechte Kern und das Mark unter allen Büchern, welche auch billig die ersten sein sollten. Und einem jeglichen Christen wäre zu raten, daß er dieselben am ersten und allermeisten lese und sich durch täglich Lesen so vertraut machte wie das tägliche Brot." *WA DB* 6:2ff. Martin Luther, "Preface to the New Testament," in Helmut T. Lehmann (ed.), *Luther's Works*, vol. 35 (Philadelphia: Muhlenberg Press, 1960), 362.

Nevertheless, among Luther's writings we find numerous sermons in which he interprets the Matthean Gospel. Last, but not least, in Luther's "Large Catechism" of 1529,[30] the interpretation of the Lord's Prayer has huge significance.[31] In his continuous reference to Matthew's *Wirkungsgeschichte* Luz has stated how important the Matthean Gospel was in Lutheran theology. Indeed, Luther has referred to various Matthean text passages—from the Sermon on the Mount and beyond—especially in tricky situations of theological conflict and debate. Matthew 5:17 played an important role in the dispute with the so-called Anabaptists. While the latter group of reformers tried to mark a basic difference between the Old and New Testament, in his 1539 treatise "Against the Antinomians" Luther insisted on pointing out the continuity with Israel in Jesus' teaching: "Christ does not only recite the Mosaic law, but interprets it [...] entirely" (III:32).[32]

How might Luther look at the contemporary state of the art in Matthean studies? Would he appreciate the current socio-religious discourse about an intra or extra muros position that was mentioned earlier? How would he interpret Mathew 5:17–20 in light of that debate? I am quite aware that my individual reading of Luther will influence preliminary answers. At the same time, this hypothetical reflection about Luther's reading in the twenty-first century can also lead to a substantial critique of current exegetical research. When thinking about Luther's possible attitude toward contemporary research quests which are already my own, I have to be prepared for no less than self-critique. This practice of self-critique may even be the most elementary part of exegetical and hermeneutical work inspired by Lutheran studies.

1. Luther would certainly have followed up various types of political readings which are applied to the Matthean Gospel. As Heinz Schilling has pointed out, Luther continuously justified his political attitude(s) with his interpretation of the gospel. Being on the Wartburg he had to deal with various kinds of revolutionary ambitions which even attracted his friend Philipp Melanchthon. However, during this time Luther became more and more a "considerate reformer of church and society, who was

---

[30] *WA* 30:1.125ff; "The Large Catechism (1529)," in Robert Kolb and Timothy Wengert (eds), *The Book of Concord. The Confessions of the Evangelical Lutheran Church* (Minneapolis: Augsburg Fortress, 2000), 377ff.

[31] Cf. also "Deutsche Auslegung des Vaterunsers für die einfältigen Laien" (1519), in *WA* 2:41.

[32] "Christus rezitiert das Gesetz Mose nicht nur, sondern legt es... vollkommen aus," *WA* 39/1:351—quote according to Luz, *Das Evangelium nach Matthäus*, op. cit. (note 5), 312.

averse against all kinds of violence."[33] In his letter to Melanchthon (13 July 1521), Luther explains this attitude as follows:

> Über die Gewalt des Schwertes denke ich noch so wie früher. Denn du scheinst mir darüber aus dem Evangelium eine Anweisung oder einen Rat zu begehren. Darin halte ich es völlig mit Dir, daß es im Evangelium weder ein Gebot noch einen Rat für ein derartiges Recht gibt. Es würde sich auch auf keine Weise ziemen, da das Evangelium ein Gesetz der Freiwilligen und Freien ist, die nichts mit dem Schwert oder mit dem Recht des Schwertes zu schaffen haben.[34]

Later in this letter Luther carefully reflects about when and why the use of the sword according to the gospel was legitimate.

2. As much as Luther privileges some New Testament writings over others he explains this with a theological argument that reveals a critical view of the Synoptic Gospels (Mark, Matthew and Luke):

> Denn wenn ich je auf deren eins verzichten sollte, auf die Werke oder die Predigten Christi, dann wollte ich lieber auf die Werke als auf seine Predigten verzichten... Weil nun Johannes gar wenig Werke von Christus, aber gar viele seiner Predigten beschreibt, umgekehrt die andern drei Evangelisten aber viele seiner Werke und weniger seine Worte beschreiben, ist das Evangelium des Johannes das einzige, schöne, rechte Hauptevangelium und den andern dreien weit, weit vorzuziehen... Ebenso gehen auch des Paulus und Petrus Briefe weit den drei Evangelien des Matthäus, Markus und Lukas voran.[35]

---

[33] Heinz Schilling, *Martin Luther. Rebell in einer Zeit des Umbruchs* (München: C. H. Beck, 2012), 252. "Die Monate auf der Wartburg [...] ließen ihn zu einem umsichtigen, allem Ungestüm abgeneigten Reformer von Kirche und Gesellschaft heranwachsen [...]."

[34] Translation of the text provided by Kurt Aland, *Luther Deutsch, Die Werke Martin Luthers in neuer Auswahl für die Gegenwart*, vol. 10, Die Briefe (Göttingen: Vandenhoek and Ruprecht, 1983), 93f., at **https://goo.gl/iogLxs** ("I continue to think about the power of the sword as I did earlier. It seems to me that you want the gospel to provide you with instruction or advice. I agree with you that the gospel does not contain any commandment or advice for such a right. It would not be appropriate since the gospel is a law to the willing and free who have nothing to do with the sword or the law of the sword" (*WA Br* 2:357–59, nr. 418 [orig. Latin]).

[35] *WA DB* 6:10. "If I should ever the renounce either Christ's deeds or sermons, then I would rather renounce his deeds than his sermons [...]. Since St. John describes only some of Christ's deeds, but many of his sermons and, by the same token, the three other evangelists describe his deeds rather than his words, the Gospel of John is the only, pleasant, correct main Gospel that is to be privileged over the

Luther's view implies that for him Matthew is primarily a gospel narrative about "deeds" rather than "words." And even the Sermon on the Mount was obviously not at the center of Luther's theology[36]—it is presumably not a key text in Lutheran tradition either.

3. At the same time, Luther reveals a quite modern point of view about what the gospel actually is about in literary terms. In his tractate, "A Brief Instruction on What to Look for and Expect in the Gospels, 1521," Luther develops his argument in two stages: First, he approaches the nature of the gospel according to its narrative quality: "Thus the gospel is and should be nothing else than a chronicle, a story, a narrative about Christ, telling who he is, what he did, said, and suffered [...] the gospel is a discourse about Christ [...]."[37] From here, Luther manages to appraise the one gospel in varying literary forms so that, secondly, Pauline letters (esp. Rom 1:1–4) as well as gospel narratives can be defined as gospel. To some extent, Luther leaves behind the gospel letter divide that has designed *Formgeschichte*, form criticism, in gospel studies over the last 100 years. Rather, Luther inspires innovative ways of, for instance, relating the Markan Gospel to Pauline letter writing and vice versa.[38] In light of Lutheran exegesis, contemporary constructs of early Christian literary history can fruitfully be reconsidered.

4. However, in the tractate mentioned above, Luther brings a third argument: Since the nature of the gospel is defined according to its narrative quality that can formally be found in the gospel as well as in letter writing, another criterion is formulated which now tends to confine the gospel in a material sense: "So you see that the gospel is really not a book of laws and commandments that requires deeds of us, but a book of divine promises in which God promises, offers, and gives us all his possessions and benefits in Christ."[39] As a consequence, Luther warns against a reading of the gospel which will soon turn the Christ figure into Moses, the lawgiver.[40] This admonition corresponds

---

three others [...]. Likewise the letters of St Paul and Peter take precedence over the three gospels Matthew, Mark and Luke." Author's own translation.

[36] Cf. Ursula Berner, "Art. Bergpredigt II. Auslegungsgeschichtlich," in *RGG⁴* 1 (1998), 1311–14, here 1312.

[37] *LW* 35, 118; *WA* 10:1.1.8ff.

[38] Cf. Eve-Marie Becker, Troels Engberg-Pedersen, and Mogens Muller (eds), *Mark and Paul, Comparative Essays Part II: For and Against Pauline Influence on Mark*, BZNW 199 (Berlin/Boston: Walter de Gruyter, 2014).

[39] Ibid., 120; *WA* 10:1.1.13

[40] *WA* 10:1.1.10f.

to how Luther in various other writings prepares the programmatic distinction between law and gospel,which can be seen as the basic paradigm of Christian theology.[41] In 1525 Luther makes it quite clear in "How Christians Should Regard Moses, 1525"

> Now the first sermon, and doctrine, is the law of God. The second is the gospel. These two sermons are not the same. Therefore we must have a good grasp of the matter in order to know how to differentiate between them. We must know what the law is, and what the gospel is. [42]

Accordingly, Luther rejects finding any nomistic, prophetic or sapiental texts in the New Testament beyond the features of gospel and history.[43] On the contrary, he insists on maintaining a basic difference between the Old and the New Testament in terms of its literary as well as its theological character.[44]

Since current trends in Matthean studies increasingly tend to read the Gospel of Matthew and its sources (especially Q) in light of its Jewish roots and settings, we might imagine that Luther would be extremely cautious and hesitant: he might fear that redaction criticism as well as literary criticism and tradition history imply and cause a turn of the Matthean Jesus from Christ into Moses. Against this background a reevaluation of Matthew's Christology (e.g., Mt 16:20) will be illuminating. The Lutheran perspective, arguing for the Christological interpretation of the gospel, might be a helpful corrective in current dilemmas of textual interpretation which are caused by the one-sidedness of socio-religious studies: Luther's quest for Christology might force Matthean exegesis once again to reflect about the origins of "Christian theology."

---

[41] Ulrich H. J. Körtner, "Art. Gesetz und Evangelium IV. Systematisch-theologisch," in *LBH* (2009/2013) 220–21, here 220.
[42] *LW* 35, 162.
[43] *WA* DB 6:2.
[44] Ibid.

Reading Matthew in Light of a (Recovered) Hermeneutic of Law and Gospel

Mark Allan Powell

Modern study of the Gospel of Matthew raises a number of hermeneutical questions that may be of particular concern to Lutherans. Many of these arise as a consequence of the attention this Gospel gives to the law, i.e., Torah.[1]

First, Matthew's Gospel makes clear that the entire law of Moses will remain in full force until heaven and earth pass away (Mt 5:18). There is no thought that believers enjoy a new dispensation in which they are no longer "under the law" (Rom 6:14; 1 Cor 9:20; Gal 3:23); rather, the expectation seems to be that followers of Jesus will exhibit a higher righteousness, obeying even the most minute commandments of Torah in a way that puts

---

[1] See especially Dale C. Allison, *The New Moses: A Matthean Typology* (Minneapolis: Fortress, 1993); Benjamin Bacon, *Studies in Matthew* (London: Constable, 1930); Günther Bornkamm, Gerhard Barth and Heinz Joachim Held, *Tradition and Interpretation in Matthew*, NTL (Philadelphia: Westminster, 1963); Blaine Charette, *The Theme of Recompense in Matthew's Gospel*, JSNTSup 79 (Sheffield: Sheffield Academic Press, 1992); O. Lamar Cope, *Matthew: A Scribe Trained for the Kingdom of Heaven*, CBQMS 5 (Washington D.C.: Catholic Biblical Association, 1976); W. D. Davies, *The Setting of the Sermon on the Mount* (Cambridge: Cambridge University Press, 1964); Terence Donaldson, *Jesus on the Mountain: A Study in Matthean Theology*, JSNTSup 8 (Sheffield: JSOT Press, 1985); John P. Meier, *The Vision of Matthew: Christ, Church, and Morality in the First Gospel* (New York: Paulist, 1979); Mathew Palachuvattil, *"The One Who Does the Will of My Father." Distinguishing Character of Disciples According to Matthew: An Exegetical Theological Study*, TGST 154 (Rome: Editrice Pontifica Università Gregoriana, 2007).

the scribes and Pharisees to shame (Mt 5:20). Becoming a disciple means being taught to obey all Jesus' commandments, which surely includes his command to do and keep everything that Moses taught (Mt 28:19–20; cf. 5:17–20; 23:2–3).

Further, Matthew's Gospel does not obviously espouse any theology of justification by grace through faith. God is merciful and willing to forgive trespasses, but the gate to the kingdom is narrow and the road that leads to life is hard (Mt 7:13–14). Trees that do not bear good fruit are cut down and thrown into the fire (Mt 7:19); God does not forgive the sins of those who hold grudges against others (Mt 6:15, 20; 18:34–35); everyone (baptized or not, believing or not) will be judged by God with the same standard they used when judging others (Mt 7:2); those who fail to take drastic measures (plucking out their eyes, severing their limbs) to ensure that they are living righteously will be thrown into hell (Mt 5:29–30; 18:8–9). Much of this is metaphorical and can be read as prophetic rhetoric, but the bottom line seems to be that the primary entrance requirement for the kingdom of heaven is not confessing faith in Jesus Christ as Lord but doing the will of God (Mt 7:21).

There may have been a time when Lutherans could have dealt with the so-called problem texts in Matthew by citing verses from other portions of Scripture that seem to clarify matters in a manner more congenial to our theology. For example, Matthew 7:21 could be domesticated by the application of John 6:29, where doing God's will means believing in Jesus Christ. But advances in exegetical science have rendered such casual solutions intolerable. Decades of historical criticism, especially redaction criticism, have left us with an almost indisputable conclusion: the author of Matthew's Gospel would not have agreed with the Apostle Paul on some fundamental matters of faith, and he would not have agreed with leaders of Lutheran churches on some key principles of Lutheran theology.

Specifically, Lutherans have wanted to read the Gospel of Matthew in light of a hermeneutic of law and gospel. But since Torah occupies so large a place in Matthew (both in terms of content and priority), the first Gospel is deemed "legalistic" and attempts to mitigate its legalism are regarded as the imposition of a foreign ideology in a manner that historical criticism will not allow. In this short article, I will propose that the solution lies in taking two steps: the first entails recovery of the hermeneutical principle of law and gospel in its most powerful, original expression, before some questionable adjustments dulled its impact. The second involves a de-throning of authorial intent as the hermeneutical key for finding authoritative meaning in Scripture. As we will see, both steps favor openness to polyvalence and recognition of the role that reception plays in the transference of meaning.

The "Lutheran error" and the Sermon on the Mount

Legalistic passages are found throughout Matthew's Gospel but they are especially concentrated in chapters 5 to 7, the section that has come to be called the Sermon on the Mount. Accordingly, this significant passage may serve as a test case for our discussion, in terms of both explicating the problem and proposing a solution. It will be best to consider the Sermon as a whole, but to focus our attention, we may think especially of the antitheses (Mt 5:17–48): here Jesus intensifies Mosaic commandments for his followers, insisting on abstention from anger, insults, lust, divorce, oath-swearing and reprisal; followers of Jesus must love their enemies and, indeed, be perfect as their heavenly Father is perfect.

It has become commonplace for modern biblical scholars to speak of "the Lutheran error" in the exposition of such texts. That phrase has caused more than one Lutheran exegete to cringe in shame at ecumenical gatherings since everyone, including Lutherans, now agrees that "the Lutheran error" is a fallacy to be avoided at all costs. The term was first used by Joachim Jeremias (a Lutheran) in what would turn out to be one of the most influential works on the Sermon on the Mount ever written.[2]

In his brief book—originally a lecture—Jeremias discussed various ways in which exegetes have sought to domesticate Jesus' ethical demands so that those demands do not need to be taken seriously. First he turned his attention to "the catholic error," according to which the demands of Jesus' teaching are understood to be applicable for a minority of Jesus' followers only: they were never intended for Christians in general, but for a super-righteous few (saints, or clergy, or those who take special vows).

But, then, in a manner more relevant to our concern, Jeremias spoke of "the Lutheran error," according to which the Sermon on the Mount is viewed as a ploy to expose the folly of works righteousness. Those who try to live in the way that Jesus demands in this Sermon will find that they are unable to do so; accordingly, they will be brought to despair and forced to abandon any hope of ever achieving righteousness through their own efforts. They will thus be prepared to hear the gospel.

Centuries of Lutheran interpretation have embraced this reading, which was especially favored by Lutheran scholasticism. According to Paul Althaus, it could stem from Luther himself, insofar as Luther claimed that Jesus' Sermon on the Mount sharpened the demands of the law to the point that "sinful man [...] simply cannot fulfill it."[3] Nevertheless, most Matthew

---

[2] Joachim Jeremias, *The Sermon on the Mount,* Facet Books (Philadelphia: Fortress, 1963).
[3] Paul Althaus, *The Theology of Martin Luther* (Philadelphia: Fortress Press, 1956), 254; cf. *WA* 39, I, 364, 374.

scholars today would insist that both Jesus and the Matthean evangelist assumed their audiences would be able to keep these demands. They would, at least, be able to do so in the only manner that would have made sense within a context of Torah-observant Judaism: they would orient their lives according to a commitment to observe the prescriptions and proscriptions of their rabbi's teaching on a day-to-day basis, asking forgiveness for specific instances of failure when those occurred.

Nevertheless, to this day, I rarely lead a program on the Sermon on the Mount among Lutheran clergy at which at least one pastor does not ask, Wasn't the reason Jesus gave this sermon to make people realize they will never be able to live up to God's demands, so that they would have to trust in justification by faith? But the answer to that question would be an unequivocal "No!" Historically, that was not the reason Jesus gave the Sermon on the Mount, nor was it the reason Matthew included this teaching of Jesus in his Gospel.

This was why Jeremias found the popular Lutheran interpretation of the Sermon so appalling: it contravened the obvious intention of Jesus, whom he took to be the author of the Sermon. The generation of redaction critics who followed Jeremias tended to regard the author of the Sermon as the evangelist who was responsible for compiling and composing the Gospel, rather than Jesus himself, but that would only relocate the objection without minimizing its substance. Neither the historical Jesus nor the Matthean evangelist ever intended for the words of this Sermon (or, specifically, of the antitheses) to be read as a prelude to a more evangelical proclamation found elsewhere. Both "authors" no doubt believed that the principal value of the Sermon was that it reveals how God wants and expects people to live. The underlying assumption is that followers of Jesus could and would live this way.

RECOVERING THE HERMENEUTICAL
PRINCIPLE OF LAW AND GOSPEL

Readings of the Sermon on the Mount such as that described above are but one example of how Lutheran interpreters have found themselves at odds with historical critical exegesis of the Bible. I suggest, however, that such problems result from a misapplication of the principle of law and gospel. That principle was never intended to be used as an exegetical tool for determining the intended meaning of texts; rather, it was articulated as a pastoral and theological principle for understanding the anticipated effects of texts.

The Lutheran idea of law and gospel is essentially an audience-oriented hermeneutical principle that celebrates polyvalence and locates meaning in reception rather than in authorial intent.[4] Of course, the principle was not articulated as such by Luther or his followers, but only the terminology I am using is anachronistic. Luther did believe and teach that the Word of God was a dynamic force that impacted hearers; he essentially equated the meaning of God's Word with the effects that it has on those who receive it. Of all the potential effects that God's Word can have, two typical effects interested Luther the most: sometimes the Word of God accuses and judges those who hear it; other times it comforts and saves them. Those typical effects of the Word of God are what Luther had in mind when he spoke of law and gospel.

In general, Lutheran theologians have recognized this. Carl Braaten says the law is that which "accuses, condemns, denounces, punishes, and kills"; the gospel is that which "comforts, strengthens, forgives, liberates, and renews."[5] At Trinity Lutheran Seminary, Walter Bouman liked to speak of law as "existential dread" and gospel as "eschatological hope." Cheryl Peterson, a systematic theologian, says "The law convicts us; the gospel delivers us." I hope we can agree that these are different ways of talking about the same reality. And while people may prefer one set of terms to another, all of these descriptions seem to cohere with what I said when speaking of Luther's view: the law accuses and judges, the gospel comforts and saves.[6]

This is the original and powerful concept of law and gospel, a Lutheran hermeneutic that focuses on the impact God's Word has on its audience. The concept underwent development, however, and some questionable adjustments to Luther's reception-oriented hermeneutic have not cohered well with modern exegesis (particularly of the Old Testament and the Gospel of Matthew). Perhaps the most insidious of these adjustments has

---

[4] See Mark Allan Powell, "Law and Gospel and the Interpretation of Scripture," in Laurie Jungling (ed.), *Lutheran Perspectives on Biblical Interpretation* (Minneapolis: Lutheran University Press, 2010), 36–58.

[5] See Carl E. Braaten, *Principles of Lutheran Theology*, 2nd ed. (Minneapolis: Fortress Press, 2007), 39. Luther himself said, "The true and proper function of the law is to accuse and to kill; but the function of the gospel is to make alive." *WA* 39, I, 363.

[6] Walther offers a somewhat more detailed listing of the effects of law and gospel. The law demands but does not enable compliance; it hurls people into despair, for it diagnoses the disease without providing any cure; and it terrifies the conscience by producing contrition and offering no comfort. The gospel creates faith, stills every voice of accusation, and transforms people by planting love in their hearts and enabling them to do good works. See C. F. W. Walther, *The Proper Distinction Between Law and Gospel* (St. Louis: Concordia, 2004; lectures given in 1864–1865), 16. Cf. John T. Pless, *Handling the Word of Truth: Law and Gospel in the Church Today* (St. Louis: Concordia, 2004), 14–15.

been the reductionist equation of "law" with biblical commandments and "gospel" with biblical promises. The damage of such a construal has been further exacerbated by a second adjustment, namely the relatively recent (Post-Enlightenment) construal of interpretation as a process for discerning authorial intent. If we can articulate a hermeneutic of law and gospel that avoids these adjustments, we may still find the principle indispensable for the interpretation of texts, including, if not especially, legalistic texts like the antitheses, the Sermon on the Mount and the Gospel of Matthew as a whole.

LAW AND GOSPEL DO NOT DESIGNATE GENRES OF BIBLICAL LITERATURE

Many people have misconstrued law and gospel as designations for two different types of biblical material. For example, in an instruction book for those new to Lutheranism, Martin Marty says, "Law represents the demands of God, and the gospel is the promises of God."[7] Marty is trying to state a complex matter in simple terms, but such a construal ultimately misses the point. When the expression "law and gospel" is taken as shorthand for "demands and promises," the theological concepts of both law and gospel end up being defined in terms of content (and, so, implicitly, in terms of authorial intention) rather than in terms of effect (and so, implicitly, in terms of reception).

It is precisely this misunderstanding of law and gospel that has created hermeneutical problems for Lutherans, who often feel compelled to make biblical texts fit into a mold that they think the Lutheran paradigm requires. We have seen one famous example in the Sermon on the Mount. Since it consists primarily of demands and commandments, Lutheran exegetes decided it must fall into the "law" half of the "law and gospel" paradigm; accordingly, it must be interpreted in accord with what the law does (accuse, judge, bring people to despair). Rightly understood, however, the principle of law and gospel does not require such interpretations. Both "law" and "gospel" elucidate potential effects of texts, effects that will usually cohere with, but need not be restricted by, the intentions of their authors.

Indeed, the Word that accuses and judges us might be anything that reveals God's majesty and holiness. Commandments often do this, insofar as they testify to God's standard of righteousness, in light of which all human endeavors are judged. That makes us tremble, but so does any revelation of who God is when presented in stark contrast to who we are: God is power-

---

[7] Martin E. Marty, *Come and Grow with Us: New Member Basics* (Minneapolis: Augsburg Fortress, 1996), 10.

ful, we are weak; God is wise, we are foolish; God is omniscient, we are ignorant; God is eternal, we are finite; God is complex, we are simple; God is magnificent, we are petty, God is love (= fundamentally unselfish), we are self-absorbed. In sum, God is holy, we are sinful. And it is not just commandments that reveal the extent to which God is so different from us (and therefore fearsome and terrifying); the Word of God always reveals this and, so, the Word of God always carries the potential to accuse us and judge us.

Of course, the Word also reveals that God comes to us, and it is not just promises that reveal this, but commandments as well. The Word of God always reveals a God who is merciful and gracious, who takes the initiative in closing the considerable gap between us, who respects our weakness, tolerates our foolishness, transcends our finitude and forgives our sins. Since the Word of God always reveals this God, it always carries the potential to comfort and save us.

Luther thought that any text could convey either law or gospel depending on the disposition of the audience.[8] The first of the Ten Commandments says, "You shall have no other gods." People who want to have other gods may hear a restrictive word that accuses them and judges them. But people who do not want to have other gods, who find the notion of multiple gods oppressive, might take comfort in the offer of Yahweh to be the only God one needs to worship or serve. Likewise, the beloved affirmations of the twenty-third Psalm will be pure gospel to those who want to be led, guided and protected by a compassionate, powerful Lord, but there are people in this world who would prefer to be footloose and fancy free, without anyone telling them where to go or what to do. To them, the recognition that they have a shepherd may come as a word of incrimination and judgment.

The Sermon on the Mount contains numerous demands, but these need not be heard by all receptors as "law"; they might just as well be heard as "gospel," e.g., as wise counsel from an all-knowing God that reveals how we can have more meaningful and fulfilling lives. Like the Torah of the Old

---

[8] So Althaus, "For Luther, then, God's word can, in the final analysis, definitely not be categorized into law and gospel. The one and the same word strikes sinful man both as law and as gospel," in Althaus, op. cit. (note 3), 264. The functions of law and gospel "are functions of the same word. They always take place concurrently" (ibid., 265). Also Lohse: "The distinction between law and gospel cannot be made once for all, but must be drawn ever anew [...]. What is further unique about Luther's distinction is that law and gospel cannot be assigned to the Old or New Testament, nor to particular biblical passages, so as to establish for all time that one text is only law and the other gospel. Most texts assigned to the law have also a gospel side, and most texts assigned to the gospel have also a law side," in Bernhard Lohse, *Martin Luther's Theology: Its Historical and Systematic Development* (Minneapolis: Fortress Press 1999), 269.

Testament, the Torah of Matthew might be received with delight, as words that are sweeter than honey and more to be desired than gold (Ps 19:10)—a far cry from words that accuse and judge. And, almost as an aside, we should note that the Sermon does contain numerous promises, but these would not always be received by everyone as "gospel." The assurances that God will provide for us (Mt 6:25–33) and answer our prayers (Mt 7:7–11) may serve to convict us of our little faith (Mt 6:30) and misplaced priorities (Mt 6:33).

LAW AND GOSPEL ARE NOT EXPRESSIONS OF AUTHORIAL INTENT

Post-Enlightenment biblical scholarship established "authorial intent" as the arbiter for determining legitimate meaning. Under the dominance of the historical critical method, Lutherans who wanted to be regarded as responsible scholars were expected to back their claim that Scripture conveys law and gospel by showing how this was in accord with the intention of the biblical authors. The situation persists to this day and, when paired with the reductionist misunderstanding of law and gospel discussed above, the task becomes (1) a demonstration that the authors of promises intended those texts to comfort and save; and, (2) a demonstration that the authors of commandments intended their texts to accuse and judge. In general, for those who have wanted to take this route, the first of these demonstrations has been easier than the second. Thus, legalistic texts, such as the antitheses in the Sermon on the Mount have become especially problematic, and some Lutherans are mocked within the guild for reading sixteenth-century theology back into first-century texts and for resorting to desperate, if not ludicrous, measures to safeguard their confessional biases from the views of biblical authors who had different agendas.

Again, the interpretation of the Sermon on the Mount Jeremias denounced may serve as an obvious example of an approach that is confessional, but is no longer regarded as critical. But we should recognize that Jeremias' objection was based entirely on the assumption that the correct meaning of the Sermon was that which its author had intended. Jeremias did not deny that the Sermon could be read in a way that exposes the folly of works righteousness, a claim that would have been existentially falsifiable. His point was that it should not be read that way, since that was not what the author had intended.

Before going further, let us note that the hermeneutical assumption that texts are correctly interpreted only when they are read in light of authorial intent should cause problems for Lutherans that go far beyond interpretation of the Sermon on the Mount. The simple fact is that the great majority of biblical texts were not intended by their authors to function as either law or gospel in the Lutheran sense of those terms. Some texts are merely informative: they were intended to relay information about practices, people, places and things. Some texts were intended to explain various puzzles, such as the reason places or people are called by various names. Some texts were intended to serve as aids in worship; some were intended to offer moral instruction, or just good practical advice. Some were intended to vilify opponents, or to advance the political careers of their authors, or to garner support for a given cause. Some texts were apparently intended to entertain readers or to evoke various emotional responses. If we were to apply our best exegetical methodologies for determining authorial intent and collect only those texts that are likely to have been intended by their authors to be heard as "words that accuse and judge" or as "words that comfort and save," we would have a much shorter Bible—an ideal Lutheran lectionary, some might think, but nothing like the canon of writings we confess to be the authoritative and inspired Word of God.

The historical critical method has served church and academy well in many ways, but it has not proved particularly helpful for preaching. Almost anyone who has taught at a Lutheran seminary is aware of the potential tension between exegetical classes and homiletical ones. In exegetical classes, students learn to interpret the text in a way that reveals the author's original intent. And in homiletical classes, those same students are urged to preach law and gospel in a manner that is faithfully evoked by that text. The problem is that, more often than not, the author's intent was not to evoke either law or gospel. But this does not mean the principle of law and gospel is flawed. Rather, the historical critical method is flawed, which is to say it is limited insofar as it can, at best, point to only one facet of meaning.

Reader-response criticism of the Bible now contends that, despite the obvious value of authorial intent in production of meaning, unanticipated responses to texts need not be deemed illegitimate. Indeed, reader-response critics have demonstrated that no church has ever actually been faithful to the hermeneutic of authorial intent that its scholars have espoused for the past few centuries. Isaiah 53 continues to be read on Good Friday, despite academic consensus that the historical Isaiah did not intend for his words to be understood as applying to a specific, future Galilean.[9] Further, New Testament authors do not apply any such hermeneutic in a restrictive manner. Where do we find Jesus or any New Testament author objecting to

---

[9] As I have explained elsewhere, if we truly embraced the hermeneutic of authorial intent that we often espouse, we would have to reject all christological interpretations of the Old Testament (including those proffered by New Testament authors). See Mark Allan Powell, *Chasing the Eastern Star: Adventures in Reader Response Criticism* (Louisville: Westminster John Knox, 2001), 176–79.

a biblical interpretation by saying that is not what Moses/Isaiah/whoever meant when they said this to their original audience? And when Paul tells the Corinthians "the rock was Christ" (1 Cor 10:4), does he really mean to say that the historical author of Exodus (or Numbers) intended for his readers to understand that the rock was a metaphor for a future Messiah?

In sum, the Lutheran hermeneutic of law and gospel does not claim to explicate meaning in terms of authorial intent, nor is its legitimacy dependent on consistency with authorial intent. Indeed, the hermeneutic of law and gospel challenges the modernist assumption that Scripture only functions properly or authoritatively when its understanding is restricted to the sense that the historical author meant to convey.

Third use of the law and didactic preaching

We have identified two questionable adjustments to the original, powerful Lutheran hermeneutic of law and gospel. The fact that these adjustments were made very early is suggested by their appearance in the Formula of Concord, which famously explains how the "law" has three uses: a political function of maintaining a semblance of order in society; a theological function of showing people their need for the gospel; and an ethical or catechetical function of teaching believers right from wrong. This assertion seems to assume two things. First, the term law is apparently being used as shorthand for "biblical commandments" and, second, the reference to function seems to imply that such texts are intended to serve in particular ways.

There has been a history of controversy in Lutheran theology over whether this "third use of the law" is actually valid. I addressed that controversy elsewhere,[10] but, in any case, it need not concern us here. What does concern us is the widespread (almost unanimous) perception in Lutheranism that the law mentioned in the Formula of Concord, the law that has three functions, is synonymous with the law in "law and gospel." If the Formula of Concord had simply said that there are three functions of biblical commandments, it is hard to imagine that there would have ever been any controversy. No one doubts that biblical commandments have an ethical and catechetical function. For example, in his section on the Ten Commandments in the "Small Catechism," Luther repeatedly asks, What does this mean? and each time he says that the meaning of the commandment is that God wants us to do or not do something; he never says that the meaning of the commandment is that we should despair of works righteousness and realize our need for the gospel.

---

[10] See Powell, op. cit. (note 4), 38–43.

But what is true of "laws" would not necessarily be true of "the law" in the broader sense of any true revelation of God, which necessarily accuses and judges but which would not necessarily be didactic or, for that matter, politically relevant. When the word law is taken to mean "anything that reveals God's otherness" = "anything that causes us to recognize our separation from God" = "anything that accuses us and judges us"—when the word law has that meaning, as it does when Luther speaks of the Word of God being law and gospel—then there can be no meaningful "third use" (hence the controversy). When we gaze in awe on God's holiness, we do not take notes regarding this or that aspect of God's divine nature that we might, with a bit more effort, be able to emulate. No, we tremble at the horrifying realization that we are not simply ignorant or ineffective or lackadaisical or unmotivated: we are, in fact, sinners, and nothing that lies within our power can change this, not even perfect obedience to all the commandments, if such were within our power.

Of course, the insight that biblical commandments have more than one function is not without merit. We might say that "the Lutheran error" in reading the Sermon on the Mount resulted from assuming that these commandments had to serve the second function when, in fact, they better serve the third. Rather than claiming Jesus or the Matthean evangelist intended the Sermon to bring people to despair of works righteousness, we may affirm that these authors intended the Sermon to serve as a moral guidebook for justified sinners. This may at first seem promising, but to my mind, it does not rescue the principle of law and gospel, but abandons it, with severe theological loss.

It may be valid to say that the demands of the Sermon can and do serve what the Formula of Concord calls the third function of the law, but saying this has almost nothing to do with understanding the Sermon or the Gospel of Matthew in light of law and gospel. It may be exegetically sound to interpret the demands of the Sermon on the Mount as moral guidelines for Christian living, and teaching the Sermon as such may make for an interesting Adult Forum or Sunday School class, but Lutherans are called to preach law and gospel—and didactic sermons that offer moral guidelines for Christian living do not fit that paradigm.

This is an important point, so let us slow down and take it one step at a time. Let us begin by recognizing that the Lutheran principle of law and gospel was developed with primary reference to preaching, not biblical interpretation. When Luther and others said that the Word of God is both law and gospel, they usually meant that God's Word ought to be proclaimed in a way that both accuses and comforts, judges and saves.[11] Of course,

---

[11] So, Althaus, "Luther's distinction is clearly related to the context of proclamation," in op. cit. (note 3), 269.

what can be said about the proclaimed Word might also apply to the written Word, and a hermeneutical principle for interpretation of Scripture may be extracted from the law and gospel insight, but there are two ways in which we might (and often do) get this wrong.

First, we ought not to allow a homiletical principle to control exegetical practice. I sometimes hear Lutheran church leaders maintain that since someone's interpretation of Scripture does not cohere with law and gospel, it must be rejected as a misunderstanding or an invalid use of Scripture. "Lutherans are always supposed to interpret Scripture in light of law and gospel," this person will say. But I would respond, "No! I disagree." What we believe, as Lutherans, is that preachers should always proclaim Scripture in light of law and gospel; accordingly, exegetical work that is intended to support proclamation should seek to interpret Scripture in that light. But the concept of law and gospel should not be employed as a restrictive hermeneutic that invalidates exegesis of Scripture for purposes other than preaching. The fact is, we study the Bible for many reasons and in many different ways. Sometimes, we simply want to know more about the ancient world: it is not wrong to learn about agricultural practices in ancient Israel, just because that has little to contribute to the proclamation of law and gospel. More to the point, exegesis of Scripture that sincerely seeks to discern the varied and contradictory intentions of diverse authors produces relevant data for catechesis and theology, and if such study is to have any integrity it must be conducted without imposition of any particular construct. Lutherans can affirm that the proclaimed Word of God always comes to us as law and gospel without contending that every text of the Bible is properly interpreted only when it reveals those aspects of God's Word.

Second, and more to the matter at hand, interpretation of Scripture that is intended to support proclamation should employ the paradigm of law and gospel. In Lutheran homiletical theory, the goal of a sermon is not to provide people with doctrinal or moral instruction: preaching is different from teaching. Thus, one should not simply preach the exegetically determined meaning of a text. An additional hermeneutical step is required, though seminaries have not done a stellar job of training people in how to take that step and many pastors do not seem to have figured out how to do it on their own. What sometimes happens is that Lutheran preachers, just like other preachers, present the exegetically determined meaning of the text as the sermon. To my thinking, this might make for a fascinating Bible study, for inspirational and provocative teaching, but it does not necessarily make for proclamation of law and gospel.

With the Gospel of Matthew, especially the Sermon on the Mount, we tend to get didactic sermons, filled with exhortations, "do's and don'ts" regarding how we should or should not live as disciples of Christ. I call these "so that" sermons. Martin Luther says in his "Small Catechism," "we are to fear and love God so that [...]" and then lots of things follow. Especially during the Series A lectionary year, I often hear didactic sermons in Lutheran churches that are basically summaries of all the "so thats,2 as the preacher tells me what people who fear and love God ought to do. The problem with such a sermon, from my perspective as a sinner in need of law and gospel, is that it assumes I fear and love God.

I tell my students at Trinity Lutheran Seminary, "Do not make that assumption! Preach the law so that I will fear God and preach the gospel so that I will love God." Then I can come to the Adult Forum and learn about the "so that's." "Further," I tell them, "Do not think that just because I feared and loved God last week, we can skip over that part and get right to the "so that's" for this week's sermon. I may be a worse sinner than you think. I know you are just trying to help me be faithful to God, and I appreciate that, but it is not what I need from a sermon. I need the Word of God to operate as a means of grace, producing in me the fear of God and the love of God every week! Law and gospel!"

Now I hope we can see why an appeal to the third use of the law does not solve the hermeneutical problems we encounter with Torah-heavy texts. It dodges those problems, ignoring them altogether. The problems associated with interpreting Matthew in light of law and gospel do not arise when teaching Scripture; they only arise when preaching it. Of course, one can use all the demands of the Sermon on the Mount in catechesis, as examples of moral instruction that fulfills an important function of biblical commandments. But that has nothing to do with preaching—and nothing to do with the Lutheran concept of law and gospel that comes into play when texts of Scripture are used for proclamation.

INTERPRETING MATTHEW (FOR PROCLAMATION) IN LIGHT OF LAW AND GOSPEL

My contention is that the Lutheran concept of law and gospel actually assumes an audience-oriented or reader-response approach to Scripture. It defines the meaning of Scripture in terms of its effect on those who receive it.

Historical critical approaches to Scripture assume an author-oriented hermeneutic: the meaning of any text is to be equated with the sense intended by its original author. Reader-response criticism, by contrast, seeks to discern the plurality of meaning that a text might generate for a variety of different readers who receive it in diverse contexts. There should be discernible trajectories between authorial intent and these diverse responses, but reader-response criticism does recognize that texts come to mean things that their authors did not specifically intend.

Reader-response criticism is often associated with either (1) a postmodern hermeneutic that denies the stability and/or accessibility of meaning, and/or (2) ideological approaches to texts (feminist, Marxist, etc.) that seek to impose lenses for understanding texts in ways that overtly reject or resist authorial intent. But, though reader-response criticism may be popular with scholars who operate with a postmodern or ideological hermeneutic, the approach itself assumes no particular epistemology. As a mode of literary analysis, reader-response criticism simply employs various strategies for discerning anticipated effects of texts on various readers and identifying factors that make certain effects likely to be realized.[12]

As an official approach to biblical studies, reader-response criticism is only a few decades old, but Martin Luther appears to have been 500 years ahead of his time. His hermeneutical principle of law and gospel seems to assume an approach to exegetical interpretation that allows for a more dynamic concept of meaning than one that defines legitimate interpretation narrowly as expressions of explicit authorial intent. Reader-response criticism offers such an approach. The reader-response critic attempts to recognize a range of possible meanings that a text might have in various contexts, and effects congruent with what Lutherans call "law" and "gospel" will typically be included within that range of possible meanings.

In my own teaching, I summarize the text-to-sermon process thus: First, Scripture should be faithfully interpreted in accordance with the historical-critical method, so as to reveal the basic intentions of its original author. Then, we may employ reader-response criticism to take a second step: drawing on insights from pastoral theology, and using gifts of discernment acquired through years of exercising empathetic, prayerful concern for other people, we should be able to discern a plurality of possible effects that the text might have on people in various contexts. From that plurality of possible effects, we should isolate potential effects that would be congruent with authorial intent, even if they go beyond the specifics of such intent. Finally, from the limited plurality of potential effects congruent with authorial intent, the Lutheran preacher will focus on those effects that are always the intended impact of any Lutheran sermon: the accusatory effects of law and the comforting effects of gospel.

Such an approach is quite different from the text-to-sermon model aligned with traditional, historical-critical exegesis, a model that seldom allows for genuine proclamation of law and gospel in the Lutheran sense and that only allows for didactic preaching of legalistic material. Historical criticism focuses on discerning the intended message of a text and, as we have seen, the intended message of many texts will not have been to

---

[12] See Powell, op. cit. (note 9).

present a word that judges or a word that saves. But the goal of reader-response criticism is to elucidate anticipated effects of a text, which usually will include meanings that fit with the Lutheran principle of law and gospel. Why? Because law and gospel are categories defined by effect, not by intention or message or genre or content.

The hermeneutical concerns raised at the beginning of this paper are mitigated when reader-response criticism is employed as an exegetical strategy for discovering how biblical texts may be proclaimed as the Word of God that speaks both law and gospel.

First, we recognize that these concerns need not surface when the biblical text is interpreted for purposes other than proclamation. The historical critical method may by applied as effectively as possible so that we can learn as much about the world of the Bible and the perspectives of the various authors. Further, since we do not equate law and gospel with genres of biblical literature, we are free to analyze all genres in light of the probable functions such genres were intended to serve. And since law and gospel is not regarded as an explication of authorial intent, we do not need to "fudge" our analysis in an effort to turn the biblical authors into anachronistic supporters of a hermeneutical principle developed in the sixteenth century.

Having dispensed with all of that, the problems only arise when we interpret texts for proclamation—and, then, they may not turn out to be problems at all.

Rigorous application of historical critical exegesis leads to the recognition that the author of Matthew's Gospel had a different understanding of the law than would be embraced by Paul or Luther. He believed that the entire Jewish law (including, I think we must assume, prescription of circumcision) would remain in full force for God's people until the end of time. He further believed that the commandments of the law, even (or especially) as interpreted by Jesus could be obeyed and, indeed, would be obeyed by most of God's people most of the time. And he believed that, while the death of Jesus on the cross had made participation in the eschatological kingdom of God a possibility for all of God's people, obedience to God's commandments was still a pre-condition for anyone to gain actual admission.

This is not the theology of the church and no one should preach it. Still, it is instructive in many ways to realize with unflinching honesty that the canon contains such diversity. Matthew's Gospel becomes a testimony to an alternative variety of the Christian faith, a highly Jewish version that is similar in some respects to movements that Paul resisted, movements that actually prompted his deepest thinking regarding the law, justification and grace. Historical-critical study of Matthew's Gospel helps us to understand Christian origins. We may benefit from this without assuming that being faithful to Scripture or believing the Bible means adopting the mindset or even the theological perspective of any one, particular biblical author.

Reader-response criticism offers a different way: being faithful to Scripture entails being affected by the texts in ways congruent with the author's intentions, albeit in ways that transcend those intentions to the extent that we are also affected by a fuller, canonical witness of Scripture and by sound theology based on that canonical witness. So, when I read the Sermon on the Mount in Matthew, I recognize that the author wants me to live in the manner so described—and I endeavor to do so. Over time, I experience some success, but much failure.

I get a pretty bad scorecard on all of the points addressed in the antitheses, and I realize it would be ridiculous to compare myself to others who may be doing no better or even worse. Jesus says the only standard for comparison is the heavenly Father (Mt 5:48), and he says this knowing full well that it means "the road is hard that leads to life, and there are few who find it" (Mt 7:14). And to remove all ambiguity as to what that metaphor might imply, he makes clear that those who do not live in the manner he describes, as I most assuredly do not, will be denied admission to the kingdom of heaven (Mt 5:20); they will be liable to judgment (Mt 5:21, 22); they will be cast into hell (Mt 5:22, 29, 30). So, what I am to do, as a Bible-believing Christian who takes these antitheses as the absolute, inspired and authoritative Word of God?

It would be dismissive and far too easy for me simply to conclude that, since Paul says I am justified by grace, it does not matter whether or not I actually live the way the Sermon on the Mount says I should live (cf. Rom 6:1). It would likewise be dismissive and far too easy for me to say that Lutheran theology tells me it is impossible for any sinful human to live this way and, so, my failure is anticipated and should not be the cause of undue alarm.

Contra Lutheran theology, the Matthean Jesus clearly does expect me to be able to live in the manner he describes and, contra Paul, he assures me that I will be damned if I do not do so. Ultimately, it is this biblical witness against Luther and Paul that drives me to despair. Indeed, I am not sure that the Lutheran principle of law and gospel would actually work if we did not have strong biblical testimony against it. That is an irony built into the canon.

I am condemned not only by my own conscience or by the law of Moses but by the Gospel of Matthew and, quite possibly, by the historical Jesus. One has not experienced the full weight of the law's condemnation until one realizes that Jesus himself endorses it: I am damned not only according to Moses, but according to the Gospel of Matthew, and according to Jesus Christ as Matthew, I suspect faithfully, presents him.

And, so, as it turns out, I am accused and I am judged and, now, I am ready to hear the gospel.

With due deference to Jeremias, I believe the so-called legalism of Matthew's Gospel does function to bring us to despair and prepare us for the gospel, but not because this was how the author intended it to function. In fact, it brings us to despair precisely because that is not how the author intended it to function!

This is consistent with the Lutheran concept of law and gospel, which was never intended as an exegetical principle for discerning the intended message of texts but as a hermeneutical principle for explicating the ultimate effect of texts. The Apostle Paul, who was no doubt Luther's primary inspiration for developing this concept, says in Romans 7 that the effect of the law is to magnify our sins in such a way that we are confronted with them: the law (in this case, as expressed through commandments) becomes the means through which sin deceives and kills, bringing death (Rom 7:7-11). But when Paul says this, he is not writing as an exegete, claiming that he has discerned the ingenious intention of Moses (or his biographers). He is simply describing the effect of God's Word on sinful humanity.

Likewise, we Lutherans may recognize correctly that the paradigm of law and gospel summarizes the effects of Scripture without assuming that those effects were explicitly intended in every instance by every author. The point is that Scripture as a whole conveys a message that accuses and condemns us, and also a message that comforts and saves us. With regard to the Sermon on the Mount and the Gospel of Matthew, it is not exegetically correct to say that Jesus preached the Sermon in order to bring people to despair or to show them their need for the gospel; nevertheless, it is hermeneutically sound to say that despair would be an appropriate consequence of receiving the text as the words of a holy God spoken to sinful humanity.

Matthew's Gospel for the Reformation: "The Messiah ... Sent and Manifested"

Timothy Wengert

The history of biblical interpretation allows us to hear voices from the past interpreting Scripture. Paraphrasing the definition of a historian proposed by the philosopher Friedrich Schlegel, the historian of biblical interpretation is a prophet looking backwards. Part of a prophet's responsibility is to debunk myths. So, before engaging in the topic itself, consider two popular myths about the Lutheran interpretation of Scripture.

First, it is not helpful to assume that early Lutherans insisted that there was always only one meaning for individual passages of Scripture. Just because a single person often wrote to a specific audience does not imply that a text has only one meaning for later interpreters to explain. Such an approach ignores several important aspects of communication. Sometimes authors meant to be obscure. Sometimes the original audience also took what the author said in different ways. Most biblical authors did not imagine they were writing to more than their first readers.

The fact that two interpreters reach different conclusions about a particular Scripture passage does not *prima facie* mean that one is wrong and the other right. Consider this example from the earliest days of the Reformation when three important Reformers met at the Torgau Castle in late November 1527 to settle differences in understanding repentance and the law.[1] At a private breakfast meeting between John Agricola and Philip Melanchthon, Agricola repeated the charge that Melanchthon and Luther disagreed in their

---

[1] For the details, see Timothy J. Wengert, *Law and Gospel: Philip Melanchthon's Debate with John Agricola of Eisleben over "Poenitentia"* (Grand Rapids: Baker, 1997), 103–38.

interpretation of Galatians 3:19, which said that the law "was added because of transgressions." Luther interpreted this verse as a kind of "second use" of the law to drive the sinner to Christ, and Melanchthon as "the first use" of the law, which keeps evil in check. Agricola insisted that Melanchthon needed to bring his interpretation in line with Luther's.

Melanchthon's response gives insight into Wittenberg's flexible approach to Scripture. Melanchthon admitted to differences between himself and Luther and preferred older interpreters to Luther. But he could not imagine how this would anger Luther.

> For there is no doubt that Paul teaches that the law has been proposed for two reasons: first, to coerce the flesh with carnal righteousness; then to terrify the conscience. I have adapted the interpretation of this Pauline text to the former effect of the law; Luther adapts it to the latter.[2]

Now, such an approach did not mean Scripture could mean anything but rather implied that one could not, from the outset, reject one interpretation simply because it differed from another. Lutherans do not accord *carte blanche* authority to Luther under the slogan: Luther said it, I believe it, that settles it. Instead, one must listen to interpreters and, as long as they do not disagree on the central witness of the entire Scripture, one can accept their arguments or propose others.

The second misunderstanding is that the early Reformers insisted on *sola scriptura*, Scripture alone, when dealing with biblical authority.[3] It turns out that, according to the "Weimar" edition of Luther's works online, the phrase appeared only twenty times in Luther's Latin works. This contrasts to *sola gratia* (120 times) and *sola fide* 1200 times. Moreover, two of the twenty are actually quotes from Luther's opponents. Both Cardinal Cajetan and Erasmus of Rotterdam agree to argue with Luther *sola scriptura*. Of the remaining eighteen, half come in passages where Luther explicitly states that he would not argue *sola scriptura*. This leaves only nine references, none of which present a generalized theory of the authority of Scripture. Instead, for the most part, Luther contrasted his position to those who claimed papal authority over Scripture.

In contrast, using a phrase developed by Melanchthon scholar Peter Fraenkel, for the Wittenbergers Scripture was the *primum et verum*, the first and true authority. This did not eliminate other authorities, including creeds or early and medieval interpreters. While these interpreters were

---

[2] Ibid., 120–21.
[3] For details, see Timothy J. Wengert, *Reading the Bible with Martin Luther: An Introductory Guide* (Grand Rapids: Baker, 2013), 16–21.

always subject to the "first and true" authority of Scripture, they nevertheless represented, as Philip Melanchthon stated in the Augsburg Confession (1530), the *testimonia Patrum*, the testimonies of our ancestors in the faith. Indeed, any interpreter from any time, but especially those to whom we accord special respect and honor, such as Martin Luther and Philip Melanchthon, are signposts and witnesses to the center of Scripture: Jesus Christ crucified and risen for the life of the world. No wonder Luther used the phrase, *solus Christus*, Christ alone, well over 500 times in his Latin works. To imagine that Luther or these early Lutherans read Scripture apart from the "cloud of witnesses" that surrounds the church misses the true heart of the Reformation and would turn Lutherans into fundamentalists.

At the very least, these two caveats warn us to be very careful about how we use Scripture. Consider the fact that, in Scripture, the very first people to quote Scripture are the man and the woman in the garden. "The woman whom you gave to be with me" (Gen 3:12) Adam sputters, quoting, as it were, from the previous chapter. "The serpent, [whom you made,] tricked me," Eve rejoins, again "quoting" the Bible. And they are quoting Scripture against God. And in the New Testament, at Jesus' temptation recorded in Matthew and Luke, the Devil also quotes Scripture. And John, not to be outdone, records Jesus' attack on the Pharisees and their quoting the Bible. "You search the scriptures because you think that in them you have eternal life; and it is they that testify on my behalf" (Jn 5:39).

THE HERMENEUTICAL AND CHRISTOLOGICAL HEART OF MATTHEW

The center and heart of Matthew's Gospel may be summarized with the word, "Immanuel," God with us. Philip Melanchthon describes Matthew in his commentary published by his student, Sebastian Froschel, in 1558:

> Always at the beginning of an exposition of books that recount the Gospel story, something must be said about the distinction between law and gospel. Then, when something has been said about the promise, it must be added that these narrations have been written so that the Apostles may be witnesses and posterity may be certain that the Messiah has been sent and manifested. Third, it may be stated that the gospel readings principally consist of these four things: 1) Stories about who Christ is and where he came from; 2) Miracles testifying that he is not an imposter but truly sent from God and that his teaching is true; 3) Sermons of the Gospel, that is, the promises, such as: "All who believe in the Son will not perish" or "Come to me, all you who labor" and similar ones concerning eternal life; 4) Sermons concerning good works, which are like sermons of the law and

interpretations of the law, and they pertain to sermons about repentance. And
the distinction between precepts and promises must diligently be observed lest
this light (that remission of sins is gratuitous) is lost.[4]

First, the distinction between law and gospel is crucial. Not only does
Melanchthon begin the paragraph by emphasizing the importance of distinguishing law and gospel, but also in describing the content of the four
gospels, two of the four points are about law and gospel. In the gospels
there are sermons about the gospel, God's promises and about good works,
which are "like sermons of the law." And he closes with the comment: "And
the distinction between precepts and promises must diligently be observed
lest this light (that remission of sins is gratuitous) is lost." When Lutherans
abandon this central hermeneutical principle of theirs, then their interpretations simply cease to be Lutheran, and they join forces with other
streams of the Christian tradition, streams that invariably emphasize the
necessity and centrality of works and law in Christian life.

Second, Melanchthon emphasizes what might be called the Christological principle of Lutheran biblical interpretation. "These narrations have
been written so that the Apostles may be witnesses and posterity may be
certain that the Messiah has been sent and manifested." He reiterates this
in the first two things that make up gospel readings: stories about who
Christ is and miracles that prove that point. Melanchthon remembers that
(to use the title of a brilliant book from the 1940s by Hoskyns and Davey),
Jesus Christ, Immanuel, is the answer to the "riddle of the New Testament."[5]

Already in 1530 Melanchthon had embedded distinguishing law and
gospel and focusing on Christ as Messiah into Article XX of the Augsburg
Confession.[6] Article XX deals with the charge that Lutherans forbid good works.
After dismissing the charge, Melanchthon restates the basic Lutheran teaching
on justification, on the nature of faith and, finally, on good works. He begins,

> In the first place, our works cannot reconcile us with God or obtain grace. In-
> stead, this happens through faith alone when a person believes that our sins are
> forgiven for Christ's sake, who alone is the mediator to reconcile the Father. Now

---

[4] *CR* 14: 543–44. The translation is from Wengert, ibid., 59–60.
[5] Edwyn Hoskyns and Francis Davey, *The Riddle of the New Testament*, 3rd ed.
(London: Faber & Faber, 1947).
[6] "The Augsburg Confession—German Text—Article XX: Faith," in Robert Kolb and
Timothy J. Wengert (eds), *The Book of Concord. The Confessions of the Evangelical
Lutheran Church* (Minneapolis: Fortress, 2000), 52–57, [henceforth: *BC*].

all who imagine they can accomplish this by works and can merit grace, despise Christ and seek their own way to God contrary to the gospel.[7]

Not only is this the first place where the document confesses justification by "faith alone," but it also speaks of Christ's sole mediation ("Christ alone"). For our purposes, however, the most important comment comes in Melanchthon's description of what happens when people claim to merit grace. They "despise Christ and seek their own way to God contrary to the gospel." The heart and soul of Lutheran interpretation of the Bible and, more specifically, of the four gospels protect reader and preacher alike against despising Christ and contradicting the gospel by proclaiming the Christological center of the text in relation to law and gospel.

Such an approach to the Gospel of Matthew frees readers from certain moralistic interpretive models and brings them back to the central task of the preacher and expositor, which is to proclaim Christ crucified and risen again "for us and for our salvation." Lutherans can best defend themselves against turning Matthew into a gospel of Christian rules and regulations by listening to Matthew's heart: This one, Christ, is Immanuel, God with us, who speaks law and gospel—commands and promises—to make us believers in him and not in ourselves.

THE HERMENEUTICS OF LAW AND GOSPEL[8]

Sometimes, Lutheran supporters of law and gospel make a completely understandable mistake. Both Martin Luther and Philip Melanchthon divide theological problems into two parts, asking first what the entity is and then what its effects are. Later Lutherans, however, often focus more on the first than the second part. That is, they first define law as commands or even imperatives and then define gospel as promises or indicatives.

But neither Luther nor Melanchthon thought that they had said anything important by separating commands and promises. The point of their hermeneutics was not determining what law or gospel is but precisely what any Word of God does to people when they hear it. Indeed, this intense listening to what God is doing to us through the Word rests at the very heart of Luther's breakthrough to a new—and remarkably old—way of doing theology. Whether one discovers that breakthrough in Luther's earliest

---

[7] Ibid., 54.

[8] See Wengert, op. cit. (note 3), 22–46, and Timothy J. Wengert, *A Formula for Parish Practice: Using the Formula of Concord in the Parish* (Grand Rapids: Eerdmans, 2006), 77–89.

lectures on the Psalms from 1513–1515, as Gerhard Ebeling does,[9] or in his defense of the Ninety-five Theses from 1518, as Oswald Bayer has,[10] makes little difference. The fact remains that Luther discovered that when interpreters encounter God's Word in Scripture, it works on them not the other way around. This did not preclude the hard work of understanding the words and context of a particular passage—what it means—but it did imply that, properly speaking, Scripture interprets us not we it.

While defending the Evangelical position on penitence in the Apology of the Augsburg Confession (September 1531), Melanchthon insists that penitence consists of two parts: repentance and forgiveness. To explain the movement from repentance to forgiveness, Melanchthon first distinguishes, as Luther had in earlier writings, between God's alien and proper work—first God reveals sin and puts to death the old creature before bringing the new creature to life. This leads immediately to a discussion of law and gospel. Here is what he wrote.

> Scripture makes a practice of joining these two things, terrors and consolation, in order to teach that these are the chief parts of repentance: contrition and faith that consoles and justifies. We do not see how the nature of repentance could be taught more clearly and simply. For these are the two chief works of God in human beings, to justify the terrified or make them alive. The entire Scripture is divided into these two works. One part is the law, which reveals, denounces, and condemns sin. The second part is the gospel, that is, the promise of grace given in Christ. This promise is constantly repeated throughout the entire Scripture [...]. For all the saints have been justified by faith in this promise and not on account of their own attrition or contrition.[11]

To see how this distinction works for Matthew, consider Jesus' statement from the Sermon on the Mount, "Whoever hates one's brother or sister is a murderer."[12] So, what does that do to the hearer? When reduced to a rule that, with enough practice, human beings can master, then one misses Christ's point and turns the entire Scripture upside down. Of course, as soon as this text reveals the truth about our human condition, which is what the law does to us, the old creature starts looking for a way out by

---

[9] Gerhard Ebeling, "The Beginnings of Luther's Hemeneutics," in *Lutheran Quarterly* 7 (1993), 129–58, 315–38, 451–58.

[10] Oswald Bayer, *Promissio: Geschichte der reformatorischen Wende in Luthers Theologie*, 2nd ed. (Darmstadt: Wissenschaftliche Buchgesellschaft, 1989).

[11] "The Apology of the Augsburg Confession," in op. cit. (note 6), 195.

[12] Martin Luther, "The Sermon on the Mount," in Jaroslav Pelikan (ed.), *Luther's Works*, vol. 21 (Saint Louis: Concordia, 1956), 74. (Here and passim author's own translation based on *WA* 32:360–541).

reducing the commandment's severity. Then, despite the text saying nothing of the kind, readers imagine that it has to do with how hard one tries or how often one does not fail. Christ's point in preaching the law is not to reduce one's discomfort but, to make matters worse, to make matters so bad that hearers are revealed for what they are: murderers. And yet, even then, the old creature grabs the text by the throat and says, Oh, not really a murderer! Or, it finds others who violate this command in worse ways and judges them. As Luther says in his sermons on the Sermon on the Mount, a series of sermons preached on Wednesdays at St Mary's church in Wittenberg in late 1530,

> See, this is that beautiful Pharisaical holiness, that can make itself pure and
> righteous, as long as it does not kill with the hand, even though the heart is
> stuffed full of anger, hatred, envy and secret, evil and murderous treachery.[13]

In Luther's day, theologians had turned this command not to hate into a counsel, which truly holy people could follow but that Christ clearly did not intend for everyone, although the medieval exegete, Nicholas of Lyra, had insisted that this command was meant for everyone. In these sermons from 1530, delivered nine years after Parisian theologians had condemned Luther for teaching the same thing, Luther could still quote their legal rule in Latin from the pulpit, "*nimis onerativum legis Christianae*" (the burden of Christian law is too much).[14] This is the way one ought to grab Christ by the mouth, master his words and make out of them what one pleases. Others simply make this into a command for outward behavior but not a matter of the heart, Luther goes on to say, similar to the adage, "forgiven but not forgotten." If Christ on the cross had used this rule when he said, "Father, forgive them," then, Luther concludes, he could just as well have remained in heaven, avoided death and simply said, "I will forgive but not forget." Against this "lazy gloss," Luther insists that what Christ is doing here is explicating the fifth commandment itself so as to eliminate all attempts at hypocrisy. This means that, for Luther, as for later Lutherans, preaching the law is never simply a matter of pointing out how one may transgress a single commandment but always pushes both hearer and preacher to consider how the first commandment, which demands faith, is also always at play, attacking our hypocrisy.

---

[13] Ibid.

[14] Ibid., 74–75. "*Haec propositio* [that the law to turn the other cheek applies to all Christians] *est falsa, legis Christianae nimium oneratiua, & sane intelligentiae scripturae aduersa.*" See *Determinatio theologice Facultatis Parisiensis upper Doctrina Lutheriana hactenus per eam visa* (Paris: Ascensio, 1521), b 4v.

Yet, this is hardly an indication of the "introspective consciousness of the West."[15] Indeed, Luther also talks about a second, higher misuse of this approach to the text: "that one tries to be saved through this command, to make satisfaction for sins and to trust in and crow about such works to God."[16] What otherwise appears to be a good work—loving the neighbor—suddenly becomes the most evil work of all. When Luther reaches Jesus' comments about "an eye for an eye," he distinguishes between what judges, as part of their official duties, may have to do in punishing a criminal, and what the Christian person, who has no right to take revenge, must do. The former has to do with jurists, "but the Gospel has no reason to concern itself with such matters but teaches how the heart stands before God. In this all should be adept, so that the heart remains pure and does not veer off into a false righteousness." Christ teaches this "so that the heart depends upon God."[17] In this world, to be sure, a Christian may stand under the emperor "but regarding his or her own person such a one is, according to the Christian life, only under Christ and not under the emperor or any other person."[18]

Luther's exposition of the Sermon on the Mount makes clear that for him, as for the other Wittenberg exegetes, the point of interpretation was not to determine *a priori* whether a text is law and gospel but rather to observe how it actually works on a person, revealing on the one hand the truth about human existence (law) and on the other the truth about God's mercy (gospel). One example of how a text can be both law and gospel, comes again in Luther's exposition of "Ask and it shall be given you." He states:

> Therefore each Christian should in the first place receive this admonition as a command [...] and know that he or she is duty bound to practice this Christian work and not behave like that farmer who said that he gives the pastor grain so that [the pastor] might pray for him, or, as some think, "What is the point of my praying? If I do not pray, others will." Christ says this so that people do not assume that prayer makes no difference for us or that it is a matter of free choice. About this I have often admonished you. In the second place, you have here a comforting promise and rich pledge that Christ attaches to prayer, so that a person can see that it really matters to God and can learn to consider our prayer as priceless

---

[15] Written as a response to Swedish students' hyper-pietism. See Krister Stendahl, "The Apostle Paul and the Introspective Conscience of the West," in *Harvard Theological Review* 56 (1963): 199–214; reprinted in Krister Stendahl, *Paul among Jews and Gentiles* (Philadelphia: Fortress, 1976), 78–96.

[16] Cf. Luther, op. cit. (note 12), 81.

[17] Ibid., 108.

[18] Ibid., 109.

and precious to God, because he so earnestly admonishes us to pray and invites and promises in such a friendly manner so that we should never pray in vain.[19]

Luther continues: "Now the dear Lord Christ knows [our situation] well and therefore, like an upright, true physician shows us a precious, good medicine [namely, prayer] and teaches us how to use it."[20]

But Luther also understands that, in the Sermon on the Mount, Christ chiefly intended to preach the law, precisely because the people in Christ's day had reduced the law to outward works. But Luther also understood that in his own day people were making human works into the way of salvation. Thus, at the very end of his exposition, in discussing Christ's speaking with authority, Luther warns against "ignorant, false preachers who conclude from Christ's words that we enter the kingdom of heaven and are saved through our works and actions."[21] What is the cure for this misinterpretation?

> It is necessary for each person to know something about the difference between grace and merit. For the two cannot exist with each other. Where a person preaches grace, that one cannot really preach merit. And what is grace cannot be merit. "Otherwise grace would not be grace," as Paul says in Romans 11:6. This is doubtless true, so that all who mix the two together confuse the people and lead both themselves and the hearers astray.[22]

Luther insists on distinguishing faith and its fruits. Regarding the common Christian name and blessings, no one is better than another. "St. Peter has no better baptism than St. Paul or a child who was born yesterday."[23] And no one hears a better gospel. When it comes to outward fruits of faith, there are clear distinctions. "Now when you want to talk about Christians or paint their picture, so you have to paint them so that there are no differences among them but so that in all things one is just like the next."[24] For Luther merit and reward in the Bible are

> pure comfort for Christians. For if you have become a Christian and you have a gracious God and forgiveness both for past sins and those that cling to you, then

---

[19] Ibid., 229–30.
[20] Ibid., 231. See also Martin Luther, "The Large Catechism—Third Part: Lord's Prayer," 1–34, in *BC*, op. cit. (note 6), 440–45.
[21] Luther, op. cit. (note 12), 285.
[22] Ibid.
[23] Ibid.
[24] Ibid., 286.

it will doubtless happen that you must do and suffer many things for the sake of your faith and your baptism.[25]

When the flesh, world or devil come calling, then, in the midst of doubts and trials Christians "must flee from them, and for strength and comfort say [to themselves], 'You are now in grace and are God's children'."[26]

THE CHRISTOLOGICAL WITNESS OF MATTHEW

For Luther and Melanchthon, Matthew did not write his gospel simply to give Christians a list of rules to follow to be good Christians. Indeed, if we look at Luther's sermons on many of the Matthean texts appointed in the standard, one-year lectionary, sermons that comprise his oft-published and imitated *Kirchenpostil*—church postil, or commentary on the gospels and epistles comprising the common lectionary—we discover that what Luther consistently finds here are invitations to faith in the savior of the world, the only Son of God. This Christological center forms the core of his interpretation of these texts.

On the Feast of the Epiphany, Luther pondered the contrast between the magis' search for a king and what they must have thought when they found Christ in Bethlehem.

O how deserted and wild everything looks at the birth of such a king! If a puppy were born, there would at least be a little bit of crying. In this case, a king is said to have been born, and yet everything is completely quiet. Shouldn't the people be singing and jumping for joy, light lamps and decorate all the streets with mayflowers and roses? O the poor king, for whom we search; O we fools, we who permit ourselves to have apes and fools as kings! Without a doubt, the magi, too, made up of flesh and blood, were not without such similar thoughts and musings and must have suffered very great struggles of faith. For natural reason can in no way persist here; it would immediately grumble and wheeze if the king were not found to meet its expectations. Reason would say, "The devil must have led me here. What kind of king is born here when everything is so quiet and appears so miserable. Does not our shepherd cry more when a child is born to him? And when a cow calves it is more widely known than this king!" See? This is what reason and nature does all of the time, and it does not go further than it

---

[25] Ibid., 290.
[26] Ibid., 290.

can feel. If it does not feel it, then it assumes immediately that God has lied and says (as Psalm 14:1 says about reason): God is absent; the devil must be here.[27]

What a remarkable reflection on the crucified Immanuel! How like Luther to see in this simple story the paradox of the "King of the Jews," a title used only here and with reference to Pilate's inscription on the cross!

In his sermon on the entry of Jesus into Jerusalem, which he preached the first Sunday in Advent and Palm Sunday, we hear Luther reflecting on Christ's humility.

> This gospel excites and requires especially faith, for it depicts Christ's gracious coming. No one may receive him or greet him except by believing that he is the man and that he comes with the intention as this gospel presents it. What is revealed in Christ is pure grace, gentleness and goodness, and whoever believes in him and holds him to be these things is saved. Consider this! He is not riding on a steed, meant for waging war; he does not come clothed in awe-inspiring robes and power, but instead he sits on a donkey, a non-warlike animal designed to help people by bearing loads and working. He does this so that he may demonstrate how he is coming not to frighten or impel or oppress human beings but only to help them, to place their loads on himself and carry them.[28]

Luther connects the lowliness of Christ's transport with his gentleness and, thus, with that central passage from Matthew 11, "Come to me, all you that are weary and are carrying heavy burdens [...]." (Mt 11:28). On the third Sunday in Advent, Luther preached on the embassy sent from John the Baptist to Jesus, inquiring whether Jesus was Messiah, as described in Matthew 11. He notes how Christ points John's disciples both to his works (the list of miracles) and his words (that the poor have the gospel preached to them). This answer reflects Isaiah 61:1–2. The first part of Isaiah's text refers to Christ's anointing.

> For the Greek word Christ means Messiah in Hebrew or Unctus in Latin and anointed one in German. One used to anoint kings and priests for their kingdom or priesthood. But Isaiah says here that God himself will anoint this anointed king and priest, not with earthly oil but with the Holy Spirit, who will rest upon him.[29]

---

[27] *WA* 10/1/1:610, 25–611, 17.

[28] *WA* 10/1/2:22, 16–26. Here and passim author's own translation. For a translation of the *Kirchenpostil* into English, see John Lenker (ed.), *The Sermons of Martin Luther*, 8 vols (Minneapolis: Lutherans in All Lands, 1904–1907; reprint, Grand Rapids: Baker, 1989).

[29] *WA* 10/1/2:152, 29–153, 2.

Luther spends most of the sermon talking not just about Christ's miracles but the gospel itself, contrasted to the law.

> This other word of God is not a law or command, demands nothing from us, but precisely when in this first word of the law such demands come to expression and are aimed at the awful misery and poverty in the heart, then God comes and offers his loving, life-giving word and promises, vows and commits himself to give grace and help so that we may come out of this misery with all our sins not just forgiven but wiped out and in addition we are given love and desire to fulfill the law.[30]

Again, Luther moves from who Christ is to the comfort he gives.

The gospel appointed for the eighteenth Sunday after Trinity, comes from Matthew 22, a reading that not only described the Pharisees' question to Jesus about which commandment is the greatest but also Jesus' silencing of them by his asking where the Messiah comes from. On the first part, Luther stresses that Christ is the only one to fulfill this very law and that only through faith empowered by the Holy Spirit are believers made new so that they can now fulfill the law through Christ alone.

> Therefore, guard yourselves against preachers of works, who go on and on saying that one must do good works in order to be saved. We, however, say, faith alone is enough for salvation. Works belong to a different category, namely to demonstrate our faith, as you have often heard me say.[31]

He summarizes the second part of his sermon by distinguishing Jesus' divinity (by which he was David's Lord) from his humanity (by which he was David's son), citing Paul's introduction to Romans 1 as one place where Paul put the two together.

The gospel appointed for the twenty-fourth Sunday after Trinity is the healing of the synagogue leader's daughter. No other sermon demonstrates more clearly the Christological heart of Luther's interpretation of Matthew. Luther began his sermon on that text with these words.

> Dear friends, you know that the gospel is nothing other than a sermon about the single person, who is called Christ. And even though many books may have been written over the years and many sermons preached by a lot of people—both heathen and Christian—even by the Mother of God, St. Peter, the angels and many other saints—but they are still not gospels. On the contrary, this alone is the true gospel: when it presents Christ to us and teaches what good things we

---

[30] *WA* 10/1/2:158, 6–12.
[31] *WA* 10/1/2:409, 15–19.

should expect from him. From time to time in the gospel something is written about John the Baptist, Mary and the apostles, but that is actually not the gospel [...] but [was written] only to show more completely where Christ came from and what his office was.[32]

Then, a bit later in the same sermon, he states,

> To this end Christ is presented to us as an inexhaustible fountain, which at all times overflows with pure goodness and grace. And for such goodness and kindness he accepts nothing, except that the good people, who acknowledge such kindness and grace, thank him for it, praise and love him, although others despise him for it. This is what he reaps from it. So one is not called a Christian because he or she does much, but because he or she receives something from Christ, draws from him and lets Christ only give to him.[33]

Christ is the "inexhaustible fountain" overflowing with goodness and grace. The believer is always and only the receiver who draws from this rich source of refreshment.

This message was constantly on Luther's lips, especially when preaching on miracle stories. Thus, in a sermon on the healing of the Centurion's servant, Luther states,

> This is the Gospel that is the beginning, middle and end of everything good and of all salvation. For we have often heard that we must first hear the Gospel, and after that believe and love and do good works, and so reverse the order from what the teachers of works do. But the Gospel is a good report, saying or acclaim of Christ, how he is all goodness, love and grace, as can be said of no other human or saint. For even if other saints have a good report and acclaim, it is nevertheless not called Gospel except where it tells alone of the goodness and grace of Christ [...]. For the Gospel builds faith and confidence alone upon the rock, Jesus Christ.[34]

This single-minded concentration on Christ has two effects. Not only does it lift each text out of its narrower context and into the context of all the gospels, each of which was clearly written to witness to Christ crucified and risen for the life of the world, but it also drives the listener to faith in that very Christ. Thus, finding "Immanuel" in a text is never simply a matter of giving the Christologically correct answer but also a matter of trust and hope in him.

---

[32] *WA* 10/1/2:429, 17–29.

[33] Lenker, op. cit. (note 28), 5:329-30; *WA* 10/1/2:430, 36–431, 3.

[34] Ibid., 2:73 (Third Sunday after Epiphany); *WA* 17/2:73, 31–74, 4.

Finally, in the sermon about "rendering to Caesar" from the twenty-third Sunday after Trinity, Luther shows his amazement at Christ's ability to withstand his enemies' attacks.

> Consequently we have here a consolation, when we are attacked; that Christ is in us and gains the victory through us. Christ is so near us that we triumph at all times through him because we are in Christ. As long as we do not have opposition around our necks, he does nothing; but when we are attacked and oppressed, then he is at hand and puts all our enemies to shame.[35]

No wonder that almost every sermon in Matthew's Gospel wraps together law and gospel and Christ's person with the bow of faith in the face of attacks. Luther consistently gets to the heart of Matthew's motivation for writing and to the heart of the hearers' needs. The result blends every possible audience for Matthew's words and unites them into one assembly, *ekklesia*, against which no evil may prevail.

Concluding remarks

In the New Testament of 1530 produced in Wittenberg, an especially surprising woodcut graces the beginning of Matthew's Gospel.[36] Following in the tradition of medieval manuscripts, the printer had prepared a depiction of the Apostle Matthew sitting at his desk writing. The angel—the first of the four beasts of Ezekiel always associated with the first gospel—holds a mirror in which the evangelist sees reflected Christ on the cross. Two chicks are at Matthew's feet, reminding the reader of that quintessential gospel picture of the mother hen gathering her chicks. But most striking of all is the face and form of Matthew himself, unmistakably depicted by the anonymous artist as Martin Luther himself. That combination: a crucified Messiah and the chicks protected under Matthew's (or Martin's) writing desk. God with us on the cross; the mother hen spreading her wings to protect the little chicks under the shadow of the gospel itself: from this picture begin all saving interpretations of Matthew. "And remember, I am with you always, to the end of the age" (Mt 28:20).

---

[35] Cf. Ibid., 5:300 (23rd Sunday after Trinity); *WA* 10/1/2:422, 34–39.
[36] Heimo Reinitzer, *Biblia deutsch: Luthers Bibelübersetzung und ihre Tradition* (Wolfenbüttel: Herzog August Bibliothek, 1983), 95–96, 110.

TEXT, CONTEXT AND TRADITION: IMPLICATIONS FOR READING MATTHEW

Roger Marcel Wanke

INTRODUCTION

Getting the best out of the Bible requires that one is a critical as well as a knowledgeable reader: critical in order to articulate relevant questions and knowledgeable in terms of the text's cultural, historical, social, political and religious background. What should determine our reading of the Bible? Is it only the text or also the reader's context that determine our reading? Or, does our theological tradition determine our reading of the biblical text? These questions relate directly to hermeneutics. Of course, the concept of hermeneutics itself is ambivalent:[1] sometimes hermeneutics is related to the text and other times to the interpreter. This constitutes one of the fundamental challenges in hermeneutics. Objectivity and subjectivity in interpretation are questioned. According to Manfred Oeming and Ulrich H.J. Körtner, objectivity and subjectivity exist in interpretation in a dialectical tension without neutrality.[2] As a result, there are many hermeneutical methods and several hermeneutical keys, although many of them end up being an end in themselves. Hermeneutical methods are the result of hermeneutical principles: the greater the ambiguity as to how hermeneutics is defined, the greater will be the plurality of hermeneutical

---

[1] Antonius H. J. Gunneweg, *Hermenêutica do Antigo Testamento* (São Leopoldo: Sinodal, 2003), 5–11.

[2] Manfred Oeming, *Biblische Hermeneutik–Eine Einführung*, 2nd edition (Darmstadt: Wissenschaftliche Buchgesellschaft, 2007), 29–30. Oeming speaks about *Entobjektivierung* and *Subjektivität*; Cf. Ulrich H. J. Körtner, *Introdução à Hermenêutica Teológica* (São Leopoldo: Sinodal, 2009), 107–108.

methods. However, plurality is not the problem. Rather, problems arise when this plurality of methods is polarized, closing itself off and assuming the right to have the final word regarding the understanding of the text. Thus, there is no biblical exegesis, but only ideological *eisgesis*.[3]

Text, context and tradition

How do we read the Bible? How should we read Matthew? Traditionally the Gospel of Matthew opens the New Testament, even though scholars generally accept that in terms of order of writing, it should come after Mark. In this traditional arrangement, Matthew becomes the prologue, an interpretive key for the rest of the New Testament. Matthew is the gospel of the kingdom of God, the presence of God in Jesus Christ. In this essay I shall attempt to show that for understanding Matthew and its relevance for the contemporary church, text, context and tradition are inseparable.

The text: A great work of intertextuality

The Gospel of Matthew begins as a book[4] that recounts the story of salvation.[5] Genealogies are stories of God's action in the lives of men and women, including their successes and failures. Like the genealogies of the book of Chronicles, Matthew also wants to point to God's salvific action in history realized in Jesus Christ.

The book of Matthew ends with the great commission (Mt 28:18–20), which points back to the beginning. Those who believe Jesus Christ to be the son of Abraham, υἱοῦ Ἀβραάμ, are part of the fulfillment of God's promises to the patriarch of Israel: "and in you all the families of the

---

[3] In order to try to balance the hermeneutical task and avoid this risk of polarization, some scholars propose a combination of methods while retaining a distinction between the methodological dimensions of hermeneutics. Udo Schnelle is one of the scholars according to who "not methodological purism of one form or another, but a convincing methodological plurality and the combination of methods prove how sensible" it is to interpret the Scriptures. Cf. Udo Schnelle, *Introdução à Exegese do Novo Testamento* (São Paulo: Loyola, 2004), 9. In this sense, Manfred Oeming distinguishes four dimensions of methodological hermeneutics: the text and its world, the author and their world, the reader and their world and the object [*Sache*] and its world. Cf. Oeming, ibid., 5–6.

[4] Βίβλος γενέσεως Ἰησοῦ Χριστοῦ υἱοῦ Δαυὶδ υἱοῦ Ἀβραάμ "An account of the genealogy of Jesus the Messiah, the son of David, the son of Abraham" (Mt 1:1).

[5] Cf. Rolf Walker, *Die Heilsgeschichte im ersten Evangelium* (Göttingen: Vandenhoeck & Ruprecht, 1967.)

earth shall be blessed" (Gen 12:3). With these words Matthew highlights that God's promise to Abraham is fully and solely fulfilled in Jesus Christ. In the Gospel of Matthew, the designation of Jesus as the son of Abraham invites the reader to remember that, in Jesus Christ, God fulfills God's mission among the nations. The one who follows Jesus Christ is a part of the families of the earth who are blessed by God. The disciple who makes disciples of all nations, teaching them the Word of God, becomes a blessing to the nations. By presenting Jesus as the son of David, υἱοῦ Δαυὶδ,[6] Matthew points to the centrality of God's Kingdom. Jesus Christ is the Messiah foretold by the prophets. Being the son of David, Jesus inaugurates the reality of God's Kingdom. His messianic ministry not only reaches his people, who are described as harassed and helpless sheep without a shepherd (Mt 9:36), but also the people of all nations, who are presented as people of great faith, who can believe because they eat the leftovers that fall from their master's table (Mt 15:27–28). Throughout the Gospel, Matthew presents Jesus as the teacher, who calls disciples to follow him, live with him and accept the new proposal for life. Jesus calls his disciples and his church, to share in his messianic ministry (Mt 10:1–11:1).

Several scholars believe it to be impossible to recognize a clear macrostructure in the Gospel of Matthew.[7] I do not intend to discuss this in any detail. Suffice it to point out that today there is a consensus in research on Jesus' five discourses throughout the gospel that are characterized as the central elements of the structure and text of Matthew. In addition to Jesus' discourses, also called sermons, we find the various narratives that basically follow the structure of Mark's Gospel.[8]

The structure of the Matthew's Gospel is an alternation between narration and sermon. Ricardo Foulkes presents the structure of Matthew extremely well, clearly demonstrating this alternation that can be presented in chiastic form.

---

[6] Cf. Georg Strecker, *Der Weg der Gerechtigkeit. Untersuchung zur Theologie des Matthäus* (Göttingen: Vandenhoeck & Ruprecht, 1962), 118–20.

[7] Udo Schnelle, *Einleitung in das Neue Testament*, 6.Aufl. [UTB1830] (Göttingen: Vandenhoeck-Ruprecht, 2007), 268; Ulrich Luz, *Das Evangelium nach Matthäus* [Mt 1-7] EKK I/1. (Zürich/ Braunschweig: Benzinger; Neukirchen-Vluyn: Neukirchner Verlag, 1985), 16–26.

[8] The structure of the Synoptic Gospels, which Matthew largely shares, can be divided as follows: a) history of the birth of Jesus; b) appearance of John the Baptist; c) Jesus' ministry in Galilee; d) Jesus' ministry in Jerusalem; e) History of Jesus' passion, death and resurrection.

1–4 Narrative of the birth of the Messiah, the beginning of the gospel
5–7 Sermon: Beatitudes, a condition of entry into the kingdom
8–9 Narration: authority of the Messiah, invitation to follow
10 Sermon: Mission's speech
11–12 Narration: rejection of this generation
13 Sermon: parables of the Kingdom
14–17 Narration: acceptance by the disciples
18 Sermon: speech to the community
19–22 Narration: authority of the Messiah, invitation to follow
23–25 Sermon: woes, entering into the kingdom
26–28 Narration: Messiah's death and resurrection

Taking the structure suggested by Foulkes into account, I have added the dimension of God's presence, which is here visible in the macrostructure of Matthew's text. At three crucial moments, mention is made of the presence of God through Jesus Christ: a) in Matthew 1:23, Jesus is designated as Emmanuel [God with us]: "Look, the virgin shall conceive and bear a son, and they shall name him Emmanuel," which means, "God is with us"; b) in Matthew 18:20, in the context of his speech on community, Jesus says: "For where two or three are gathered in my name, I am there among them"; c) and, in a special way, the presence of God is mentioned at the end of the gospel in the great commission in Matthew 28:18–20:

And Jesus came and said to them, "All authority in heaven and on earth has been given to me. Go therefore and make disciples of all nations, baptizing them in the name of the Father and of the Son and of the Holy Spirit, and teaching them to obey everything that I have commanded you. And remember, I am with you always, to the end of the age."[9]

Thus, we can clearly see that Matthew intends to show that God is present in Jesus Christ (Mt 1:23), through the church (Mt 18:20), and in the whole world (Mt 28.18-20).

The text of Matthew can be considered a great work of intertextuality,[10] because it is marked by a number of references to other books of the Bible.

---

[9] For Udo Schnelle Matthew 28:18–20 is the theological and hermeneutical key for an objective understanding of the entire work of the Gospel of Matthew. Cf. Schnelle, op. cit. (note 7), 272–73.
[10] On intertextuality, see Julia Kristeva, *Semiotike: Recherches pour une sémanalyse* (Paris: Seuil, coll. Tel. Quel., 1969); Julia Kristeva, *Die Revolution der Poetischen Sprache* (Frankfurt a.M.: Suhrkamp, 1992; James E. Porter, "Intertextuality and the Discourse Community," in *Rhetorick Review,* vol. 5, no. 1 (1986); Umberto Eco,

In Matthew we can clearly identify intertextual relationships with the Old Testament in the way in which the literary works intersect. The famous dictum, *sacra scriptura sui ipsius interpres* (sacred scripture interprets itself), dating back to the Reformation, is affirmed. Today, we can say that, not only Matthew, but the whole Bible is an intertextual book. Speaking of biblical hermeneutics therefore means pointing, among other things, to this internal interpretation of Scriptures. Both Matthew and Luther make us look to the Scriptures as an intertextual rather than a contextual book.

Matthean research has pointed to two forms of intertextuality. The first refers to the clear literary dependence on Mark's Gospel, which can be considered Matthew's main literary source. According to Ulrich Luz, "He also made use of the Sayings-Source or 'logia document' Q, a written-out but no longer extant collection of Jesus' sayings arranged in groups by topic together with a few stories."[11] Luz says that "in theological terms this means that he combined Jesus' ethical message about the kingdom of God with the story of God's action in Jesus. Thereby, this becomes the announcement of grace."[12]

The second form of intertextuality found in Matthew's Gospel is known in research as "fulfillment citations" (*Erfüllungszitate*),[13] corresponding to the following passages in Matthew: 1:22f; 2:15; 2:17f; 2:23; 4:14–16; 8:17; 12:17–21; 13:35; 21:4f; 27:9f; 27:35 *varia lectio*. Most often, the formulation of these passages points to the promise and fulfillment of Old Testament prophecies: "All this took place to fulfill what had been spoken by the Lord through the prophet" (Mt 1:22). Thus Matthew makes clear his understanding of the *Heilsgeschichte* (salvation history). There is considerable discussion around Matthew's use of the Old Testament. Despite the exegetical problems that arise from such discussion, all the Old Testament passages Matthew uses point to the manifestation of God's presence in the history of God's people.

THE CONTEXT: CONTEXTUALIZATION OF THE GOSPEL

Text out of context is always a pretext. This is one of the basic rules of exegetical methodology. How can we describe the context for which Matthew wrote

---

Die Grenzen der Interpretationen (München: Dtv, 1992); Umberto Eco, *Lector in fabula. Die Mitarbeit der Interpretation in erzählenden Texten* (München: Dtv, 1990).
[11] Ulrich Luz, *The Theology of the Gospel of Matthew* (Cambridge: Cambridge University, 1995), 6–10; Schnelle, op. cit. (note 7), 270–72.
[12] Luz, op. cit. (note 7), 26-27: "Theologisch heißt das: Er hat die ethische Verkündigung Jesu vom Gottesreich an die Geschichte von Gottes Handeln mit Jesus gebunden. Dadurch wird sie zur Verkündigung der Gnade."
[13] Cf. Strecker, op. cit. (note 6).

his Gospel? We will work on the generally agreed assumption that the Gospel of Matthew was written between the years 80 and 90 AD in the region of Syria (cf. Mt 4:24).[14] The context for which Matthew wrote was a troubled one. Feldmeier,[15] explaining the situation of the recipients of Matthew's Gospel, speaks of two threats. One refers to the external situation of the Matthean community and the other to the internal situation within the community. Like most early Christian communities, the life the Matthean community was marked by distress and difficulties. Social rejection and discrimination were part of daily life and Feldmeier also points to the Jewish threat around the Matthean community. He uses the term *Ausgrenzung* (limitation, exclusion, isolation). The more established the Christian community became, the more it lost its links to Judaism. With this schism arose the need theologically to rework the new identity and legitimacy for the Christian community of Jewish origin.[16]

But the Matthean community was also fraught with internal difficulties and Feldmeier highlights two internal problems that threatened the existence of the Matthean community. Matthew introduces the term "of little faith." Normally the New Testament differentiates between faith and disbelief, but Matthew distinguishes between little faith and faith. Feldmeier cites Matthew 14:28–31 where Peter is called a man of little faith when he cried out as he began to sink in the Sea of Galilee.[17] Feldmeier therefore concludes that the Matthean community had to fight on two fronts:[18] externally the church needed to legitimize its existence before a Judaism increasingly established and signed in the Torah. Internally, it needed to confront those who questioned the validity of the Torah and to affirm the Christian faith and life based on the teachings of the Torah. Matthew contextualizes the Scriptures into this troubled context.

The tradition: a contradiction of traditions?

Like any other evangelist, Matthew preserves a strong Jewish–Christian tradition while featuring a large opening to the church's universal mission

---

[14] Cf. Schnelle, op. cit. (note 7), 399. Reinhard Feldmeier, "Die synoptischen Evangelien," in Karl-Wilhelm Niebuhr (ed.), *Grundinformation Neues Testament* 3. Aufl. [UTB 2108] (Göttingen: Vandenhoeck & Ruprecht, 2008), 82–83; Pablo Richard, "Evangelho de Mateus: uma visão global e libertadora," in *RIBLA*, nº27 – v.2 (1997), 7 [159]–28 [180].

[15] Feldemeier, ibid., 85–88.

[16] Ibid., 86.

[17] Ibid., 87: "Der Jünger, der nicht mehr allein auf Jesu Wort vertraut, sondern vom Meister weg auf die anstürmenden Gefahren sieht, wird von Furcht übermannt und versinkt in den Fluten. Eben dieses Verhalten wird hier von Jesus als 'Kleinglaube' getadelt."

[18] Ibid., 88.

to all nations. Are these two positions in contradiction? How can the two be related to each other?

For Gunneweg, Matthew clearly shows that the new salvation in Christ was already announced in the Old Testament. He unfolds the prophetic evidence and reflects on it theologically. The fulfillment citations in the Gospel of Matthew are the expression of a systematic attempt to present the Christ event as a whole, in all its details, as the fulfillment of Old Testament prophecy and Scripture in general.

Besides a focus on the Jewish nation, Matthew also has a strong openness toward the mission among the nations. The church of Jesus is to be the salt of the earth and light of the world (Mt 5:13-16). The disciple must do mission because this is the essence of the church. This church is not the Kingdom of God here on earth, but must live discipleship that produces fruits of righteousness. That means reaching other nations. It is curious that Jesus called Peter the man of little faith (Mt 14) soon after having told the Syrophoenician woman, "Woman, great is your faith!" (Mt 15). Like Paul, Matthew legitimizes mission among people without minimizing the value of the Torah. Therefore, there is no a contradiction of traditions. For Udo Schnelle[19] it is clear that the Torah, which is at the center of Jewish tradition, does not stand alone in contradiction to Jesus. Rather, Jesus is presented by Matthew as one who teaches the Torah. This is the hermeneutical key to understand the Christian in Matthew, both the Christian of Jewish origin (Mt 5-7), and that of other nations (Mt 28:20).

THE IMPLICATIONS OF READING MATTHEW

I would like to point to what the reading of Matthew implies in terms of our our own contexts. I shall begin with my own context, Brazil.

What can we learn from the Matthean community and the way in which the Gospel of Matthew emerged? For my Brazilian context the Gospel of Matthew is more than relevant. Our difficulties are comparable to those facing the Matthean community, both externally and internally. I shall briefly refer to some parallels between Matthew's and my own Brazilian context.

Externally: even in such a highly religious country as Brazil, which almost daily produces new churches and religions,[20] the legitimacy and existence of the church in general and, specifically, the Lutheran church are being questioned. The Lutheran church in Brazil is a minority church

---

[19] Schnelle, op. cit. (note 7), 429-30.
[20] Cf. José Arilson Xavier de Souza, *Religião: Um tema cultural de interesse geográfico. Revista da casa da geografia de Sobral*, v.12, nº1, 69-80 (2010), at **www.uvanet.br**.

and as such it has to reinvent itself time and again. It is aware that it cannot win the religious competition, but does not let itself to be deceived. Matthew's words that Jesus Christ is present when two or three are gathered in his name motivate Lutherans in Brazil not to be discouraged from God's mission and task. To read that the Kingdom of God is like a mustard seed challenges Lutherans time and again when they look for small signs through evangelism, diakonia, koinonia and celebration in community in Brazil.

Internally: men and women of little faith are part of the church in general. Jesus criticizes his disciples for having little faith. In Brazil, as all over the world, practical atheism is a growing phenomenon. Practical atheists claim to be Christians but live their lives as if God did not exist. Some people do not necessarily remain members of their churches of origin and there is considerable migration between the churches. This migration, in my view, is the result of the absence of biblical and theological education in the communities as well as a crisis of confessional identity. The new generation of Lutherans needs to understand what being Lutheran·implies in this present context. Furthermore, contempt for the law, which is equal to sin, seems to be growing and it appears to be politically incorrect to speak of sin in the church. The validity and relevance of the Scriptures is questioned not only within but also outside the church. What seems generally to determine hermeneutics in contemporary Brazil is not the Scripture but the context. We learn from Matthew and Luther that context does not determine the action of God and the church in the world since the gospel is God's action in this world and in the church. If the context becomes normative then the text of Scripture ceases to be the norm. In Brazil, there seems to be a conflict between text and context. The hermeneutical circle seems to be a circle rather than a square.

The problem does not lie in the reading and contextualization of Matthew or the lack thereof. In communities of the Evangelical Church Lutheran Confession in Brazil (IECLB), the pastors who follow the texts provided in the common lectionary for 2013–2014, preached twenty-three texts on the gospel of Matthew. The problem in Brazil is that neither the Old Testament, nor the law or the prophets are being read. In Brazil, I see two phenomena in relation to the use of the Old Testament. On the one hand, there is what I have called neo-Marcionism (a rejection of the Old Testament as promulgated by Marcion, a second-century theologian considered heretic by the mainstream church). Interestingly this has occurred in the historic churches, including the Lutheran church, where the Old Testament remains more or less only a part of the content for Sunday school or biblical stories during children's services. On the other, neo-Pentecostalism spiritualizes and completely debases the Old Testament. A good example is the opening of the Solomon's temple of the Universal Church of the Kingdom of God in São Paulo, which can seat 10 000 people. Its bishop, Edir Macedo, is considered the "high priest" of this church. How can we speak of the kingdom of God in Brazil, if one of the biggest internal threats to the church is a church itself? It looks as if churches, such as the Universal Kingdom of God which, in complete contrast to Luther's theology of the cross, proclaim a theology of prosperity, define how the Kingdom of God is defined in Brazil today.

I am convinced that even though people come from different contexts the issues that affect them are comparable. It would be beneficial to speak from a global perspective, especially on those issues that affect all Christians and pertain to building the communion. What would such a global reading look like?

In this respect, the statement made by the Second LWF International Hermeneutics Conference on the Psalms is very helpful:

> As Christian readers of the Bible we affirm that God speaks to us through the Holy Scripture. The process of understanding a biblical text reaches its goal, when the text becomes effective in the lives of the reader and listener.[21]

This same assumption should be applied in relation to the Gospel of Matthew and guide our reading of Matthew because "the Lutheran hermeneutics proceeds from reading, listening and understanding and aim toward the verification of the biblical texts in daily life" and "Lutheran hermeneutics speak prophetically for the transformation of the self and the world."[22]

How can we read the Gospel of Matthew today? I think Matthew and Luther have many things in common. I would like to highlight some of them and propose some ways for reading the Gospel of Matthew today with Matthew and with Luther.

Read Matthew and the Bible as a whole: Matthew and Luther reveal a deep knowledge of the Scriptures.[23] Matthew stands out among the evangelists in his affirmation of what the law and the prophets said. As we know, the Reformation was, above all, about interpreting Scripture. Luther calls his lectures *lectura in Biblia*. Ulrich Luz writes that "the Gospel of Matthew invites reading from beginning to end."[24]

Read Matthew with the Old Testament: Matthew and Luther held the Old Testament in high regard. While for Matthew this was obvious, because

---

[21] At **www.lutheranworld.org/content/resource-summary-statement-second-hermeneutics-conference-psalms**.

[22] Ibid.

[23] Of course we must make a distinction here. For Matthew the Scriptures referred only to the Old Testament. For Luther, the term refers to the two Testaments of the Christian tradition.

[24] Luz, op. cit. (note 7), 2.

the Old Testament was his Scripture, this has not always been so obvious throughout the history of the church. However, with the Reformation one thing became quite clear: Judaism can exist without the New Testament, but Christianity cannot exist without the Old Testament.

Read Matthew as a dialectical book of the Kingdom of God: Matthew and Luther point to the centrality of the Kingdom of God, both in the worldly and the eschatological dimension. This aspect is of fundamental importance and a major challenge today when it comes to what I call the polarization around the eschatological Kingdom of God. For Matthew and Luther, the Kingdom of God comes from God. Jesus Christ is the promised Messiah and the one who has all authority in heaven and on earth. Therefore, the Kingdom of God is not realized with the church that is only the instrument of God's universal mission. However, the church of Jesus Christ has the privilege of being called by God to manifest the signs of God's Kingdom in this world. The kingdom of God is not some political or economic ideology which can be associated with one political movement or another. It is something that draws near wherever God's reign is experienced in faith—it is already here but also still on its way. This dialectical reading of the Kingdom of God is present in Matthew and Luther.

Read Matthew as a Christological interpretation of Scripture: Matthew and Luther share a common hermeneutical assumption regarding the Christological center in the interpretation of Scripture. At this point, both present a challenge to modern exegesis since they do not have the same modern assumptions informing contemporary interpretation of the Scriptures. However, a Christological reading of the Scriptures is not exclusive. In this sense, I refer to the statement by the Second International Hermeneutics Conference that reads:

> Lutheran readings include Christological interpretation of the Psalms. A Christological reading of the Psalms means to understand more deeply who Christ is for us today in light of the Psalms and the New Testament. In this we share the experience of Martin Luther, for whom the Psalms deepened and extended his understanding of Jesus Christ. Jesus Christ is the symbol of the human condition in the presence of God, which we share and agree on; hence we read the Psalms in light of Christ rather than simply looking for references to Christ.

And

> The characteristics of Luther's way of interpreting the Psalms was first to insist on the historical meaning of the texts; second, that all biblical texts refer to Christ; and third, that the first interpretation of the Psalms is the difference of

the killing letter and the life-giving spirit (cf. 2 Cor 3). The killing letter is not inspired by the life-giving spirit. For Luther, "the life giving power is the spirit of the biblical texts that is the divine spirit."[25]:

This view is also applicable to Matthew. We need to read the Gospel of Matthew as he wants it to be read. Luther's Christological hermeneutics was neither novel nor original. Already during the Middle Ages there had been a Christological interpretation of Scripture. The difference is that at the time it had pointed to a theology of glory while Luther's interpretation points to the theology of the cross.

Read Matthew as a didactic book: Matthew and Luther are essentially didactic in their approach. Both Matthew's exegesis and Luther research exhibit a strong teaching potential. Matthew presents Jesus as master and allows us to recognize his teaching competence.[26] Luther follows in Jesus' footsteps, showing the pedagogical nature of the church in the world.

Read Matthew as a book of the church: Matthew and Luther interpret Scripture for the church. In today's exegesis the ecclesiological character of Matthew's Gospel is undisputed. The Word of God is always *extra nos* (out of us), *contra nos* (against us) and *pro nos* (for us).

Read Matthew as a book of transformation: Matthew and Luther see the gospel's transforming power in the world. They show us what it means to be rooted in the Word and engaged in the world.

READING MATTHEW AS A BOOK OF THE PRESENCE OF GOD IN JESUS CHRIST

As has been mentioned above, the presence of God is one of the central themes of both Matthew's and Luther's theology.[27] The author of the Gospel of Matthew points to the centrality of God's presence. He writes in a context marked by difficulties and conflicts prompting the question of where God is. For this, the author reinterprets the tradition in which he lives. It is the perspective of God's presence, evident in the structure and message

---

[25] Op. cit. (note 21).

[26] Schnelle, op. cit. (note 7). 429.

[27] See David D. Kupp, *Matthews's Emmanuel Divine Presence and God's People in the First Gospel* (Cambridge: Cambridge University Press, 1996).

of the Gospel of Matthew, which will make a difference in the mission of the church as it faces the challenges of today's world.

Here I would like to mention briefly some texts from the Gospel of Matthew, in which we can clearly note the centrality of God's presence in the Gospel and then look at its implications for the contemporary context:

- Jesus Christ is the Emmanuel, the Messiah, God with us (Mt 1).

- The magi, representatives of wisdom in the world, bow before the scandal of the manger. The *Deus absconditus* is not only on the cross, but also in the manger. In the poverty of the manger, God reveals Godself to us (Mt 2).

- In the Sermon on the Mount (Mt 5–7), living according to the Torah implies living *coram Deo* (before God). This involves knowing what foundation the disciple builds on.

- Jesus calms two storms. In Matthew 8:23–27, he is asleep inside the boat. In Matthew 14, Jesus left the disciples to go alone to the other side of the Sea of Galilee because he wanted to pray. The little faith of the disciples is the result of experience with the *Deus absconditus* that turns into admiration before the power of the *Deus revelatus*.

- Soon after preaching his sermon on mission (Mt 10), Jesus sends the disciples and accompanies them to their cities (Mt 11:1). The ministry of the church can count on the presence of the Lord of the church.

- Matthew defines the missionary ministry of the church as the ministry of the Good Shepherd. This becomes evident in Matthew 9:35–38 and Matthew 18:10–14. In Matthew 11:1, Jesus not only sends his disciples, but also goes along with them.

- The parables of the kingdom (Mt 13) make it clear that this kingdom is absconditus (the kingdom is hidden). We recognize the presence of God in the fruits of this kingdom. We can only see the signs of God's Kingdom.

- The presence of God is evident among the Gentiles with the Jesus' tour into the Syrophoenician region (Mt 15). The great faith lies with the Gentiles. This can be seen with the woman of Canaan.

- In his transfiguration, Jesus himself experienced the presence of God, confirming his saving plan on behalf of God's people and humanity (Mt 17).

- In the daily life of Jesus' community God is present, even if there are only two or three people gathered. It is the invocation of God's presence through the name of Jesus Christ, which guarantees God's presence in the church in this world (Mt 18).

- In his prophetic sermon (Mt 24-25), Jesus makes clear who is in control of history (see Rev 4-5). Even in a world marked by disaster and injustice he has the last word.

- While Jesus experienced the Deus absconditus on the cross, saying, "*Eli, Eli, lama sabachthani?*" and after experiencing his own death, the curtain hanging in the Temple was torn in two from top to bottom, revealing the throne of the *Deus revelatus* (Mt 27).

- Finally, as the resurrected, Jesus promised to be present in the world for whose salvation he died. He sent his disciples to teach all that he had commanded (his sermons) and all the great saving acts of God (narratives). Thus Matthew ends his Gospel as he began, with the genealogy, now no longer the people of Israel, but of disciples who make the new people of God.

In a world where some people say that God is nowhere there is the voice of the Gospel of Matthew that tells us that God is now here. Therefore, *tolle lege,* take up and read.

Sermon on the Mount

How Do We Deal with a Challenging Text?

Bernd Oberdorfer

What does taking the Bible "literally" mean?

We are accustomed to emphasize the *sola scriptura* as a crucial indicator of our Lutheran identity and gladly repeat Luther's critique of the medieval hermeneutics of the "fourfold meaning of the Scripture" and his insistence on the "literal sense" as the only reliable method to unfold the "real" meaning of the holy words. In our discussions, we therefore take it for granted to remain on the safe side by referring to the Bible as "so it has been written" (Mt 2:5).

Yet, what in general terms appears to be simple is rather complicated when we get more specific, such as when it comes to interpreting particular phrases, chapters or books of the Bible. Certainly, Luther's intentions are quite clear: He wanted to prevent that the Bible is read arbitrarily. He wanted to give the Bible the chance to speak for itself, as it were, not to be forced to fit into a framework of human categories. He wanted interpretation to be *exegesis*, not *eis-egesis*. For example, in the debates on the Holy Supper, he accused Zwingli of obscuring the clear sense of the biblical *est* by introducing rational reflections on whether or not it is possible for Christ to be present in the holy bread and wine and altering that clear sense by claiming that *est* means "signifies" instead of simply maintaining "is." However, apart from the fact that also Zwingli sought to discover the real meaning of Christ's words, it is evident that Luther's insistence on the "is" was also an interpretation and thus implied presuppositions that were not simpy "in" the text.

It is clear that Luther's understanding of the "literal sense" differs significantly from what most of us intuitively think of as the "literal sense."

For example, Luther claimed that, taken literally, the Psalms were Christ's prayer book. It is well known that Luther concentrated on the "literal sense" of the Bible on the correspondence of Christ and faith. According to the famous formula *"Was Christum treibet"* (what promotes Christ's cause) the real sense of the Bible is to evoke the faith in Christ or, more precisely, faith in being justified by God for Christ's sake through faith alone. To Luther, this is the criterion for evaluating biblical texts and qualifying them if they contradict justification by faith alone. For Luther, taking the Bible "literally," therefore means something other than receiving every single phrase as the Word of God. Therefore, even if interpretation means *ex-egesis* of a God-given meaning rather than *eis-egesis* of human concepts, it implies and requires human activity: the activity of understanding.

From a systematic perspective, Luther's insistence on the *"Was Christum treibet"* reminds us of the crucial fact that a biblical text is not adequately understood unless it is integrated into a coherent theological framework, one that is deeply influenced by basic religious convictions and theological traditions. There is, however, also a second determinant of understanding to be reckoned with which I shall call "cultural plausibility" (*lebensweltliche Plausibilität*). In other words, a biblical word must be plausible in a pragmatic sense. It must be able to give a realistic orientation in life and therefore not contradict basic convictions of life and reality or basic norms and standards of morality. Or, more exactly, a biblical word can actually transform basic convictions of life and reality or basic norms and standards of morality, but these transformed convictions and norms must, in a pragmatic sense, be plausible themselves.

In light of these factors, the Sermon on the Mount in Matthew 5–7 is a particular challenge for interpreters, especially Lutheran interpreters.

The Sermon on the Mount: a challenge for Lutheran hermeneutics

First, Christ's radical demands have always both fascinated and challenged. While, time and again evoking the impression that they give a clear and convincing picture of how life should be, they also lead us to ask, How, if at all, can they be complied with? And, apart from these pragmatic questions, we could pose the more profound question of whether we should actually wish that these demands were obeyed and complied with? Is it, for instance, responsible behavior in every case to "turn the other cheek" instead of striking back? Could there not be situations where this might lead to "not being of assistance to a person in danger"? Would this not contradict basic Christian charity?

Second, especially for Lutherans, the Sermon on the Mount raises an additional hermeneutical problem: If, according to Lutheran theology, the core message of the gospel is justification by faith alone, how should we deal with the fact that Jesus in the Sermon on the Mount presents himself as a legislator and even sharpens the laws and commandments of the Ancient Covenant? Even the "do not worry" (Mt 6:25–34) is an imperative. Yet, was it not Luther's basic theological insight that Christ does not encounter us as a legislator and judge but, rather, a redeemer; not as a demander but a giver?

Third, the Sermon on the Mount seems to indicate an intrinsic contradiction in the Bible itself. Whereas Paul emphatically calls Christ "the end of the law" (Rom 10:4), in Matthew Jesus insists that he has "come not to abolish but to fulfill [the law]" (Mt 5:17) and announces that "until heaven and earth pass away, not one letter, not one stroke of a letter, will pass from the law until all is accomplished" (Mt 5:18).

Thus, we have to face at least a threefold tension:

• Between Jesus' radical commandments and our moral responsibility

• Between Jesus as legislator and as redeemer

• Between Matthew and Paul.

These questions are not introduced into the text from outside but emerge in the process of reading and understanding the text itself. Thus, they cannot be ignored in the name of a seemingly "literal understanding." The challenge is to develop a coherent interpretation that reflects the inner-biblical tensions as well as the theological framework and the cultural plausibility.

How does Luther deal with this challenge? How does he interpret the Sermon on the Mount?

LUTHER ON THE SERMON ON THE MOUNT

I will start with some general hermeneutical reflections and then focus on a series of Luther's sermons on the Sermon on the Mount which was published in 1532.

A LUTHERAN INTERPRETATION OF THE SERMON ON THE MOUNT? PRELIMINARY REMARKS

Luther research concurs that Luther was confronted with two ways of interpreting the Sermon on the Mount, which he both strongly rejected.

On the one hand, the medieval tradition which understood Christ's radical commandments as *consilia evangelica,* relevant only to a monastic élite of "perfect Christians," whereas "normal" Christians were simply obliged to respect the norms of the Decalogue. On the other, the so-called *Schwärmer,* left-wing reformers, who claimed that the Sermon on the Mount was the binding norm for the life of a Christian community and therefore abstained from social life, rejected state authority and disregarded the economy, etc. According to Luther, the "monastic way" was wrong to restrict the commitment of the Sermon to a small number of Christians, ignoring that there is no "two-class Christianity." The left-wing reformers were wrong to expand the Sermon's validity to becoming a binding rule for every aspect of Christians' social behavior and ignoring the fact that we still live in an unredeemed world with the need to safeguard social security by means of politics and the police. In theological terms, the first contradicted the idea of the basic equality of all Christians grounded on baptism, the latter missed the elementary distinction of the two realms.

Thus, *via negationis* (by way of negation), we can get a preliminary idea of how Luther himself would interpret the Sermon: Luther would emphasize that Christ addressed all Christians without exception, and would insist that Christ did not want to exempt Christians from the duties of social life, including the enforcement of law and order.

But this seems to lead to contradictions. While Christ's commandment to abstain from revenge and violence and to "turn the other cheek" to the violent evildoer applies to every Christian, it is not supposed to prevent Christians from stopping evildoers, if necessary by using violence.

We are all familiar with the instruments Lutherans have developed to overcome this dilemma. First, we could refer to the doctrine of law and gospel and presume that Luther interprets the Sermon on the Mount within the horizon of the *usus theologicus* or *usus elenchticus,* a Reformation concept that suggests that ethical imperatives serve to emphasize the need for grace. This means that the law functions primarily to reveal to us that we have not complied with it. In the mirror of the law we recognize ourselves as sinners. One could conclude that, in the Sermon on the Mount, Jesus radicalized the law so that we are sensitive to our subtle sins: even if we are not guilty of explicit adultery for instance, we cannot proudly absolve ourselves of having disregarded God's commandment to beware of adultery. We cannot save ourselves by fulfilling God's law; we are in need of being saved by Christ. So, indeed, the Sermon on the Mount would be valid for all Christians, but only in a negative sense: proof of that, as Paul puts it, is that "all have sinned and fall short of the glory of God" (Rom 3:23). This apparently is the classical "Lutheran way." Yet, as we will see, surprisingly enough, Luther, in his interpretation of the Sermon on the Mount, uses this argument very cautiously. For Luther, the commandments of the Sermon actually have a positive function for the orientation of Christian life.

But, if so, then the only consistent way of dealing with the Sermon seems to be the puritanical, pacifist option of the left-wing reformers: no state, no violence, no compromise with the "world." This, however, was not the Lutheran way. This leads us to Lutheran theology's second tool to deal with the dilemma mentioned above: the doctrine of the two realms, the realm of faith and the realm of the world. According to this doctrine, Christians are citizens of both realms (both are realms of God). As individuals, Christians are citizens of the realm of faith: trusting that God has liberated them by grace and thus given them everything that they need both for their temporal and eternal existence. They no longer have to care for themselves, can refrain from striking back, answer hate with love, share with the poor, etc. As social beings, members of society, however, Christians are citizens of the realm of the world and have the duty to commit themselves to defend the neighbor against aggression, to participate in public administration and to fulfill public functions as judges, council members, military officers, etc. All this includes the willingness to use violence. From this perspective, the Sermon on the Mount only addresses the citizens of the realm of faith, but does not apply to the citizens of the realm of the world.

In his interpretation of the Sermon, Luther repeatedly draws on this argument. He emphatically claims that in this Sermon Jesus did not want to tell the disciples how to rule a state or run a business and is convinced that Jesus's demand to "turn the other cheek," did not exclude the use of violence in order to defend executing a public function. In his opinion, using the Sermon in order to promote pacifism constitutes an abuse.

According to Luther, the Sermon is addressed to every Christian, but only insofar as they are individuals, i.e., a citizen of the realm of faith.

While this interpretation is consistent it is obviously also ambiguous and might easily be misread. If, for instance, the Sermon does not serve as a moral blueprint for social life, does it then have any use with respect to moral discernment? What does it mean that the Sermon addresses the Christian as an individual? Does it only refer to the private sphere? What are the limits of this private sphere? The individual's body and soul? Their family? Their non-professional lives (friendship, leisure, hobbies)? One's behavior in this sphere obviously has implications for social life. For instance, if one lends someone money and does not ask for it back then this could affect the family. The same goes for not defending oneself. It is therefore hardly possible to draw a strict line between the individual sphere, in Luther's words of the *Christperson* (Christian person), and the social sphere, the *Weltperson* (worldly person). Therefore, an alternative interpretation would be to define the realm of faith as a general intrinsic habitus of selflessness that shapes and orientates the individual's private life as well as their social life. Then, again, it is difficult to imagine what the impact of the habitus of loving one's enemy might be on the behavior of a judge, political leader, soldier, CEO of a company, etc. Might not the many critics of Lutheranism be right who claim that the Lutheran doctrine of the two realms restricts the impact of faith on the individual's inner life (*Innerlichkeit*) and has no relevance for social life, thus isolating faith from life? If this were true, the Sermon on the Mount would lack any ethical significance. To answer this question, we have to scrutinize Luther's way of dealing with this challenging text.

Luther's exegesis of the Sermon on the Mount

It is helpful that we have a comprehensive exegesis of the Sermon on the Mount by Luther himself. In 1532, Luther published a series of sermons in which he continuously interpreted the full text of Matthew 5-7.[1] Luther regularly preached these sermons on Wednesdays while he stood in for the Wittenberg pastor Johannes Bugenhagen during his absence from November 1530 to April 1532. There is no original manuscript as such; the publication results from the notes of a listener (Georg Rörer). For the book version, however, Luther added a preface in which he declared that he was "very happy to see the publication."[2] These "three chapters of St. Matthew which St. Augustine calls 'The Lord's Sermon on the Mount' [are] such common sayings and texts that are used so often throughout Christendom."[3] Therefore Luther wishes that "the true, sure, and Christian understanding of this teaching of Christ" be "preserve[d],"[4] which he is quite confident to deliver in these sermons. According to Luther, to promote this truth is particularly important because "through his apostles the wicked devil has managed so cleverly to twist and pervert especially the fifth chapter, making it teach the exact opposite of what it means."[5]

How does the devil manage this? And who are his "apostles"? On the one hand, "the vulgar pigs and asses, the jurists and sophists, the right hand of that jackass of a pope and of his mamelukes"[6] have claimed that Matthew 5 does not apply to all Christians but serves "merely as advice to those who want to become perfect."[7] Because, therefore, the twelve "evangelical counsels" are

---

[1] Martin Luther, "Das fünffte, Sechste und Siebend Capitel S. Matthei geprediget und ausgelegt (Wittenberg 1532)," in *WA* 32, 299-544.
[2] *WA* 32, 299. Jaroslav Pelikan (ed.), *Luther's Works*, vol. 21 (Saint Louis: Concordia Publishing House, 1956), 3.
[3] Ibid.
[4] Ibid.
[5] Ibid.
[6] Ibid.
[7] *WA* 32, 300; *LW* 21, 4.

not compulsory for the vast majority of Christians, Luther concludes: "I call that forbidding true and fine good works—which is what these vulgar asses and blasphemers accuse us of doing."[8] And he regards himself as a defender of Christ's word—that not a single dot and iota of God's law shall be altered or qualified until it is all fulfilled. On the other hand, "the new jurists and sophists, the schismatic spirits (*Rottengeister*) and Anabaptists"[9] refer to Matthew 5 when teaching "that it is wrong to own private property, to swear, to hold office as a ruler or judge, to protect or defend oneself, to stay with wife and children."[10] By puzzling them (as well as the Catholics), the devil manages "that they do not recognize any difference between the secular and the divine realm, much less what should be the distinctive doctrine and action in each realm."[11] And Luther proudly adds that "[t]hank God, we can boast that in these sermons we have clearly and diligently shown and emphasized this (difference)."[12]

These words give a precise idea of Luther's hermeneutical perspective on reading the Sermon on the Mount. According to Luther, Jesus aims to show what to teach and to do ("doctrine and action"), but we will only understand this adequately if we respect the difference between the two realms.

Since I cannot give a full picture of Luther's exegesis in this essay I shall focus on some characteristic examples of how Luther deals with the text. I shall concentrate of his reading of Matthew 5, which he highlighted as the most relevant chapter in Matthew.

MATTHEW—NOT JOHN AND PAUL

It is interesting to see that Luther clearly distinguishes between the different biblical books; they vary in character and emphasis and focus on different aspects of God's revelation and not every book gives a comprehensive picture of the Christian doctrine as a whole. Luther reflects on the specific character of Matthew by commenting on Matthew 5:16 "let your light shine before others, so that they may see your good works and give glory to your Father in heaven." Obviously this emphasis on "good works" is a challenge. Luther comments that this statement:

> is in accordance with St. Matthew's way of speaking; he usually talks this way about works. Neither in his Gospel nor in those of the other two evangelists, Mark and Luke,

---

[8] Ibid.
[9] *WA* 32, 300; *LW* 21, 5.
[10] *WA* 32, 301; *LW* 21, 5.
[11] Ibid.
[12] Ibid.

> do we find such a great emphasis upon the profound doctrine of Christ as we do in St. John and St. Paul; instead, we find them talking and exhorting about good works.[13]

And Luther adds:

> Of course, it is appropriate that in Christendom both should be preached, yet each in keeping with its nature and value. First and highest is the proclamation about faith and Christ, then comes the emphasis upon works.[14]

He continues:

> The evangelist John discussed the chief article thoroughly and powerfully, and hence he is properly regarded as the highest and foremost evangelist. For this reason, Matthew, Luke, and Mark considered and emphasized the other issue, to make sure that it was not forgotten. On this issue, then, they are better than John while he is better than they on the other one.[15]

However, the two aspects must not be isolated from each other. Luther insists: The "statements and instructions about works" must "always be connect(ed) [...] with faith" and be "incorporate(d) (*verleibet*) [...] in it, making them a result and a concomitant of faith,[16] praised and called 'good' for its sake."[17] Luther argues thus in order not to understand the "good works" of Matthew 5:16 as "the sort of faith-less works that the good works of our clergy have been until now, but [...] the sort of works that faith performs and that are impossible apart from faith."[18] Luther even claims that Jesus speaking of good works here refers to the "exercise, expression, and confession of the teaching about Christ and faith, and the suffering for its sake."[19] The acts of confessing the faith, according to Luther, are the "light" Christians "shine with before the people." From these "first and foremost" works then follow the "'works of love' which shine, too, but only insofar as they are ignited and sustained by faith."[20]

With this interpretation, Luther respects the specific character of St Matthew, but relates Matthew's emphasis on good works to what he calls the "chief article": the faith. Yet, it is important to see that he does not do

---

[13] *WA* 32, 352; *LW* 21, 65.

[14] *WA* 32, 352–53; *LW* 21, 65.

[15] *WA* 32, 353; *LW* 21, 65.

[16] "[...] *aus dem glauben und jnn den glauben gehen*," "go from the faith into the faith"–quite certainly an allusion to Romans 1:17.

[17] *WA* 32, 353; *LW* 21, 65.

[18] Ibid.

[19] Ibid.

[20] *WA* 32, 353; *LW* 21, 66.

that without reference to the concrete text: not the good works as such but, rather, the faith, which becomes visible within and through them, is the "light" that "shines before the people."

THE BEATITUDES

From a Lutheran perspective, we might expect that Luther reads the Beatitudes (Matthew 5:3–11) as an introduction which frames Christ's sharp words on the law with words of grace and benedictions: God gives, before he demands; the "indicative" of the gospel prevails over the "imperative" of the law. Or we would expect him to emphasize the spiritual dimension of the Beatitudes, stressing, for example, the "poor in spirit" of Matthew 5:3 or interpreting the "hunger and thirst for righteousness" of Matthew 5:6 as an expression of justification by faith.

Surprisingly, this is only partly true. Of course, Luther emphasizes that Jesus begins with the promise of the "kingdom of heaven." He comments on Matthew 5:3:

> This is a fine, sweet, and friendly beginning for His instruction and preaching. He does not come like Moses or a teacher of the Law, with demands, threats, and terrors, but in a very friendly way, with enticements, allurements, and pleasant promises." [21]

And Luther claims that Jesus strictly contradicts the Jews, because "the essence of their teaching was this: 'If a man is successful here on earth, he is blessed and well off'."[22] According to Luther, this ideology of prosperity is also supported by the "Turks."[23] and "the whole papacy."[24] So it was necessary that in the beginning Jesus turned the disciples' minds away from "mammon" and to the "kingdom of heaven." Yet, he declines that all Christians have to be poor and "none of them (dare) have money, property, popularity, power, and the like."[25] A worldly authority cannot do without these worldly goods, and to have them is "not wrong in itself" but rather "God's gift and ordinance."[26] And, conversely, "physical poverty is not the answer (*leiblich arm sein thuts nicht*),"[27] because there is "many a beggar

---

[21] *WA* 32, 305; *LW* 21, 10.
[22] *WA* 32, 305; *LW* 21, 11.
[23] *WA* 32, 306; *LW* 21, 11.
[24] *WA* 32, 306; *LW* 21, 12.
[25] *WA* 32, 307; *LW* 21, 12.
[26] Ibid.
[27] Ibid.

[...] more arrogant and wicked than any rich man."[28] So, in God's view, it is not decisive whether we are rich or poor. Rather "before God, in his heart, everyone must be spiritually poor. That is, he must not set his confidence, comfort, and trust (*Trotz*) on temporal goods, nor hang his heart upon them and make Mammon his idol."[29]

But, in his interpretation of Matthew 5:5 ("Blessed are the meek, for they will inherit the earth"), Luther emphasizes that this verse is complementary to the word of being "spiritually poor," because it entails "a promise about this *temporal* life and about possessions *here on earth*."[30] However, Luther asks, "how does being poor harmonize with inheriting the land?"[31] He argues that "inheriting the land" does not mean that everyone is promised a parcel of land ("otherwise God would have to create more worlds"[32]) but, rather, that "God confers possessions upon everyone in such a way that He gives a man wife, children, cattle, house, and home, and whatever pertains to these, so that he can stay on the land where he lives."[33] Luther comments that because these earthly goods are gifts of God, Christ not simply blessed "the poor," but the "spiritually poor," in order to show that the promise to "inherit the earth" does not contradict the blessing of the "poor."[34]

But why are the "meek" promised to "inherit the earth"? Luther hurries to explain, "that Christ is not speaking at all (here) about the government (*Obrigkeit*) and its work (*Amt*)."[35] Because it is the government's work "to bear the sword [...] for the punishment of those who do wrong [...], and to wreak a vengeance and a wrath that are called the vengeance and wrath of God."[36] According to Luther, Christ is here "only talking about how individuals (*einzele personen ... fur sich*) are to live in relation to others, apart from official position and authority."[37] As is well known, Luther distinguishes office (*Amt*) and person. In this sermon, he maintains that "we have two different persons in one man":[38] in the one person,

> we are created and born, according to which we are all alike [...] But once we
> are born, God adorns and dresses you up as another person. He makes you a

---

[28] *WA* 32, 307; *LW* 21, 13.
[29] Ibid.
[30] *WA* 32, 315; *LW* 21, 22, author's own emphasis.
[31] Ibid.
[32] Ibid.
[33] Ibid.
[34] Cf. *WA* 32, 316; *LW* 21, 22.
[35] *WA* 32, 316; *LW* 21, 23.
[36] Ibid.
[37] Ibid.
[38] Ibid.

child and me a father, one a master and another a servant, one a prince and another a citizen.[39]

This second person, Luther continues, "is called a divine person," because it "holds a divine office."[40]

The demand to be "meek" does not apply to this public person, because as public persons we have to adapt to the rules of the institutions we play a role in and are not allowed "meekly" to abstain from executing our duty if this requires to be hard and to use physical power. So, Christ's word seems to be irrelevant in terms of our public roles. However, Luther warns us not to confuse the two persons: not only to avoid mixing the moral categories of private life into the ethos of the public person, but also the other way round, to abstain from introducing the instruments of power, which are legitimate in the public sphere, into the ethos of the private person.[41] Thus, indirectly, Christ's demand to be "meek" also has an impact on the public person in so far as strictly limiting the use of power to the requirements of the respective public role. In other words: the individual is called to give space to their private person by not letting the habitus of the public person dominate their lives as a whole.

In this context, it is interesting to see how Luther tackles Matthew 5:9: "Blessed are the peacemakers, for they shall be called the children of God."[42] Because of Luther's well-known notorious words in the Peasant Wars—he encouraged the authorities to use the sword against the peasants claiming they would use "God's sword"—we might expect him to spiritualize the demand to "make peace." But he does not. From the beginning, he emphasizes,

the Lord here honors those who do their best to try to make peace, not only in their own lives but also among other people, who try to settle ugly and involved issues, who endure squabbling and try to avoid and prevent war and bloodshed. [43]

"Blessed are the peacemakers," that means,

anyone who claims to be a Christian and a child of God, not only does not start war or unrest; but he also gives help and counsel on the side of peace wherever he can, even though there may have been a just and adequate cause for going

---

[39] Ibid.
[40] Ibid.
[41] Cf. *WA* 32, 316f; *LW* 21, 23.
[42] *WA 32,* 330–334; *LW* 21, 39–44.
[43] *WA* 32, 330; *LW* 21, 39.

> to war. It is sad enough if one has tried everything and nothing helps, and then he has to defend himself, to protect his land and people.[44]

Luther harshly criticizes "quarrelsome young noblemen who immediately draw and unsheathe their sword on account of one word."[45] They should not be called "'Christians' but 'children of the devil'."[46] He emphatically demands that every Christian who is "the victim of injustice and violence," does "not immediately start getting even and hitting back," but "to think it over, try to bear it and have peace."[47] And even if he fails, he is not entitled to take revenge but is supposed to leave it to "law and government in the country" that is "ordained to guard against such things and to punish them."[48] In any case, Luther admonishes Christians actively to commit themselves to peace and reconciliation. He literally calls disturbing a peaceful community by spreading bad rumors or lies the work of the *"diabolus."*[49]

This emphasis on active commitment is striking in Luther's interpretation of Matthew 5:6: "Blessed are those who hunger and thirst for righteousness, for they shall be satisfied."[50] Clearly Luther states that "'Righteousness' in this passage must not be taken in the sense of that principal Christian righteousness by which a person becomes pious and acceptable to God (*frum und angenem ... fur Gott*)."[51] According to Luther, the Beatitudes

> are nothing but instruction about the fruits and good works of a Christian. Before these must come faith, as the tree and chief part (*heubtstuck*) or summary of a man's righteousness and blessedness, without any work and merit of his; out of which faith these items all must grow and follow.[52]

Thus, righteousness here means "the outward righteousness before the world, which we maintain in our relations with each other."[53] A "righteous and blessed" person therefore is someone "who continuously works and strives with all his might to promote the general welfare and the proper behavior of everyone and who helps to maintain and support this by word

---

[44] *WA* 32, 330; *LW* 21, 40.

[45] *WA* 32, 331; *LW* 21, 40.

[46] Ibid.

[47] Ibid. "[...] *das du denckest und trachtest, wie es vertragen und fride werde,*" different translation: "consider and endeavor how to reconcile and establish peace."

[48] Ibid.

[49] Cf. *WA* 32, 332; *LW* 21, 42.

[50] *WA* 32, 318–321; *LW* 21, 26–29.

[51] *WA* 32, 318; *LW* 21, 26.

[52] Ibid.

[53] Ibid.

and deed, by precept and example." [54] It is interesting that Luther particularly stresses the "hunger and thirst for righteousness." Christ, he says, wanted to indicate that realizing righteousness requires "great earnestness, longing, eagerness, and unceasing diligence"[55] because the obstructive forces of the devil and the world interfere with the realization of righteousness which easily leads to resignation. Quoting the proverb "despair makes a man a monk,"[56] Luther explicitly criticizes monastic life as escapism resulting from resignation and vehemently appeals to Christians actively to participate in the struggle for "outward righteousness."

CONCLUSION

After having provided a few examples of how Luther understood the Sermon on the Mount, let me conclude with the following remarks on Luther's hermeneutics:

- At least to me it is surprising how clearly Luther reads the Sermon as an instruction for Christian life. The *usus elenchticus* does not play a crucial role. Thus, according to Luther, the Sermon is not a utopian text as it were but, rather, it is relevant to Christians' everyday lives.

- Moreover, it is surprising that Luther does not exclusively emphasize an ethos of passion, e.g., of suffering injustice and leaving it all to God's providence but, rather, supports an ethos of action, e.g., of struggling for outward righteousness.

- Luther reflects on the specific character of a biblical book. Biblical books may differ in focus, perspective and emphasis. We should not expect a single text to give the whole picture. It is important for the interpreter to get an idea of the text's genuine profile. Luther, therefore, distinguishes Matthew from John and Paul by emphasizing his focus on the works.

- Luther respects the specific character of the text, but does not isolate it from other aspects of the Christian doctrine which are tackled more intensively in other parts of the Bible. He integrates the "principal article" of (justification by) faith into his interpretation of the Sermon

---

[54] Ibid.
[55] *WA* 32, 319; *LW* 21, 27.
[56] Ibid.

on the Mount, saying it speaks of the "works of faith." Nevertheless, this is not a simple *eis-egesis*. He does not simply read the "principal article" into the text, but tries to find evidence in the text allowing for his interpretation.

- By reading the Sermon as an instruction for Christian life, Luther has to deal with the challenge that some of Christ's commands seem to contradict basic, intuitive common sense and morality. In my paper, I refer to this as the dilemma of cultural plausibility. Luther faces this dilemma by claiming that the Sermon does not go to the public person who is called to safeguard the social order and therefore cannot abstain from using (or at least threatening with the use of) violence. According to the hermeneutical focus of this paper, I will not go deeper into the question of whether this is a convincing answer. I would rather like to suggest that cultural plausibility is an essential dimension of biblical hermeneutics in general. Our reading of biblical texts is deeply influenced by what we imagine to be culturally plausible or implausible. And this can change. For instance, when about 100 years ago the conviction that women should not be admitted to academic education lost its cultural plausibility in Europe and North America this changed the reading of biblical texts that were formerly used to restrict the access of women to public preaching and religious leadership. It is wrong to criticize that as surrendering to the zeitgeist. Rather, it is a permanent task of theological hermeneutics to draw attention to this dimension in order to create the space for dealing with it in a reflected, responsible way.

Matthew and the Hermeneutics of Love

Oda Wischmeyer

At first sight, it is probably justice rather than love that we associate with the Gospel of Matthew. There are indeed only a few passages where Matthew touches on the topic of love, *agape*. But these texts belong to the important statements on love in the New Testament, and probably the most important or at least intriguing of these texts, the commandment of love of one's enemy, is to be found in the Sermon on the Mount (Mt 5:43–48).

In the following, I shall demonstrate how, in the Gospel of Matthew, "*agape* towards the neighbor" and "*agape* towards the enemy" work together as hermeneutical clues.

Foundations or Israel's legacy

> Matthew's general message of love is based on two Old Testament commandments: "You shall love your neighbor as yourself" (Mt 19:19; 22:39) and "You shall love the Lord your God with all your heart, and with all your soul, and with all your mind" (Mt 22:37).

The commandment to love the neighbor belongs to Leviticus 19, a chapter that is part of an ancient body of laws on holiness, covering a collection of various commandments concerning right behavior in Israelite society. The general character of these commandments is partly social-ethical and partly more juridical in the narrow sense. To love one's neighbor as oneself means fair and constructive conduct toward one's fellow Israelites or not to harm a fellow Israelite. The "neighbor" is each member of the legal community of the people of Israel. Similarly, the commandment to love the God of Israel includes a strong legal aspect. According to its place in the second sermon of Moses in Deuteronomy 6:4, which recalls God's revelation at Mount Horeb, the commandment is an expression of the theology of the covenant and demands loyalty of the people of Israel toward their God.

The semantic field of the Hebrew word *ahab*, to love, includes different aspects that are held together by the basic meaning of a strong commitment toward others. In combination with the commandments, *ahab* expresses a strong bond, combining responsibility and obedience, while in the books of the Prophets *ahab* is used in a religious context in the sense of the God of Israel's passionate love for God's people. In the Song of Songs the word *ahab* is used to express erotic love and sexual desire.

Addressed are individual Israelites: adult Israelite men whose responsibility before God Moses emphasizes once more in his second sermon. The commandments do not demand or prescribe particular feelings, but what they ask for is responsible behavior beyond individual emotions. It has frequently been criticized that this commandment demands love. Can emotions be demanded? However, this kind of *ahaba* can be "required," because it is understood as an ethical act, both toward God and the fellow Israelites. The realm of the commandments is not a private one but, rather, the public sphere of "Israel" understood as a social and legal community. It is this field of public religious and interpersonal social behavior that, in Israel, is defined as realm of *ahab/ahaba*, of love.

Originally, both commandments were independent of each other. They are not referred to elsewhere in the Hebrew Bible and, also in the Torah, do not have particular significance but coexist with other similar, more or less important, social and religious rules. The commandments are meant to provide the Israelites with perfect rules of conduct in their relationship with God and their fellow Israelites.

Matthew's hermeneutics, or Torah
and love of the neighbor

At first sight, Matthew 22:34-40 seems to repeat two sentences that belong to the vast array of Old Testament religious and ethical rules and instructions. True as this may be, we have to look carefully at the way in which Jesus quotes these. A scribe asks Jesus which is the most important law in the Torah and Jesus answers by quoting together two, originally independent, commandments.

Three points are important for interpreting this text. First, Matthew does not quote from or refer to the Torah or Septuagint as Paul does in Romans 13:8–10 or the author of the Letter of James in 2:8. Rather, what Matthew actually transmits in Matthew 22:37–39 is a quote from a Jesus logion (sayings of Jesus), in particular one of the core components of the earliest Christian

Jesus tradition that had already been recorded by Mark. Matthew read it in Mark or heard it recited by early Christian apostles or teachers in community assemblies and included it in his narrative of the gospel. According to these traditions, the evangelist lets Jesus quote Torah in connection with answering the question regarding the highest commandment.

Second, interestingly enough, Jesus does not answer by quoting one commandment, but by combining the commandment to love the God of Israel with the commandment to love one's neighbor, a combination that is not itself rooted in the Torah and therefore is frequently understood as a new ethical rule. Scholars have long argued for and against the originality of the Double Commandment of Love or Great Commandment since already in Mark 12:30f we find proof of the combination of these two sentences. We can only make certain assumptions as to how Jesus taught Torah interpretation and have no evidence that Jesus was the first to combine the two commandments and thereby to create the dual commandment to love God and neighbor. Besides, the issue of originality is perhaps not quite as important as some New Testament scholars think. At least, the point of Mark's text, the *Vorlage* or prototype for Matthew, is not Jesus' originality but the consensus between Jesus and the scribe. The Synoptic Gospels underline this consensus between Jesus and the teacher of Torah and Luke, in particular, emphasizes the consistency between the "Jewish" interpretation of the Torah and Jesus' answer by reversing roles between Jesus and the scribe. Here it is the scribe who answers and quotes the dual commandment, while Jesus is the person who asks the questions (Lk 10:25–28). Nevertheless, the evangelists are convinced that the two commandments of love are of key importance for Jesus' teaching on ethics (Lk 10:25–28).

Third, while Matthew depends on Mark and Mark depends on the earlier Jesus tradition, Matthew adds his own interpretation in 22:40: "On these two commandments hang all the law and the prophets."

It is in this phrase that Matthew provides the early Christian communities with a general hermeneutical rule for their reading of the Torah and I would therefore like to look at this rule in more detail by comparing the closing sentences of the synoptic passages. Mark underlines that there are no principal differences between the hermeneutics of the Torah of Jesus on the one hand and that of the scribe on the other. From this perspective, the Torah and its interpretation must not constitute an obstacle for fellow Jews to follow Jesus in discipleship. So, Jesus assures the scribe, "You are not far from the kingdom of God" (Mk 12:34).

In accordance with his ethical approach, Luke goes beyond the dual commandment, in particular beyond the commandment to love the neighbor, which he believes to be somewhat unclear or weak. The scribe's question, Who is my neighbor? gives Luke the occasion to transmit the parable of the Good Samaritan in which loving the neighbor is spelled out as showing mercy (*eleos*): "The one [the neighbor] who showed mercy on him" (Lk 10:37).

It is evident that the three evangelists interpret the Jesus tradition of the dual commandment differently. By and large, Mark is interested in building a bridge between the scribe's and Jesus' interpretation of Torah or, rather, to demonstrate that Jesus is the perfect teacher of Torah. Luke aims at reinterpreting and affirming love as mercy, and it is only Matthew, who in his interpretation of the Jesus tradition and Mark, deduces a specific Jesus hermeneutic regarding Torah.

And, surprisingly, Matthew's hermeneutic corresponds exactly to Paul's interpretation of the commandment to love one's neighbor. Paul writes in Romans 13:9–10:

> The commandments, "You shall not commit adultery; You shall not murder; You shall not steal; You shall not covet"; and any other commandment, are summed up in this word, "Love your neighbor as yourself."

These sentences are proof of Paul's deep interest in what I like to call the hermeneutics of love. In Romans 13 his main topic is not love as such as for example in 1 Corinthians 13 but, rather, the argument that loving the neighbor means fulfilling the Torah. This argument implies a certain freedom in dealing with the commandments of the Torah in detail and opens the door to a new ethical culture of loving each other (not "the neighbor" but "each other") that is different from the commandment in Leviticus. The argument in Romans 13 no longer relates to Israel, but to the Christ confessing communities that were founded by Paul and other missionaries. Their relationships within the communities, the *ekklesiai*, are characterized by brotherly and sisterly love. The same applies to Matthew, who in Matthew 23 confronts the social behavior, viz. living according to the instructions of the Torah, and the inner attitude toward justice, mercy and faithfulness (Mt 23:23; see also Mt 23:28). Matthew could also have added love of one's neighbor. This is the case in Matthew 24:12 which echoes Paul's vision of love as the communities' ethos: "And because of the increase of lawlessness, the love of many will grow cold."

The author of the Letter of James thinks along another line when he quotes Leviticus 19:18. His argument runs contrary to Paul's in Romans 13. James first praises his audience for loving their neighbor: "You do well if you really fulfill the royal law according to the scripture, 'You shall love your neighbor as yourself' " (Jas 2:8). He continues: "For whoever keeps the whole law but fails in one point has become accountable for all of it" (Jas 2:10).

The author calls the Love Commandment the "royal law," possibly because of the Jesus tradition of the dual commandment, but at the same time makes clear that every other commandment, at least those that belong to the

Decalogue, have the same dignity and carry the same weight as the commandment to love the neighbor. Therefore, the perfect "royal law" (Jas 2:8) is only one among other important commandments. To James's mind, love of the neighbor does not fulfill the commandments of the Decalogue as Paul states in Romans 13 and therefore is not understood as a hermeneutical rule for interpreting Torah like in Matthew 22. Contrary to Paul and Matthew, James argues traditionally, sticking to the way in which Israel understands Torah and its commandments: every single rule is of equal in importance.

INNOVATION, OR JESUS TRADITION (Q)

We have followed part of the path of the Old Testament tradition of two Love Commandments up to Jesus' dual commandment in the Synoptic Gospels and their interpretation, especially in Matthew 22. We will move from the perspective of continuity to addressing the issue of innovation in the Jesus tradition according to sayings source Q focusing, in particular, on Matthew 5:43f. In Matthew 5:43–48 the evangelist composes the last of five antithetic saying units, the nucleus of which is the commandment to love one's enemy:

> You have heard that it was said, "You shall love your neighbor and hate your enemy." But I say to you, Love your enemies and pray for those who persecute you, so that you may be children of your Father in heaven; for he makes his sun rise on the evil and on the good, and sends rain on the righteous and on the unrighteous. For if you love those who love you, what reward do you have? Do not even the tax collectors do the same? And if you greet only your brothers and sisters, what more are you doing than others? Do not even the Gentiles do the same? Be perfect, therefore, as your heavenly Father is perfect.

Again, Jesus quotes Leviticus 19:18, but this time in a way that is quite different from Leviticus 22:39. And again, it is especially the way of quoting the Jewish tradition that matters here: "You have heard that it was said, 'You shall love your neighbor and hate your enemy' "(Mt 5:43).

With this ambivalent opening phrase Jesus already addresses the distance he keeps to the Torah in this pericope. The wording of the second part of the quote then illustrates well the disregard with which Jesus reads Leviticus 19:18 here. Unauthorized and arbitrarily, Jesus alters the wording of the commandment to love one's neighbor by adding the opposite part of the rule. Contrary to Matthew 22:39, he does not respect the constructive meaning of the commandment, but reveals the—at least potentially—destructive implications of the rule. In what follows, Jesus caricatures the commandment by maintaining that "neighbors" are friends ("those who love you"). As I have pointed out, in Leviticus 19 "neighbors" are not friends but to be understood as fellow Israelites. However, Jesus' criticism of the one-sidedness of the commandment of loving one's neighbor is not as unfounded as one may think when we read, for example, Sirach 12:1-18, especially verses 4 and 6:

> Give to the devout, but do not help the sinner (v. 4).
> For the Most High also hates sinners and will inflict punishment on the ungodly (v.6).

Even more remarkable than Jesus' polemic against the Love Commandment is Matthew 5:47 where Jesus argues against mere sisterly and brotherly love. It is most intriguing that Jesus more or less equates sisterly and brotherly love with "pagan" polite behavior, because, what Jesus actually criticizes, is exactly the culture of loving each other that I have defined earlier as the new ethical culture of the Christ confessing communities. As I mentioned earlier, Matthew is very critical of the brotherly and sisterly love of the communities (Mt 24:12), and the same applies to the author of the first Johannine letter's polemic against the lack of brotherly and sisterly love in his communities. Hence, the fifth antithesis meets neither the commandment of love of one's neighbor nor brotherly and sisterly love. Instead, it is stated here that perfect behavior is only characterized by loving one's enemy.

Perfection is a common motive in early Christian literature. It is not only familiar to Matthew (Mt 19:21), but also part of Paul's parenetical advice as we learn from Romans 12:2 and Philippians 3:15 and it is frequently used by the author of the Letter of James.

In the following I shall discuss only two aspects of the fifth antithesis. First, the issue whether loving one's enemy is to be considered as the core component of Jesus' ethical teaching (e.g., Ulrich Luz) since his original contribution to ethics in general is highly controversial and cannot be discussed here. Only one comment on this issue: in his ethical advice in Romans 12:17–21, Paul quotes Proverbs 25:21f, "If your enemies are hungry, give them bread to eat; and if they are thirsty, give them water to drink."

The general ethical demand to treat an enemy as a human being is rooted in the Old Testament and, from the very beginning, a part of early Christian ethics without particular reference to Jesus and the Sermon on the Mount. And, the sayings source, source Q, transmits only the admonition to love one's enemies, without the critical and polemical aspects that are added by Matthew in his antithesis. Therefore, love of the enemy, not criticizing love of the neighbor, belongs to the central ethical demands of the earliest Christian movement.

Second, this observation brings us back to Matthew who framed the antitheses. In Matthew 5 we not only find a very different understanding of love than in Matthew 22 but also a second hermeneutical rule. By framing the antitheses Matthew leaves the realm of the contemporary Jewish hermeneutics of the Torah. Regardless of whether or not Jesus himself was the originator of the demand to love one's enemy, it goes without saying that from Matthew's perspective the love of one's enemy was the last and most perfect of Jesus' new commandments that were compiled by Matthew into a coherent ethical compendium in chapter 5 of his gospel. Matthew constructs Jesus as the only teacher of Torah who develops a new hermeneutic of perfect justice according to Torah (Mt 5:20) or, more precisely, the inner tendency of Torah, against the misinterpretation by the scribes who did not know the real meaning of the commandments. The result is an ethical concept that oscillates between the radicalization and internalization of the Old Testament commandments. On closer inspection, Matthew's hermeneutic is no longer a hermeneutic of merely interpreting Torah, but a new and independent Jesus hermeneutic by which Matthew intends to establish Jesus' authority as the perfect teacher: "For I tell you ... ."

MATTHEW'S HERMENEUTICS AGAIN, OR TORAH AND "LOVING YOUR ENEMY"

This then raises the question of how one should judge Matthew's tendency to prefer the love of the enemy to the love of one's neighbor. What kind of hermeneutical implications are connected with Matthew's interpretation? And is what we observe in Matthew a kind of clash of different interpretations of Torah or of Jesus traditions or of the Jesus tradition against Matthew's own interpretation? First of all, Matthew is concerned with two closely connected topics: Torah as the guiding principle of ethical behavior, and the hermeneutics of Torah. And his own intention is to narrate the story of Jesus as the perfect teacher of Torah, both from an ethical and a hermeneutical perspective. Matthew shares Paul's basic hermeneutical insight that Torah is said for Israel: "Now we know that whatever the law says, it speaks to those who are under the law" (Rom 3:19).

I have already pointed out that Matthew constructs and narrates Jesus as a teacher of Torah. The figure of Jesus as Matthew narrates it reinterprets Torah *intra muros*, viz. for Israel, by radicalizing and internalizing the Old Testament commandments. But, at the same time, in the exaggerated formulation of the antitheses Matthew creates something like a new ethos: love of the enemy against love of the neighbor or brotherly and sisterly love. Here we find Matthew's own *extra muros* view, that is to say the view of a member of a Christ confessing community who writes his Jesus narration in light not only of chapter 16, but also of chapters 24 to 28. As far as I understand the Gospel of Matthew, it is the author's dual perspective that leads to Jesus' different kinds of interpretation of Torah and the Love Commandment. His severe criticism of the scribes' interpretation of Torah and, similarly, of the concept of brotherly and sisterly love are obviously not only the result of the so-called parting of the ways between the synagogues and the *ekklesiai*, but also Matthew's experience in Christ confessing communities, such as Luke's reinterpretation of love as mercy.

Love of one's enemy may sound exaggerated, but this kind of love has a significant potential of its own: against blood vengeance, against zealots, against all kinds of hatred, in particular against results of religious hatred and an *intra muros* mentality that is hostile toward foreigners who are regarded as enemies. The latter for example applies to new political movements in several European countries that pretend to feel threatened and attacked by immigrants. The fifth antithesis is right in claiming that love of one's neighbor does not explicitly exclude some of these practices. Love of one's enemy works as a criterion of difference in the field of interpretation of the Love Commandment and, in so far, is to be regarded as the second hermeneutical rule of love in the Gospel of Matthew.

Luther's interpretation, or perfect love as a distinguishing mark

Martin Luther interprets the Gospel of Matthew as the gospel of love. His sermon on the first antithesis of the Sermon on the Mount (Mt 5:20-26) gives an example of his reading of the Gospel of Matthew. Luther opens up his sermon by underlining that the antithesis is to be understood not as law, but as gospel:

> In diesem *Evangelium* lehrt unser lieber Herr Jesus Christus die christliche Liebe, die wir untereinander haben sollen, und zeigt das Gegenteil oder die Hindernisse an, die solche Liebe zu hindern pflegen, und will uns lehren, dass wir uns nicht dünken lassen, wir hätten die christliche Liebe, wenn wir an diesen Stücken sind, die er hier aufzählt.[1]

And Luther ends his sermon by stating:

---

[1] Martin Luther, "Sechster Sonntag nach Trinitatis: Matth. 5,20-26," in Kurt Aland (ed.), *Luther Deutsch, Die Werke Martin Luthers in neuer Auswahl für die Gegenwart*, vol. 8, Die Predigten (Göttingen: Vandenhoek and Ruprecht, 1965), 298 (= *WA* 37, 111–115, 111) ["In this Gospel, our Lord Jesus Christ teaches Christian love which we shall have for one another, and points to the opposite and to the obstacles that hinder such love. He wants to teach us that we should not pretend already to have the real Christian love when we do those things that he enumerates here," author's own translation]

Darum lasst uns aus diesem Evangelium lernen, daß jedermann rechtschaffen in der Liebe sei.[2]

Luther does not expose the problems of the antitheses—Torah rigorism or Jesus' originality or possible anti-Judaism—neither does he discuss whether Matthew intends to improve the Jewish understanding of Torah or to introduce Jesus' perfect interpretation. Instead, Luther reads the whole Sermon on the Mount as *euaggelion* according the opening phrase of the Beatitudes: "Blessed are you [...] ." What New Testament exegesis may perhaps learn from Luther is the fact that texts need interpretation, even texts of the New Testament, even texts of the Sermon on the Mount. Whether we read these texts as *euaggelion* or as a strict ethical rule is up to us. Controversy over texts is a necessary part of belonging to religions such as Judaism, Christianity or Islam. We have to struggle to find the better argument in interpreting the text, for the better hermeneutics and for rules of application. For the Lutheran church, Luther's claim of reading the antitheses as love texts remains crucial.

Let me refer briefly to another interpretation of Matthew 5 by Luther[3] where he gives a detailed analysis of the Sermon on the Mount, and focuses especially on the scope of loving one's enemy. He clearly distinguishes between the obligation to love the enemy on the one hand and theological disagreement on the other:

> I shall willingly serve you, but not in order to help you overthrow the Word of God. For this purpose you will never be able to persuade me even to give you a drink of water. In other words, our love and service belong to men. But they belong to God above all; if this is hindered or threatened, love and service are no longer in place. For the command is: Yous hall love your enemy and do him good. But to God's enemies I must also be an enemy, lest I join forces with them against God.[4]

---

[2] Ibid., 303. ["Hence, let us learn from this gospel that everybody be honest in love," author's own translation].

[3] Cf. Martin Luther, "The Sermon on the Mount," in Jaroslav Pelikan (ed.), *Luther's Works*, vol. 21 (Saint Louis: Concordia Publishing House, 1956). This is an English translation of a collection of sermons on the Sermon on the Mount that Luther gave from 1530–1532 in Wittenberg and which were already edited in 1532 (cf. *WA* 32, 299-544).

[4] Martin Luther, "The Sermon on the Mount and the Magnificat," in *LW* 21, 121-22; cf. *WA* 32, 400, "Gerne wil ich dir dienen, aber nicht dazu das du Gottes wort wilt umbstossen, da soltu mich nicht zu bringen noch vermoegen das ich dir einen trunck wassers solt geben. Summa, menschen sol man lieben und dienen, aber Gott uber alles, das wo man die selbe hinderen odder weren wil, da gilt keine liebe noch dienst mehr, Denn es heisset: deinen feind soltu lieben und guts thun, Aber Gottes feinden mus ich auch feind sein, das jch nicht mit jn widder Gott anlauffe."

Luther clearly differentiates between the private attitude toward an enemy and the spiritual or ecclesiastical ministry, the latter of which does not demand love.

LOVE INSTEAD OF HATE, OR IMPLICATIONS AND CONSEQUENCES OF MATTHEW'S HERMENEUTICS OF LOVE FOR THE ABRAHAMIC RELIGIONS

The investigation of Matthew's hermeneutic of Jesus that is to be defined as a hermeneutic of love is not only of exegetical, and that means of inner theological relevance. In light of the current international policy, especially religious policy in the Middle East and in parts of Africa, love should be regarded and esteemed as the first criterion of difference that can be a solid assessment of the understanding of who the religions are and what kind of ethical values and behavior in everyday life they stand for. Churches, in particular the Roman Catholic Church, aim at establishing a situation of dialogue and partnership between the so-called Abrahamic religions. At this point we can leave aside the issue of whether the monotheistic religions in particular are inclined to use force, as some scholars such as Jan Assmann argue. Friedrich Wilhelm Graf, on the other hand, denies Assmann's hypothesis by pointing to the so-called polytheistic religions such as Hinduism that combine intolerant nationalism with religious violence. At any rate, a real partnership can only be established on the basis of the shared belief that it is with love, not with hate, that we must face one another. According to the Sermon on the Mount, love refers not only to the people of one's own church or religion, but also to those of different religions that are regarded as strange and perhaps even as "wrong" from one's own point of view. The greatest benefit of Matthew's hermeneutics of love and Luther's interpretation is the insight that we have to distinguish between our own deep religious beliefs and convictions on the one hand, and the people who do not share our beliefs or belong to another religion that calls into question or denies our belief on the other. What love of the enemy means is not to share different opinions and religious beliefs, but to love the persons who maintain these beliefs. It is hermeneutics or this art of distinction or *discretio* that we are taught by Matthew and by Luther.

Perfection of Christian Life in the Face of Anger and Retaliation. Martin Luther's Interpretation of the Sermon on the Mount

Hans-Peter Grosshans

For Lutheran theology, the interpretation of the Jesus' Sermon on the Mount has always been somewhat of a challenge. Taking seriously its lofty moral ambitions has often come into conflict with the Lutheran emphasis on justification by faith alone. Therefore, in Lutheran theology the Sermon on the Mount was often used merely to convict people of their sins, viz. Jesus' counsels in the Sermon on the Mount were taken to show that we cannot fulfill divine law and must therefore be continuously aware of being sinners. However, we cannot in fact find such an understanding in Luther's interpretation of the Sermon on the Mount. Luther was convinced that Christians should live according to how Jesus told them to in the Sermon on the Mount. This understanding is consistent with the hermeneutics which, from the beginning, he had developed in his public teaching. From 1513 onwards, in his first lectures on Psalms, Luther had begun to redefine the way in which Holy Scripture was to be interpreted.[1] Increasingly he emphasized

---

[1] Cf. Hans-Peter Grosshans, "Luther's Early Interpretation of the Psalms and his Contribution to Hermeneutics," in Kenneth Mtata, Karl-Wilhelm Niebuhr and Miriam Rose (eds), *Singing the Songs of the Lord in Foreign Lands: Psalms in Contemporary Lutheran Interpretation*, LWF Documentation 59 (Geneva/Leipzig: The Lutheran World Federation/Evangelische Verlangsanstalt, 2014), 19–32; for an outline of Lutheran hermeneutics, cf. Hans-Peter Grosshans, "Lutheran Hermeneutics: An Outline," in Kenneth Mtata (ed.), *You have the Words of Eternal Life—Transformative Readings of*

the literal sense of biblical texts over and above their spiritual interpretation; oriented his interpretation to Jesus Christ as the main scopus of biblical texts; operated with the difference between killing letter and life-giving spirit (law and gospel); envisaged the situation of the true reader and interpreter to be one of being "before God" and aimed at an existential verification, a verification of the biblical texts in the life of those who try to understand them. In his extensive study on an evangelical interpretation of the gospels, Gerhard Ebeling shows that after 1525 Luther more or less abandoned allegorical interpretations and that we can find allegorical interpretations of only four of his texts.[2] From 1530–1532 Martin Luther continuously preached on the Sermon on the Mount in Wittenberg. In his interpretation of Matthew 5 especially we can observe that Luther firmly resisted all temptation to resort to the easier spiritual interpretation and to propose specific spiritual forms of life in which the ideal of a perfect Christian life may be realized. Furthermore, Luther did not interpret Jesus' counsels in Matthew 5 as "laws," which human beings cannot fulfill and therefore show that all human beings are sinners. Instead, he understood Jesus's teaching in Matthew 5 to be the "gospel" that includes Jesus's counsels to his disciples and to all believers for a perfect Christian life and which are therefore valid and relevant for every Christian's daily life. According to Luther's understanding, especially Matthew 5 has to be verified in light of the concrete and complex lives of all ordinary Christians, who listen to it and try to understand it. Luther's model for a perfect Christian life, which he developed based on a literal interpretation of the biblical text, is very down to earth. The idea of a perfect Christian life, which is proposed in Matthew 5, is not meant to be realized in specific spiritual forms of life, but amidst the realities of Christians' secular lives and its challenges.

In the following essay we shall first take a close look at Martin Luther's interpretation of the antithesis concerning retaliation (Mt 5:38-42). Secondly, with Luther, we shall consider some consequences for ecclesiology and finally draw two conclusions.

Luther's interpretation of the antithesis on retaliation

In our daily lives there are many reasons for anger and retaliation. For Christians being persecuted for righteousness' sake or the sake of one's faith can give rise to such strong emotions as anger and seeking retaliation or revenge. This seems only natural. However, contrary to such natural instincts, Jesus

---

the Gospel of John from a Lutheran Perspective, LWF Documentation 57 (Geneva/Minneapolis: The Lutheran World Federation/Lutheran University Press, 2012), 23–46.
[2] Gerhard Ebeling, Evangelische Evangelienauslegung. Eine Untersuchung zu Luthers Hermeneutik (Tübingen: Mohr Siebeck,[3]1991).

told this disciples: "But I say to you, Do not resist an evildoer. But if anyone strikes you on the right cheek, turn the other also; and if anyone wants to sue you and take your coat, give your cloak as well; and if anyone forces you to go one mile, go also the second mile" (Mt 5:39–41). The overall subject of the "antitheses" is perfection—as we read in the last verse of Matthew 5: "Be perfect, therefore, as your heavenly Father is perfect" (Mt 5:48).

Luther never gave an academic lecture on the Synoptic Gospels. We know his interpretation of the Sermon on the Mount only from his sermons, which he gave from 1530–1532 in Wittenberg and which were edited already in 1532.[3] In the introduction to the publication of these sermons on Matthew 5-7 Luther pointed to the difficulties of arriving at a true interpretation, especially of Matthew 5. According to Luther's understanding, some interpreters' claim, namely that "Christ does not intend everything He teaches in the fifth chapter to be regarded by His Christians as a command for them to observe,"[4] is wrong. The consequence of such a misinterpretation had been the invention of twelve *consilia Evangelii* (evangelical counsels)—understood as being recommendations based on the gospel that were not valid for all Christians, but only for those, who want to be more perfect than other Christians.

In the sixteenth century, the way in which the evangelical counsels were understood in terms of the perfection of Christian life and the question of where ordinary Christians can find orientation as they strive to lead a perfect Christian life was one of the major differences between the denominations. In Article XVI of the Augsburg Confession, "Concerning Civic Affairs," we find a critique of the position that a perfect Christian life can only be realized through a monastic life. According to this understanding monastic life orients every ordinary Christian's life.[5]

---

[3] Cf. Martin Luther, "The Sermon on the Mount," in Jaroslav Pelikan (ed.), *Luther's Works*, vol. 21 (Saint Louis: Concordia Publishing House, 1956). We have around 1000 of Luther's sermons that are relevant for his interpretation of the Synoptic Gospels. Luther gave these sermons following the normal order of pericopes, but also in his series of sermons on Matthew 5-7, 11-15 and 18-24. We have these sermons in the form of transcripts by listeners or in manuscripts, which have been further worked on by others and are not always reliable. Cf. Ebeling, ibid., 11-47. For a further survey on Luther's interpretation of the Synoptic Gospels, with a different emphasis see W. von Loewenich, *Luther als Ausleger der Synoptiker* (München: Kaiser Verlag, 1954). The publication of Luther's sermons on Matthew 5-7, preached between 1530 and 1532, is based mainly on transcripts, which may have been in part rewritten by the transcribers and editors. So the text may not always be one hundred percent Martin Luther's. But Luther acknowledged the publication as his own text by writing an introduction to it.
[4] *LW* 21, 3.
[5] "Concerning civic affairs they teach that lawful civil ordinances are good works of God and that Christians are permitted to hold civil office, to work in law courts, to decide matters by imperial and other existing laws, to impose just punishments,

At the time, the evangelical counsels were part of the teaching of a logical discipleship of Christ and understood to be the charismatic expression of Christian perfection. Moreover, they were understood as the norms of a perfect Christian life, which was made possible by divine grace (that is, not resulting from human nature). According to traditional teaching these evangelical counsels—chastity, poverty and obedience—are not necessary to gain eternal life. Eternal life is gained through baptism and faith and the evangelical counsels are recommendations for those who want to be perfect. The biblical basis for this is found for example in Matthew 19:1ff. (chastity); Matthew 19:16ff. (poverty); Matthew 20:26 (obedience).

Protestant Christianity has redefined and substituted these ideals of monastic life, which functioned (and in some parts of Christianity still function today) as a model and general orientation for every ordinary Christian who wants to strive for perfection. The idea of perfection was not given up by Reformation theology, but the old ideals were redefined and replaced by others. Chastity was replaced by marriage and family; poverty was replaced by professional work, diligence and property in civil society; obedience was replaced by appreciation and acknowledgment of the laws based on freedom and justice. Consequently, for Protestant Christians the affirmation of secular life and an active participation in the political, civil and economic orders became an expression of their spirituality and their theology. From this perspective a perfect Christian life is realized. The Protestant redefinition of the evangelical counsels did and does not abandon the ideal of perfection and the ambition to strive for a perfect Christian life. But the perfection of a Christian life is seen differently to the old monastic ideal.

When in his interpretation of Matthew 5–7 Martin Luther talks about evangelical counsels, then the above mentioned context and discussion are addressed. In Luther's opinion Roman-Catholic theologians used passages in

---

to wage just war, to serve as soldiers, to make legal contracts, to hold property, to take an oath when required by magistrates, to take a wife, to be given in marriage. They condemn the Anabaptists who prohibit Christians from assuming such civil responsibilities. Because the gospel transmits an eternal righteousness of the heart, they also condemn those who locate evangelical perfection not in the fear of God and in faith but in abandoning civil responsibilities. In the meantime the gospel does not undermine government or family but completely requires both their preservation as ordinances of God and the exercise of love in these ordinances. Consequently, Christians owe obedience to their magistrates and laws except when commanded to sin. For then they owe greater obedience to God than to human beings (Acts 5[:29]." "The Augsburg Confession—Latin Text—Article XVI: Civic Affairs," in Robert Kolb and Timothy Wengert (eds), *The Book of Concord. The Confessions of the Evangelical Lutheran Church* (Minneapolis: Fortress Press, 2000), 49f.

Matthew 5 in a similar way to the texts in Matthew 19 and 20. On the basis of the Sermon on the Mount they formulated twelve evangelical counsels,

> twelve bits of good advice in the Gospel, which may be kept by anyone who pleases if he wants to attain a perfection higher and more perfect than that of other Christians. Thus they have not only made perfection as well as Christian salvation dependent upon works apart from faith, but they have even made these works optional. I call that forbidding true and fine good works.[6]

Luther then lists these twelve evangelical counsels:

> Do not requite wrongdoing! Do not avenge yourself! Offer the other cheek! Do not resist evil! Give your cloak along with your coat! Go the second mile! Give to everyone that asks! Lend to him who borrows! Pray for your persecutors! Love your enemies! Do good to those who hate! Do the other things that Christ teaches here![7]

Luther believes this command to apply to all Christians.[8] For him, theologians who teach that Jesus taught and advised something that should and could not be realized by every Christian pervert Jesus' teaching. The contrary is true: "Thus you may preserve in its purity the teaching of Christ in this chapter of Matthew."[9] We can see here, that Luther is challenged by an interpretation that, according to his understanding, is wrong: a centuries-long, widespread interpretation of Matthew 5 in the Roman-Catholic Church that the evangelical counsels mentioned in the Sermon on the Mount are not meant to be realized by ordinary Christians. They are only optional counsels for those who not only want to gain eternal life in heaven, but also to strive for perfecting their Christian life in especially cloistered forms of life.

Luther also opposed the position held by the Spiritualists and Anabaptists and Enthusiasts. According to Luther they teach, "that it is wrong to own private property, to swear, to hold office as a ruler or judge, to protect or defend oneself, to stay with wife and children."[10]

Luther believed that both the theologians of the established Roman church and the theologians of the new Enthusiast and Spiritualist move-

---

[6] *LW* 21, 4.

[7] Ibid., 4.

[8] Luther accused especially the theologians in Paris of saying, that "Christian teaching would have much too hard a time of it if it were loaded down with things like this," ibid., 4.

[9] Ibid., 5.

[10] Ibid., 5.

ments made the same mistake: "they do not recognize any difference between the secular and the divine realm, much less what should be the distinctive doctrine and action in each realm."[11]

Luther makes this difference and its consequences clear in his sermons and interpretations. For him it was a struggle to find the pure Christian teaching. He believed that suppressing good works (which he wanted to stimulate) or inventing wrong "good" works and to make up a holiness as it was observed among monks and Enthusiasts or, in more general terms, a holiness and a perfection of Christian life for Christians who "have laid claim to a more perfect station in life than other Christians"[12] would pervert pure Christian teaching. Luther clearly sees that all such claims have been put forward on the basis of Matthew 5. But according to Luther's understanding there is only one Christian ethics: one and the same ethics applies to all Christians, whatever they are.[13]

In his interpretation of Matthew 5, Luther reorganizes Christian ethics and the idea of a perfect Christian life. We shall now have a closer look at Luther's interpretation of Matthew 5:38–42, which is about retaliation. In this antithesis Jesus went far beyond the old law. "You have heard that it was said, 'An eye for an eye and a tooth for a tooth.' But I say to you, Do not resist an evildoer. But if anyone strikes you on the right cheek, turn the other also"

---

[11] Ibid., 5.

[12] Ibid., 6.

[13] Luther opposed the idea that one ethic applies to Christians who live in the secular world and another to those who are priests or monks or are in the one or other way especially "called" by God into a special state. Similarly, he opposed the idea that priests and monks have a "higher" or more holy occupation than those who undertake "worldly" jobs. In "On Monastic Vows, 1521" Luther rejected the spiritual status accorded to monks. With reference to 1 Corinthians 7:20, "Let each of you remain in the condition in which you were called," Luther argued that normal working people undertake tasks that are approved by God and good in themselves. For Luther, a "calling" does not constitute to be called out of the world but to be called into service in the world where one is needed. All work, however, should be undertaken as a work of love and done in order to honor and serve God, while recognizing the contribution one is making to other people. The office of the priest is, essentially, not different from that of the road sweeper—both are undertaking worthwhile and important tasks in the service of God and society at large. Whether or not a person does their job well can be judged by reason and by worldly standards of measurement—what it means to work successfully and well will depend on the chosen career or calling but success in this task is to be measured by ordinary human means and not by appealing to theological or spiritual principles. Having said this, there is a spiritual dimension to all work since it is undertaken in the service of God and out of love for one's neighbor. As Luther said in a sermon: "If everyone were to serve their neighbor then the world would be full of worship" (WA 36: 340,1 2–13, author's own translation).

(Mt 5:38-39). The rule "an eye for an eye" constituted an enormous progress in the history of justice and law. Blood revenge (vendetta) was replaced by punishment commensurate with the injustice committed such as the rule of Lamech, "I have killed a man for wounding me, a young man for striking me" (Gen 4:23). Now Jesus questions this rule: an eye for an eye—not more. If somebody strikes you, do not take his life—like Lamech—and do not give him a strike in return, but show him the other side of your face as well.[14] In his interpretation Luther first noted, that "this text has [...] given rise to many questions and errors among nearly all the theologians who have failed to distinguish properly between the secular and the spiritual, between the kingdom of Christ and the kingdom of the world."[15]

In respect to hermeneutics it is interesting to see that in his interpretation of Matthew 5:38-42 Luther introduced a doctrinal concept already at the beginning. His emphasis on the literal sense of the text obviously did not mean merely repeating what was written or taking the first understanding of a text to be its true meaning. Some conceptual decisions are necessary in order not to misunderstand some biblical texts and, referring to the above mentioned biblical text, not to produce only counterfeit saints, that is, saints in outward works. One of the major problems Luther saw in the understanding of Mosaic law in Exodus 21:24 (an eye for an eye), was that people took this text and applied "it to themselves, though it was addressed only to the government. They took it to mean that every individual had a right to wreak vengeance on his own behalf, taking an eye for an eye."[16]

Luther understood Jesus' teachings differently.

> He is not tampering with the responsibility and authority of the government, but He is teaching His individual Christians how to live personally, apart from their official position and authority. They should not desire revenge at all ... restraining the vindictiveness not only of their fist but also of their heart, their thoughts, and all their powers as well. In other words, what He wants is a heart that will neither be impatient nor wreak vengeance nor disturb the peace.[17]

---

[14] Jesus then used three more examples with the same logic. "If anyone wants to sue you and take your coat, give your cloak as well; and if anyone forces you to go one mile, go also the second mile. Give to everyone who begs from you, and do not refuse anyone who wants to borrow from you" (Mt 5:40-42).

[15] *LW* 21, 105.

[16] Ibid., 106. In Luther's opinion the mainstream teaching at his time claimed "that revenge and self-defence were proper against violence," at least for ordinary Christians, but not for monks and priests.

[17] Ibid., 106.

Luther asked, if then a person must "suffer all sorts of things from every-one, without defending himself at all? Has he no right to plead a case or to lodge a complaint before a court, or to claim and demand what belongs to him?"[18] If this question has to be answered in the affirmative then, accord-ing to Luther, a "strange situation would develop. It would be necessary to put up with everybody's whim and insolence. Personal safety and private property would be impossible, and finally the social order would collapse."[19]

Luther was critical of the idea generally to apply monastic ethics to all aspects of the life of all Christians. For Luther the implication of such a (monastic) Christian ethics, namely Christians cloistering them-selves away in their own ecclesial and moral world in order to separate themselves from the secular world, was wrong as was the message that a perfect Christian life is only possible separate from the profane world in special—sub-cultural—forms of life.

Luther was furthermore critical of the idea of drawing political conclu-sions from the evangelical counsels in the Sermon on the Mount as he had seen Thomas Müntzer do. Luther acknowledged the motives and interests of people like Müntzer. "They see that the world at large, and particularly their own government, is being so poorly managed that they feel like jumping in and taking over."[20] But for Luther it was wrong to make the evangelical counsels to be laws of the world and to define profane punishment for not obeying them. So Luther's advice was, to "leave these things to the care of those who are authorized to distribute property, to do business, to punish, and to protect."[21]

Luther believed that "the Gospel does not trouble itself with these matters. It teaches about the right relation of the heart to God, while in all these other questions it should take care to stay pure and not to stumble into a false righteousness."[22]

According to Martin Luther it makes a huge difference whether some-thing concerns only my own life and interests or if it concerns others I am in relation with.

> [I]f someone asks whether a Christian may go to court or defend himself, the answer is simply no. A Christian [...] belongs to kingdom or realm where the only regulation should be the prayer (Matt. 6:12): "Forgive us our debts as we forgive our debtors." Here only mutual love and service should prevail, even toward people who do not love us, but who hate us, hurt and harm us. It is to

---

[18] Ibid., 107.
[19] Ibid., 107.
[20] Ibid., 107–108.
[21] Ibid., 108.
[22] Ibid., 108.

these Christians that He says they should not resist evil, that they should not even seek revenge, but that they should turn the other cheek to an assailant.[23]

But a Christian never lives in isolation but together with other people and within a society. Every Christian has a role within the society and Luther opened his reflection on this role by asking:

> May a Christian be a secular official and administer the office and work of a ruler or a judge? This would mean that the two persons or the two types of office are combined in one man. In addition to be a Christian, he would be a prince or a judge or a lord or a servant or a maid - all of which are termed 'secular' persons because they are part of the secular realm. To this we say: Yes; God Himself has ordained and established this secular realm and its distinctions, and by His Word He has confirmed and commended them. For without them this life could not endure. We are all included in them; indeed, we were born into them even before we became Christians. Therefore we must also remain in them as long as we are on earth, but only according our outward life and our physical existence.[24]

According to Luther's model, in their individual lives Christians are only responsible to Christ and without obligation to any other authority.

> But at least outwardly, according to his body and property, he is related by subjection and obligation to the emperor, inasmuch as he occupies some office or station in life or has a house and home, a wife and children; for all these are things that pertain to the emperor. Here he must necessarily do what he is told and what this outward life requires. If he has a house or a wife and children or servants and refuses to support them or, if need be, to protect them, he does wrong. It will not do for him to declare that he is a Christian and therefore has to forsake or relinquish everything.[25]

What may be right in respect to oneself—for example, to accept and suffer violence—may be wrong if applied to one's responsibilities for others. I cannot advise somebody else to turn the other cheek or to throw their cloak away with the coat. In this context, Luther used the example of the legend of a saint, who let the lice nibble at him and refused to kill any of them on the basis of this text from Matthew, being convinced that he had to suffer and should not resist evil. So, surely this responsibility for others also applies to oneself when it comes to one's self-preservation.

---

[23] Ibid., 108–109.
[24] Ibid., 109.
[25] Ibid., 109.

Because life is complex, Luther discussed in detail a Christian's own interests, when they suffer injustice. For him, immediately striking back is not possible for a Christian, but he was open to the possibility of taking one's case to court, if one is unable or unwilling to stand the injustice one suffers. However this should only be done in order to seek justice, not revenge. If the attitude in the heart is to use the law for one's own "protection and self-preservation against violence and malice [...] you are not doing wrong."[26] Consequently it is alright for a Christian—according Luther—to go to court and to sue against injustice or violence. The only advice Luther gives here is not to do this with a false heart that would not only seek justice or protection, but also an advantage or revenge. If the heart is not pure, then the relation to God is affected. If a Christian fights publicly or in court against injustice or violence—which they or somebody else may suffer—they should do this only with the intention "to maintain the right and to avoid the wrong, out of a genuine love for righteousness."[27] In fact:

> we are not compelled or obliged to let every insolent person run rampant all over the place and to take it silently without doing anything about it - not if we can follow orderly procedure in defending ourselves. [...] We must not sanction a wrong, but we must testify to the truth. In opposition to violence and malice, we certainly may appeal to the law.[28]

Luther summed up his considerations on the role of the Christian in the secular world and the challenges arising from being faithful to the commandment of Jesus "Do not resist one who is evil" in Matthew 5:39 as follows: "A Christian may carry on all sorts of secular business with impunity—not as a Christian but as a secular person—while his heart remains pure in his Christianity."[29] In respect to Matthew 5:39 Luther paradoxically concluded,

> A Christian should not resist any evil; but within the limits of his office, a secular person should oppose every evil. ... The rule in the kingdom of Christ is the toleration of everything, forgiveness, and the recompense of evil with good. On the other hand, in the realm of the emperor, there should be no tolerance shown toward any injustice, but rather a defense against wrong and a punishment of it, and an effort to defend and maintain the right.[30]

---

[26] Ibid., 111.
[27] Ibid., 111.
[28] Ibid., 112.
[29] Ibid., 112.
[30] Ibid., 113.

In respect to hermeneutics it is interesting to note that Luther explicitly queries whether one really has to take seriously the literal formulation of the text in Matthew 5:39. This becomes important in light of who is addressed in Jesus' recommendation, "do not resist one who is evil." Jesus used the second person plural: you. He was not addressing everybody and saying that generally there should be no resistance against one who is evil. It is "you," the disciples of Christ, who should not resist one who is evil. Jesus' counsel is directed at the personal sphere rather than secular government. Jesus' disciples should leave the resistance to evil to secular institutions while maintaining a strong interest in and support for strong institutions in a society resisting injustice and evil and securing justice and peace. However, in respect to themselves, their individual "I"-perspective, Christians should not encounter those who are doing evil and injustice with anger and revenge but, rather, preserve a pure and friendly heart in respect to them.

Luther would not have had the impact he had on his fellow people, if it were not for the fact that the whole situation was (and often still is) more tricky, because there are more subtle forms of doing injustice and evil than directly striking someone in the face or taking away their coat or other property. Luther was well aware that courts and politics were used by people to betray others or to impropriate somebody's property. In such cases injustice happens with the support of the law and political institutions.

> Thus a person may seek an injunction against you before the law as if he had a good claim against you, when what he really wants is to make you surrender your own property. This is what Christ calls 'taking your coat' before the court, when someone denies you the right to your own property; then you must not only suffer injustice innocently, but you must also be adjudged guilty as though you were in the wrong.[31]

The law, which was intended to protect the pious and the powerless, was and continues to be misused and within the legal system there are—at least in Luther's opinion—too many people who, in the first instance, seek their own advantage, "who turn and twist and misuse the law to support their own whims. [...] Nowadays nothing is so common as making right wrong and wrong right."[32] Luther articulated his fear, that especially pious Christians will suffer from this situation, because with their pure hearts they easily fall victim to all those who play their evil games with them.

---

[31] Ibid., 114.
[32] Ibid., 114.

According to Luther, Jesus warned his Christians to prepare themselves to suffer from such a situation of evil.

Solidarity in persecution and suffering and resisting anger and retaliation as a mark of the church

In his interpretation of Matthew 5, Luther's considerations on Christian perfection were mainly related to the life of a Christian as an individual in their personal and public life. But, in his other texts, we find similar ideas related to the church, especially concerning anger and retaliation. Luther considers not to give room to anger and retaliation, even in cases of unfair und unjust suffering and persecution, as a mark of the true church: the church which is faithful to its Lord Jesus Christ.

In his later writings, Luther formulated new marks of the church in addition to those in the Nicene Creed[33] or the Augsburg Confession.[34] In "On the Councils and the Church, 1539" he formulated seven marks of the church, arguing against a profane understanding of the church—in the sense of the church being an important organization within society, contributing for example to the homogenization of a society. For Luther this would not be the "holy Christian church" or the "holy Christian people." He believed living a holy life to promise "that a Christian holy people is to be and to remain on earth until the end of the world. This is an article of faith that cannot be terminated until that which it believes come, as Christ promises,

---

[33] The traditional four marks of the church are formulated in the Nicene Creed: "We believe [...] in one holy, catholic and apostolic Church." Oneness, holiness, catholicity and apostolicity are attributes of the church, who is the body of Christ and the people of God (to use two major definitions of the church in the New Testament). They are attributes of God's acting, which creates the church and preserves it. For the understanding of these four marks of the church, see Eberhard Jüngel, "Belief in the One Holy, Catholic and Apostolic Church," in Hans-Peter Grosshans (ed.), *One Holy, Catholic and Apostolic Church. Some Lutheran and Ecumenical Perspectives*, LWF Studies 01/2009 (Geneva/Minneapolis: The Lutheran World Federation/Lutheran University Press, 2009), 21-32; Hans-Peter Grosshans, "Introducing the Theme: The One Holy, Catholic and Apostolic Church as Realized in Lutheran Churches," in Hans-Peter Grosshans and Martin L. Sinaga (eds), *"Like Living Stones." Lutheran Reflections on the One Holy, Catholic and Apostolic Church*, LWF Studies 02/2010 (Geneva/Minneapolis: The Lutheran World Federation/Lutheran University Press, 2010), 11-20.

[34] According to CA 7 the church, which is the congregation of the believers, has two essential characteristics: an adequate teaching of the gospel and the right (that is: in correspondence with the gospel) to administer the sacraments. These two essential marks of the Church in CA 7 are the minimal requirements for a social and spiritual body to be identified as church.

'I am with you always, to the close of the age' (Mt 28:20)."[35] Luther asked how an ordinary person can "tell where such Christian holy people are to be found in this world."[36] He then formulated seven marks of the church that identify the true church on earth (and so distinguishes the true from a false church). These marks take up the well-known marks of CA 7 and start with the possession and preaching of the holy Word of God and then go on to the administration of the sacraments of baptism and the altar. As a fourth mark Luther mentions the office of keys: the practice of forgiving sins, followed by the calling and consecration of ministers (and perhaps further offices), the Lord's Prayer, public worship and songs.

> Seventh, the holy Christian people are externally recognized by the holy possession of the sacred cross. They must endure every misfortune and persecution, all kinds of trials and evil from the devil, the world, and the flesh [...] by inward sadness, timidity, fear, outward poverty, contempt, illness, weakness, in order to become like their head, Christ. And the only reason they must suffer is that they steadfastly adhere to Christ and God's word, enduring this for the sake of Christ, Matthew 5:11, "Blessed are you when men persecute you on my account." They must be pious, quiet, obedient, and prepared to serve the government and everybody with life and goods, doing no one any harm. No people on earth have to endure such bitter hate [...]. In summary, they must be called heretics, knaves, and devils, the most pernicious people on earth, to the point where those who hang, drown, murder, torture, banish, and plague them to death are rendering God a service. No one has compassion on them; they are given myrrh and gall to drink when they thirst. And all of this is done not because they are adulterers, murderers, thieves, or rogues, but because they want to have none but Christ, and no other God. Wherever you see or hear this, you may know that the holy Christian church is there, as Christ says in Matthew 5:11-12, "Blessed are you when men revile you and utter all kinds of evil against you on my account. Rejoice and be glad, for your reward is great in heaven." This too is a holy possession whereby the Holy Spirit not only sanctifies his people, but also blesses them.[37]

With two references to the Beatitudes in Matthew 5, Luther identifies the persecution Christians suffer to be a mark of the church. Luther saw himself and the Reformation churches in the tradition of the early church that suffered heavy persecution. But it is not only in persecution and discrimination that the true church can be recognized; it is also in the reaction to this by not striving for revenge, but in accepting suffering for the sake of Christ.

---

[35] *LW* 41, 148.
[36] Ibid., 148.
[37] Ibid., 164f.

In his highly polemical writing, "Against Hanswurst, 1541," Luther argues against the accusation that he and others founded a new church and are therefore schismatics and heretics who have fallen away from the holy church. Luther wanted to show that on the one hand the churches of the Reformation "have remained faithful to the true ancient church, indeed, that we are the true ancient church" and, on the other, "that you have fallen away from us, that is, the ancient church, and have set up a new church against the ancient one."[38] Luther's formulation of the marks of the church in "Against Hanswurst" takes a specific direction: the marks of the church show that the church of the Reformation corresponds to the early and original church. Consequently, Luther shows that the papal church is a new church by pointing to the many inventions the Roman Catholic Church made since the times of the apostles. At this point, Luther repeats the marks of the church from "On the Councils and the Church" adding some new ones. Marks 9 and 10 then read as follows: "[N]obody can deny that we experience the same suffering [...] as our brethren in the world. We are persecuted in every place, strangled, drowned, hanged, and tormented in every way for the sake of the word." [39]And,

> nobody can deny that we have not shed blood, murdered, hanged, or avenged ourselves in return, as we could often have done could still do. But as Christ, the apostles, and the ancient church did, we endure, admonish, and pray for others. And, indeed, we do this publicly in church, in the litany and in sermons, just as Christ our Lord did and taught and as the ancient church also did, so that in this we all act according to the ancient practice of the ancient church.[40]

Here Luther repeats that he, as well as many other reformers who wanted to be faithful to the gospel and to Jesus Christ, suffered in similar ways to Jesus Christ and the persecuted Christians in the first centuries of the church.

We find the most drastic example of this understanding in Martin Luther's first song written in 1523 that describes the way in which, during his time, the established powers persecuted, killed and turned into martyrs faithful Christians. This was the case on 1 July 1523, when on the market square in Brussels two young Augustinian monks from Antwerp, Heinrich Voes and Johann Esch, were burnt to death after having been charged with adhering to Martin Luther. The first two verses of Luther's ballad read as follows:

---

[38] Ibid., 194.
[39] Ibid., 197.
[40] Ibid., 198.

A new song now shall we begun,
Lord, help us raise the banner
Of praise for all that God has done,
For which we give Him honor.
At Brussels in the Netherlands
God proved Himself most truthful
And poured His gifts from open hands
On two lads, martyrs youthful
Through whom He showed His power.

One was named John, a name to show
He stood in God's high favor.
His brother Henry, well we know,
Was salt of truest savor.
This world they now have left behind
And wear bright crowns of glory.
These sons of God had fixed the mind
Upon the Gospel story,
For which they died as martyrs.[41]

Today we still witness the suffering and persecution of faithful followers of the gospel. And suffering and persecution are not always inflicted by non-Christians but also by people and organizations that claim to be Christians and to be church. The suffering and persecution, experienced not only by Luther but also by fellow Christians such as the two Augustinian monks burnt publicly because they had sympathized with Luther linked the Reformation churches directly with the ancient church and made them direct followers of the Christian church as it had existed from its beginning in Jesus Christ and the apostles.

In this experience of suffering and persecution—for the sake of righteousness—Luther also saw the reality Matthew envisaged in the Beatitudes in Matthew 5:10–12 and in other parts of the sermon of the Mount.

Summary

One is a Christian because one belongs to Jesus Christ. As an individual I am responsible to Jesus Christ for all my life. The "heart" is the symbolic expression of the individual's center. Therefore Jesus Christ lives in the heart of a Christian, and purity of the heart is a prerequisite for being Christian. But

---

[41] *LW* 53, 214.

individual Christians ("I") are also related to other people whom they refer to with the personal pronouns "you" and "he, she, it" and plural "you" and "they." These relations have to be lived out differently to the relationship to oneself. In relations to others a Christian is responsible for their welfare, justice and peace. In relation to oneself one does not have the same responsibility; in fact, a person is a Christian because they trust that Jesus Christ is fully responsible for their sake. However, Christians are not only "I" in relation to Jesus Christ but also "we." Because they belong to Jesus Christ, they can refer to themselves in the plural, as "we." As "we" they share all the characteristics that characterize the individual Christian existence. If one of the "we" suffers, they all suffer. Furthermore, they share fundamental beliefs and the same idea of a perfect Christian life. Therefore, not to seek revenge and retaliation for injustice, suffering and persecution also characterize the community of Christians. Not every Christian has to experience injustice, suffering and persecution and to struggle with the emotions of anger and retaliation and to resist them. This is a mark of the church because in the "we" of the Christians all feel the injustice one of them experiences; all suffer if one suffers; all are persecuted if one is persecuted. And, similarly, every Christian has to combat their emotions of anger and retaliation and resist them.

The model that Luther developed to understand Matthew's evangelical counsels, especially in Matthew 5, could be read as a commentary on Matthew 10:16b "so be wise as serpents and innocent as doves," a counsel Jesus gave to his disciples when he sent them out. The Greek word used here implies a specific form of wisdom: prudence. In classical Greek philosophy this comprises intellectual and emotional wisdom, which a person needs in every situation: no two situations are the same and every situation is more or less complex. Pretending to realize a perfect Christian life by eliminating the diverse plurality of life situations and their complexity by Christians cloistering themselves in strictly ordered forms of life does not secure perfection. It is similar to the attempt to secure a perfect life by forcing everybody by law and public force into specific forms of life in order to reduce the diversity and complexity of life. Such reduction of complexity and diversity is not only inhuman but also an illusion. According to Luther, Christians with pure heart and only good intentions should be prudent in all their contacts with other people. As Luther maintains, "be prudent in your contacts with other people."[42]

To retain the idea of perfecting Christian life, Luther distinguished between the secular and divine realms. It is in the interface between both realms and their respective responsibilities, in which Christians live, that a perfect Christian life becomes possible.

---

[42] *LW* 21, 118.

On Loving your Enemy

THE SECRET LINK BETWEEN FAITH AND LOVE: LUTHER ON THE BEATITUDES (MT 5:43-48)

Vítor Westhelle

INTRODUCTION

"These are three things, so to speak, which every good preacher should do: First, he takes his place; second, he opens his mouth and says something; third, he knows when to stop."[1] These are words with which Luther opens his commentary on the Sermon on the Mount. And he follows his own counsel, at least up to step two. It is only some 300 pages later that he finally tries to accept his third piece of advice and stop: "Let this be sufficient on the matter,"[2] he concludes. But something about this text is disturbing. It lacks the craftsmanship and flourishes of Luther's other texts.

Luther's Sermon on the Mount is a transcript from the Wednesday sermons he delivered between 1530 and 1532. He was filling in for Johannes Bugenhagen—Luther's pastor in the city church of Wittenberg—while he was out of town implementing the Reformation in Lübeck. Questions remain about the accuracy of these transcribed sermons and how well they present the nuances and subtleties of the Reformer's theology. Yet, there is no reason to assume that the recorders were untrustworthy. Even if the manner in which the text tries to convey some of the subtleties in Luther's thought and theology can be questioned, the topics are generally consistent with other works that Luther penned himself. Clumsy expressions notwithstanding,

---

[1] Martin Luther, "The Sermon on the Mount," in Jaroslav Pelikan (ed.), *Luther's Works*, vol. 21 (Saint Louis: Concordia Publishing House, 1956), 7.
[2] Ibid., 94.

the language broadly follows his style, and the prose bears the imprint of Luther's theology. This is supported by the fact that the Reformer himself authored the preface to the published edition of these sermons. This is as good an imprimatur as any.[3]

Addressing the hermeneutical conundrum

Harald Diem's dissertation on Luther's two kingdoms notion employs Luther's interpretation of the Sermon on the Mount in Matthew as the gauge for accessing Luther's hermeneutical principle.[4] It serves as a guide for interpreting the relationship between the faith that the Scriptures attest to, and the ethical demands implied there. Diem sees this sermon as paving the way for assessing Luther's distinction of the two kingdoms as an interpretative principle that links faith and love, but does not confuse them. Avoiding an allegorical interpretation, Luther finds in the Sermon on the Mount a distinction between dimensions of competence, or realms of truth-speaking, which are not transferable from one to the other. They are distinct and not to be confused or separated.

The terms that refer to these two realms or dimensions are not consistently used by Luther. In German *Reiche* and *Regimente,* normally used to designate the "doctrine," suggest a clear distinction between conceptual schemes. One finds its source in the Augustinian two cities, and the other in the medieval two swords distinction. But this is not that simple for in Latin the term for both is only *regnum.*[5] The picture gets even more complicated by the fact that Luther uses many other metaphors and concepts to frame the same distinction.[6] To avoid unnecessary disputes over nomenclature it is proper to call it a distinction of regimes and thus to avoid the trap of a vitiated dispute over terminology, lest we be distracted from the

---

[3] Note the pertinent comment by Jaroslav Pelikan regarding this issue in ibid., XX–XXI.

[4] Harald Diem, "Luthers Lehre von den Zwei Reichen untersucht von seinem Verständnis der Bergpredigt aus," in Gerhard Sauter and Johannes Haun (eds), *Zwei-Reiche-Lehre Luthers* (Munich: Chr. Kaiser, 1973), 1–173. The original publication is from 1938 and he is not to be confused with his older brother, Hermann Diem, who wrote *Luthers Predigt in den zwei Reichen* (München: Chr. Kaiser, 1947).

[5] For a comprehensive account of the history of the doctrine, see Ulrich Duchrow, *Christenheit und Weltverantwortung: Traditionsgeschichte und systematische Struktur der Zweireichelehre* (Stuttgart: Ernst Klett, 1970)

[6] See Gustaf Törnvall, *Geistliches und weltliches Regiment bei Luther* (München: Kaiser, 1947), particularly 44, 94–95, where he lists some thirty-eight different expressions to point to the different regimes.

very distinction to which these terms point to, namely the relationship of incommensurable values.

These different values are expressed in the simultaneous affirmation of the tradition ("you have heard") and the apparent supersession ("but I tell you"). But then, while raising the bar on demands and ethical commands, he radically sharpens the contrast between obligation and the gift freely bestowed without a demand. The blessings are bequeathed to people, in particular life conditions without any relationship to duties. They are given to the poor, the meek, the hungry, the peacemakers, etc. Here the difference between gift and task is drastically highlighted. More than a difference, a disturbance is introduced, since the relationship is not cancelled. Rather, the system of causality is suspended. One is blessed for one's condition in life, not for achieving it.[7]

Being blessed is caused neither by love nor does it bring about love in any positive causal sense i.e., in its philosophical reception of some-thing being posited. Instead, blessedness is the negative condition of the possibility for love to take place, because those described as blessed are neither subjectively nor objectively entering into a circular economy of reciprocity and bartering. They can love and be loved without a quasi-commercial transaction. Blessedness belongs to the *vita passiva*; it does not posit anything but is pure receptivity. Love, on the contrary, posits something. Love expresses itself objectively in action; it belongs to the *vita activa*. But then, what about love as a command in general and love of the enemy in particular? How can it be issued as a positive command when its conditions of possibility are negative? Or are they? If faith cannot be predicated on duty, how can the love command be at all linked to it? Can there be love without faith or vice-versa? Or can faith at all demand love? In other words, the problem that Luther faces is to explain how faith and love relate. How can faith that is purely receptive and the source of all blessedness yield love that is active without destroying itself in work righteousness? Kierkegaard writing about duty in general phrased it with precision: "The duty becomes duty by being traced back to God, but in the duty itself I do not enter into relation to God."[8] If there is a relationship, it is a one-way street. This also means that the issuing of the love com-mand is divine, but its execution does not bring us closer to God. Phrasing

---

[7] Note that the apparent exception is the reference to the peacemakers (*eirēnopoioi*). But Matthew's Gospel was written for a context after the destruction of the temple, which suggests that a peace*maker* is one who loves peace and is at ease under the most adverse circumstances, not a militant pacifist in an active protest.

[8] Søren Kierkegaard, *Fear and Trembling, and Repetition,* ed. and transl. Howard V. Hong and Edna H. Hong (Princeton: Princeton University Press, 1983), 68.

it more precisely, the fulfillment of the law takes us into the world. Yet, Christologicallly this move into the world, into materiality is to encounter God *sub contraria specie*.

The merit of Harald Diem's work was to show that the key to opening up the apparent maze or labyrinth of Luther's thoughts on the issue was a hermeneutical one.[9] How do we read the Scriptures? Who is addressed? And to which of life's stations does it pertain? Does it speak to us in our nudity when we are as we are, without pretense, without representation, exposed and utterly vulnerable? And then, when does it speak to us when we are dressed up, wearing the outfit proper to the office we occupy? In other words, how does Scripture address us when we put up a persona, the mask we wear when performing the task to which we are called? When we perform a duty, when we answer a call, we are not simply ourselves, exposed and bare, because we must carry out the obligations entailed in the calling we have, the mask we wear: the soldier, the peasant, the banker, the carpenter, the mother, the clerk, the politician, the lawyer, the teacher, the priest and so forth, in their station in life. Love as expressed positively in daily life conforms to the conditions of possibility within the constraints of institutional life where our calling takes place. But given those constraints, is love possible at all, particularly the love of the enemy? In this regard Luther is Pauline to the core by sustaining the incommensurability of faith and love

The Sermon on the Mount exemplifies the distinction between two sets of injunctions, which we find in the Bible by presenting them in relation to each other. The first is the Beatitudes themselves, the gift that is given and in faith received. The other is the commandments. One does not invalidate the other, but if the latter addresses the office, the Beatitudes address the bare self, the naked self, the self that is held in secrecy as in the bareness of the heart. "And your father who is in secret and sees in secret will reward you," as the saying is repeated three times in chapter 6 of the Sermon on the Mount (Mt 6:4, 6, 18). It functions as a trustworthy mantra that one may know by heart, even and because its meaning is not evident to our common earthly (rational) experience.

The context in which this call for secrecy appears is relevant. One refers to giving alms to the poor; the other two times are in reference to devotional practices, praying and fasting. One refers to the expression of love toward the neighbor and the other two, which apparently references religious practices, are still expression of worldly love in keeping the

---

[9] See Johannes Heckel, "Im Irrgarten der Zwei-Reiche-Lehre: Zwei Abhandlungen zum Reichs- und Kirchenbegriff Martin Luthers," in *Theologische Existenz Heute* 55 (1959), 343–45.

ecclesia in its right place as a space to worship, demarcated from socio-political and economic transactions. But even this expression of love is not to enter into a relationship to God, but to preserve in the world the space of Shabbat. However, it is interesting to note that these three "good works" comprise for Luther the whole scope of good works. Luther subjects the text of Matthew to his own systematic purposes.

> For these three good works include just about all the rest. The first means that we do all kinds of good works toward our neighbor; the second means that we are concerned about all sort of needs, both public and private, and that we bring them before God; and the third means that we discipline our body. As they have shamefully misused both almsgiving and praying by seeking not God's glory but their own praise through it, so they misused and perverted fasting.[10]

That Luther sees these three good works as a summary of all reveals the triadic structure of Luther's thought on the spheres that comprise earthly existence. Alms giving concerns human sustenance and is a perversion of the economic dimension when used to enhance one's control over the means of subsistence. Praying, particularly the emphasis Luther gives to its public character, refers to our vested needs to advertise what we want accomplished publicly. Here prayer is not used as a religious rite belonging to the ecclesial sphere, but rather it is employed in its political use! What finally follows, fasting, refers properly to the emptying of oneself for God to see, but keeping it a secret to other humans.

God is the one who sees in secret, which means that God can see what humans cannot see. For love to be real and not merely sentimental, it needs to show itself, be visible. However secrecy is required for this love not to become work righteousness. Love needs to be hidden with regard to its source (the doer), but visible and to be seen and received by the beloved. This is precisely the meaning of the saying in Matthew 5:16, "let your light shine before others, so that they may see your good works [...] ." Indeed, the affirmation of visibility is emphatic. However, the decisive point is the ending of the verse in which those who see the good work "give glory to your Father in heaven." In other words, it does not say: "so that they may thank you." The secrecy by hiding the agent protects faith from entering the economy of reciprocity.

This secrecy creates an emptiness that eludes the sight and thus offers itself as the receptacle of blessedness, as it also disguises a gesture of love by preventing it from being directly reciprocated. So is the love of the enemy. If seen by the adversary as a gesture of the opponent, it would

---

[10] *LW* 21, 155; *WA* 32, 428, 11ff.

cancel itself out. The gaze must be redirected toward God. *Coram mundo* enmities and hatred will continue until *coram deo* we acknowledge the good deed and give glory to God. This is *metanoia*. This is the singular reason why the love of the enemy does not stretch love to its implausible most demanding extreme. Love of the enemy is the litmus test of any love, its secret heart, the naked core of love itself.

What humans naturally see belongs to the created world that extends itself in time and space. Humans are to administer it as public persons fulfilling a calling through labor, political action and observing the Shabbat. We find in Luther the distinction between the realm of hearing (*Hörreich*) and the realm of seeing (*Sehereich*).[11] That faith comes by hearing is a statement that in the visible realm corresponds to love. This love grows out of what is heard, but as a love its vector is toward what is seen. Love needs to empty itself of the lofty assurances of faith's blessedness in order to become love in its concrete and tangible expression in finite existence. But to be concrete/actual love, above all, love of the enemy, it must be "shown" by it not being displayed. Only under this condition of secrecy will it bring effective results. It needs to be a secret love. Only a love that is real and concrete, but kept in secret as to its doer, fulfills the commandment of love. And it does so by redirecting the gaze from things visible to the glory of God. This is the reason why only a blessed one can love the enemy. Only those who refuse to use their love as a bargaining chip truly love.

To display to others the love for an enemy is likely to be a Trojan horse; it carries in its belly the venom disguised in a glamorous appearance. The poison comes along with the display and is effective because of the seductive glamour of the display.

The legend of the Greek gift is the counter-narrative to the secrecy of the Sermon on the Mount. To display love for an enemy is likely to be a Trojan horse. The poison comes along with the display. Against this backdrop, we can make sense of Jesus' injunction in the Gospel of Luke 14:26: "Whoever comes to me and does not hate father and mother, wife and children, brothers and sisters, yes, and even life itself, cannot be my disciple." Only in this hatred can true altruistic, unselfish love manifest itself. As Kierkegaard himself recognizes, "this is a hard saying," but true in keeping both, faith and love, without confusing them and thus betraying both.[12]

Here we find the crucial point. True love is presence; it cannot be represented. However this hiding of presence requires representation, as

---

[11] For this terminology and several other expressions used by Luther to address the distinction of regimes, see Törnvall, op. cit. (note 6); see also David Löfgren, *Die Theologie der Schöpfung bei Luther* (Göttingen: Vandenhoeck & Ruprecht, 1960).
[12] Kierkegaard, op. cit. (note 8), 72.

much as a gift calls for a wrapping (Luther: *involocrum*). Luther faces the conundrum of affirming the finitude of love in its worldly endeavors and in the visibility of its expressions or representations, while also affirming its universal claims and acknowledging love's infinite enabling source. In his commentary on the Sermon, Luther is grappling for language to convey the *est*, his signature concept, without erasing the difference nor accepting a form of gradation between the finite and the infinite, as if the richer the wrapping the closer it is to the present it envelops.[13] Luther was particularly concerned about distancing himself from the standard medieval interpretation of the Sermon's radicalization of duty as counsels (*consilia*) for some and not precepts for all. He was, at the time of his sermons, suspected of theologically caving into Rome's stance. And he wants his position to be made clear.

FAITH AND LOVE

What is the connection between faith and love, two of the three traditional cardinal virtues of 1 Corinthians 13—which Luther also affirmed—namely, faith, hope and love? Luther's task is to explain the relationship between the undetermined faith that belongs to the *vita passiva* and the love that is determined and active, and shows itself. This is the reason why it should be kept in secret (*en tō kryptō*). It is not invisible. It is a question of authenticity. This is the point: love is to be kept from sight, so that the act seen by the receiver is an authentic gift rather than an object of barter. And the Father who sees in secret will reward the giver.

This is not the economy of circular exchange, which happens when the subject of the act of mercy is rewarded by displaying the act in the open as propaganda. This reward from the "Father" who sees in secret is absolute surplus value, because the reward of publicity is sacrificed when love is kept out of sight, yet all the same visible only *in abscondito*! This is how love of the enemy needs to proceed. It is a secret love of the pure heart that dispenses mercies without necessarily ceasing outward hostility. Love appears here as a disruption in the circular economy of exchange. The exchange becomes asymmetric. The gift bestowed by secret love disrupts the economy and yields no compensation, except by the One who sees in secret and to whom alone glory is due.

---

[13] These two fronts are identified as the "enthusiast," who defended the identity of Christian life and worldly existence, and the "Roman" gradation, which treats some moral demands as counsels for some people and other demands into precepts that all are to keep. See Diem, op. cit. (note 4), 22.

The Sermon on the Mount is not to be taken as counsel or advice for the few who want to achieve perfection while remaining at most a desideratum for the average Christian. This is one motif that the Reformer repeats over and over again to counter the contiguity between heaven and earth in which the difference is not a matter of gradation, an axiological ordering between lower and higher and higher and lower, as he accuses the systems of knowledge and power of doing in his day. Luther opens the preface that he himself wrote for the publication of his transcribed sermons, attacking the difference between *praecepta legis* and *consilia evangelica* and ordering them so that the counsels are seen "merely as advice to those who want to become perfect."[14] No, he says. The distinction is not the one between different classes or castes of people; it is a distinction within the person, between the heart and the deed. To use Luther's expressions, one being *coram deo*, and the other *coram hominibus/mundo*. What bridges the two is kept out of sight, is kept in secret, for the eyes of the one who sees in secret only.

Communio

The theology behind the Reformer's stance is twofold. First, the person is simultaneously a Christian and a worldly person but, nonetheless, one person. Here Luther's understanding of the *communicatio idiomatum*, as expounded in "The Councils and the Church, 1539" in particular, is of paramount importance. The person of Christ cannot be divided, and neither can the Christian, in whom Christ indwells. "Wherever you place God for me, you must also place the humanity for me."[15] For him, anthropology recapitulates theology. Hence he states plainly and clearly that these injunctions are not advice "to be kept by anyone who pleases."[16] They are commandments given to the whole human person as a Christian.[17] Loving one's enemy means what it says, it demands what it asks. But, in so much as the divine is encrypted, secretly held, in the frailty of the flesh to be the gift, so is the love of the enemy possible as long as it remains a secret gift. In short, love of the enemy is the often missing link in Luther studies between grace and love, faith and work/law.

Secondly, Luther is quite aware of the imperious character of Jesus' radicalizing of the law, apparently stretching it to the breaking point. And

---

[14] *LW* 21, 3–4; *WA* 32, 299–301.
[15] *LW* 37, 219; *WA* 26, 261ff.
[16] *LW* 21, 4; *WA* 32, 300, 1–5.
[17] *LW* 21, 4; *WA* 32, 299–301.

somehow he delights in it, for it plays along with his theological program of letting God be God and the human truly human. Yet, this is the point, the two are in communion, they communicate their properties, their *idiomata*, to each other in the singularity of the person. Neither the Roman canonists nor the enthusiasts understood that. The former, by turning it into mere advice "obliterate" it; the latter try to organize the whole of life with these commandments as if they belonged to the organization of social existence, as if infinitude could be conquered, while it is already a given.[18] "Thus the devil blows and brews on both sides so that they do not recognize any difference between the secular and the divine realm,"[19]—the enthusiasts by collapsing the difference, the Papists by rationally ordering them axiologically. The whole commentary on the Sermon in Matthew hinges on this distinction. But how do we proceed from here? Luther is aware of the hazards of navigating between the Scylla of Rome and the Charybdis of enthusiasm.

The injunctions of the Sermon on the Mount neither abolish the law nor substitute for it. It also does not establish a different social sphere for which it becomes valid. It is legislation valid neither for the *ecclesia* nor for the *oeconomia* or the *politia*. It is not valid in any of these spheres or institutions. However, it does actuate itself in these institutions not being a dispositive of them. How does it actuate itself? This is the formulation of the problem: if the radicalizing of the law exceeds the law, how does it encroach on the law? It does by hiding the gift under the law. The law is love's camouflage. One does not see this love, but faith tells the tale.

Rhetorical device

Diem's early work on the two kingdoms, using this Sermon as narrated by Matthew, presented it as Luther's hermeneutical proposal to avoid the intricacies of medieval semantics and the figurative rendition of difficult biblical texts. Consider the love of the enemy as in the passage of the Sermon on the Mount that is being addressed. This entails a complicated argument if not an inconsistency in Luther's writing.

After all that is said about the *sensus literalis*, we are here faced with the unavoidable problem of the use of figurative language. Luther's critique of the *quadriga* with its three figurative senses (allegorical, tropological and anagogical, to which the literal sense was a fourth) comes up because he claims that the Sermon on the Mount applies to all Christians—and not

---

[18] Ibid., 5; *WA* 32, 300–301.
[19] Ibid., 5; *WA* 32, 301, 3–6.

only to the monks or other particular groups of people. However, he also said that many other things do not apply. He uses the example of the lepers. Upon healing them, Jesus orders them to show themselves to the priests and make a sacrifice (Lk 17:14). The example of Jesus ought to serve us, says Luther, but not his command.[20] What is the difference between that passage in Luke, where Jesus' command is not to be followed, and the commands of the Sermon on the Mount, from which no one is excused, even when they cannot be completely fulfilled? Was this a way of circumventing the pertinence of the Sermon on the Mount for every Christian, by just changing the medieval distinction between religious and secular by replacing them with the distinction between intention and act?

Luther himself insisted that even if the whole Scripture was the Word of God, not everyone was addressed by it. It is God's Word, "that is true; we cannot deny it, but we are not the people," he insisted in the sermon "How Christians Should Regard Moses, 1525."[21] Furthermore, in addition to using the *quadriga* himself on occasion,[22] he is known for his appeal to figurative language, and he praised in particular what he regarded to be the most beautiful use of such a rhetoric device in the Scriptures: synecdoche. Synecdoche is the rhetorical figure by which the whole expresses a part, or a part the whole. "Synecdoche, to be sure, is a most sweet and necessary figure of speech and a symbol of God's love and mercy," claimed the Reformer.[23]

However, immediately after he discusses the biblical usage of synecdoche, he notes that he does not recall "seeing any scriptural texts which use that form of synecdoche in which a universal expression stands for the particular."[24] Only the reverse is the case. For example: "God loves the world" is a universal, thus it is literal; as a synecdoche it refers to God's love for a particular people or person. When synecdoche is used it is the particular that receives a universal signifier. This means that a universal is evoked but it pertains to the particular. Luther said that this is exemplified "sometimes when He [God] is said to strike and destroy," and "one is not to understand that He strikes all or completely annihilates, for He touches the whole when he touches a part."[25] What is the implication of this for the discussion here?

Luther's use of synecdoche, restricting its application in biblical interpretation to cases in which the particular is referred to by the whole, already gives us a clue to understanding the universality of love, even if

---

[20] *LW* 35, 174; *WA* 16, 393.

[21] *LW* 35, 161–74; *WA* 16, 363–93.

[22] E.g., *WA* 4, 14–15; 55/I, 4, 3–18.

[23] *LW* 32, 169f.

[24] Ibid., 170.

[25] Ibid., 170.

in its manifestation it remains partial. To use the example of the command given to the lepers to present themselves to the priests and make a sacrifice, to make it a universal precept to all would be an incorrect use of the synecdoche, to take a particular case and universalize it.

LOVE'S LABOR'S LIMITS

The Sermon on the Mount offers the Reformer a unique understanding of what is entailed in love of the enemy. As in all the other injunctions, it starts with an appeal to the law or customs ("You have heard that it was said ..., but I say..."). Luther is quick to note that this reference to the hatred of enemies is not found anywhere in the Scriptures. Nevertheless, "scattered" references infer it. Stretching such inference by assuming its legitimacy is, for the Reformer, wrong. So, in order to get the intention of the law it was stretched to the extent of loving one's enemy. However this law, if prescribed without further ado, would turn out not only to be impossible to fulfill, but also irresponsible. And so he asks:

> What is to be said about the fact that the Scriptures often talk about holy men cursing their enemies, even about Christ and his disciples doing so? Would you call that blessing their enemies? Or how can I love the pope when every day I rebuke and curse him—and with good reasons too?[26]

This leads to two problems. First, Luther applies these words to all Christians, for it is the gospel, thus it is for all.[27] Here he does not let anyone off the hook, whereas, as we have seen above, many other passages he deemed not applicable to all. Secondly, he recognizes that Christians are unable to fulfill Christ's commandments, not due to moral weaknesses (even though those weaknesses apply), but because our calling to serve in the divinely ordained institutions would not allow us even to try to fulfill them outwardly. It is irresponsible to apply them to our calling in the household (*oeconomia*), in the government (*politia*) and even in the church (*ecclesia*).

So, how do we get out of this imbroglio? We have to remember that we are here talking mainly about the Beatitudes, about being blessed. This is the framework of this chapter, which starts with the description of the blessed and continues with the contrasting "you have heard ... but I say to you." Furthermore—and this brings us back to the use of the synecdoche—while love of the enemy is a gesture of universalizing love, the concrete and particular form

---

[26] *LW* 21, 119; *WA* 16, 363–93.
[27] *LW* 35, 171; *WA* 16, 363ff.

in which this love is manifested is limited by circumstances, which means that its employment is restricted to particular expressions or gestures of love. Inconspicuous as these gestures might be, particular are they in their manifestation. Thus here is the synecdoche: the part touches the whole. This particular form in which love expresses itself may be used, by figurative transference (synecdoche), as love universal, always limited to the constraints of the earthly kingdom where love displays itself. It is confined and conforms to the size of the masks we wear, adapted to the instruments we employ.

This means that we are called to be holy *coram mundo,* where we are entrusted with responsibilities that definitely require work and law in the service of love in sanctification. No one is exempt from this responsibility. But we are blessed *coram deo* for the faith that by grace reaches us when we relinquish any attempt at confusing blessedness and holiness, or seeing the two as stages in an ascending scale. Luther saw the confusing of the two in the enthusiasts' attainment of perfection; the progression on the gradation toward sainthood was seen as the stance of the medieval Roman church.

Spheres and regimes

Here Luther insists on another distinction that not only discerns or discriminates among the orders,[28] but distinguishes realms that are not symmetrical alternatives. These are the earthly and the spiritual realm, which Luther, also called *inter alia* kingdoms, governances.[29] The amount of literature on the so-called "Two Kingdoms Doctrine" produced between the 1930s and the 1960s is immense.[30] However, in order to clarify the challenge of interpreting the Beatitudes, it is sufficient to indicate some guiding marks. First, although it relates to the three spheres or instituted orders, the distinction of regimes belongs to a different order of discourse. The institutions belong to a form of discourse that is not properly or uniquely theological, because it intersects with philosophy *lato sensu,* to

---

[28] *Vult Deus esse discrimina ordinum* (*WA* 44, 440, 25).

[29] The terms that refer to these two realms are not consistently used by Luther. While in German *Reiche* and *Regimente* suggest a clear distinction between conceptual schemes, in Latin the term for both is only *regnum*. For the best description of the formation of these two traditions, see Duchrow, op. cit. (note 5); see particularly his main thesis on 440. To avoid unnecessary disputes over nomenclature it is proper to call it a distinction of regimes.

[30] See Vítor Westhelle, "The Dark Room, the Labyrinth, and the Mirror: On Interpreting Luther's Thought on Justification and Justice," in Joseph A. Burguess and Marc Kolden (eds.), *By Faith Alone: Essays on Justification in Honor of Gerhard O. Forde* (Grand Rapids: Eerdmans, 2004), 316–31.

include politics, economy, sociology, anthropology, etc. However, Luther's distinction of regimes is strictly theological. Here Christology is the determining factor. It pertains to Luther's understanding of the relationship of Christ's two natures, without separating or mixing his understanding of the *communicatio idiomatum,* as referred to above. Like Christ, so are Christians, as "little Christs," simultaneously and totally in the flesh and in matter and, by grace, partakers of the divine. The reality is one, as the finite is capable of the infinite, but the perspective from which we look at it differs. It is as different as it is to look at the same crystal from different facets, yet it is the same crystal, to use Luther's simile.[31]

The Beatitudes describe those whose situation is one that goes against the ways of the world or who resists to its ways by not following them: The poor, the weak, those who mourn a loss, the hungry, the merciful, the pure in heart, the peaceful, the persecuted all those characterized by negative characteristics, adverse features. These characteristics do not apply to the orders of creation characterized by such positive features as having nourishment, reproductive rights, protection and leisure. The household or the economy has to feed the people and not let them hunger, the government has to defend the weak even by engaging in war, and the church's calling is to enrich the people spiritually by preserving the dignity of the Shabbat and providing space for learning the Word preached and for leisure, to be at ease receiving God's very presence.

BLESSED AND HOLY

In his "Confession Concerning the Lord's Supper, 1528," Luther makes this distinction between the blessed and the holy, which ought not to be forgotten because it applies precisely to the problem we are trying to resolve: "For to be holy [*heilig*] and to be saved [*selig*/blessed] are two entirely different things. We are saved [*selig*] through Christ alone; but we become holy both through this faith and through these divine foundations and orders."[32] As a Christian one is not excused from participating in any or all the divinely

---

[31] Luther loved this image of the crystal and played with the sound of the word when speaking about Christ. The idea is that the omnipresence of Christ is something we perceive only in one of its dimensions or facets at a time. See *LW* 37, 224; *WA* 26, 337. Niels Henrik Gregersen, "Natural Events as Crystals of God–Luther's Eucharistic Theology and the Question of Nature's Sacramentality," in Viggo Mortensen (ed.), *Concern for Creation: Voices on the Theology of Creation* (Uppsala: Tro & Tanke, 1995), 143–55.

[32] *LW* 37, 365; *WA* 26, 505, 18–20.

instituted orders as Luther states in the Confession of 1528: "But the holy orders and true religious institutions established by God are these three: the office of priest, the estate of marriage, the civil government. All who are engaged in [...] these are engaged in works which are all together holy in God sight."[33]

This brings us back to the question about the connection between the two—the holy and the blessed. Simply put, can one be blessed and saved without being holy or saintly? Or the reverse, can one be holy without being blessed? Luther admitted that there was a lot of holiness among the pagans, without being blessed thereby. There is some form of causal relationship implied here. But if there is holiness without confessing faith in Christ, this would break down the union of natures (*unio hypostatic*). The same would be the case if there were the possibility of being blessed without producing holy works. There is enough in Luther's writings to corroborate these possibilities as the emphasis in the *sola fide* and the invectives against works and law. These seem indeed to corroborate this breaking down of the union, which is only mildly assuaged by the metaphor of the tree and its fruits. But even this analogy breaks down because one might conceive of a tree without a fruit, but never the fruit without a tree.

The dilemma will not be resolved by finding in Luther's writings arcane redeeming quotes concerning questions of justice or prophetic denunciations against the powers of oppression. These indeed are plenty, but so are also many terrible things he said and wrote. Instead, we need to take Luther to the root of his theology, radicalizing him and then drawing the consequences that he should have drawn even when they turn against him.

Love's labor's won

Luther makes a surprising move right after identifying the orders as the spaces in which to exercise holiness. Instead of remaining close to the expression of love as it is shown within the instituted orders or hierarchies, he adds a vague reference to the "order of Christian love." This "order" is not a hierarchy or institution, which has attributes like those Luther used to describe, the three classical orders or spheres he inherited from medieval times and ultimately from Aristotle's distinction of human faculties in *The Metaphysics*.[34] What is this order that is not covered by the established institutions in which holiness inscribes itself? Luther goes on to say:

---

[33] *LW* 37, 365; *WA* 26, 504, 30ff.
[34] See Vitor Westhelle, "Power and Politics: Incursions in Luther's Theology," in Christine Helmer (ed.), *The Global Luther: A Theologian for Modern Times* (Min-

> Above these three institutions and orders is the common order of Christian love, in which one serves not only the three orders, but also serves every needy person in general with all kinds of benevolent deeds, such as feeding the hungry, giving drink to the thirsty, forgiving enemies, praying for all men on earth, suffering all kinds of evil on earth, etc. Behold, all of those are called good and holy works. However none of these orders is a means of salvation.[35]

In medieval theology there were "seven acts of mercy," consisting of those six listed in Matthew 25:35–36 (feeding the hungry, giving to drink to the thirsty, welcoming the stranger, clothing the naked, visiting the sick and the prisoner) plus the burying of the dead. But forgiving one's enemy or suffering all kinds of evil was not among them. Luther does not use these acts as extra ingredients that are added to improve our chances of salvation, but as an excess in the sanctifying regime. Faith remains the unconditional gift. Tenuous as it might seem, there is a link that connects faith and love, blessedness and holiness, which the eyes cannot behold, yet the ears hear. It is the tale of a secret love, the love of the enemy. That was God's love, secret, *absconditus* in the cross for us who crucified God.

The small act of forgiving an enemy, in an inconspicuous merciful gesture toward a foe, above all if it is kept secret, is love and love of the enemy. It is this frail gesture that in synecdoche touches the whole that is expressed by the incarnation (Jesus is the synecdoche for the whole of creation). One extraordinary gesture of kindness, be it almost insignificant, fulfills the commandment of universal love. A meek gesture of love covers a multitude of sins (1 Pet 4:8). The synecdoche gives expression to this while respecting the limits of the flesh, as it also remains an endless duty.

What the Reformer was trying to express is akin to Carl Schmitt's reminder that, in modern languages (German or English), *echthros* (as in Matthew) is not *polemios* in Greek, or *inimicus, hostis* in Latin.[36] Following Matthew, the reference here is to enemies in a private and not a political sense. For Luther, however, the distinction that Schmitt makes so adamantly is blurred in the fluidity of the rhetorical use of figurative language. One's vocation calls for political craftiness. The enemy is not reduced to an adversary who can be "loved" in a stoic detachment that for Schmitt would make politics possible. The enemy remains an enemy, while a gesture of love disturbs the logic of hatred without legislating itself as a new politics.

---

neapolis: Fortress, 2009), 284–300.

[35] *LW* 37, 366; *WA* 26, 505, 11–16.

[36] Carl Schmitt, *The Concept of the Political* (Chicago: The University of Chicago Press, 2007), chapter 3.

The novelty in this move is that the excess in the realm of holiness does not add to the realm of blessedness. In fact, the procedure is one of subtraction. By the simple fact of not enforcing the means of carrying out hatred and reacting to persecution, love makes its meager appearance in an open space for blessings to blossom. This is why, for Luther, love of the enemy comes together with prayer for those who persecute.

Blessedness belongs to the one who loves and forgives the enemy in the heart, even if the person remains a foe in the temporal sphere. It is through the synecdoche that the two denotations of enmity are connected. So the Pope, the Turks, the enthusiasts and the usurers, could be met with fantastic accusations of being the devil, and all the filthy language that Luther could think of (and not much did he miss from the scatological lexicon). The reason is his use of the synecdoche. But in the earthly regime they were secular, worldly adversaries to be met according to the rules of the ecclesio-politico-economic sphere. This earthly regime has rules, duties and laws that set demands for the sake of justice and peace. But to this minimal demand in the administration of the earthly spheres, Luther calls also for a surplus that exceeds the demands of those spheres. This excess is the decisive element in Luther's "political theology." The love of the enemy is the cipher of this excess which is its victory, even if no bigger than a mustard seed. Even if there is no positive causality between love and faith, love of the enemy releases, *via negativa*, a space of peacefulness for the Word to be heard in the chambers of faith.

The Reformer, it has been often repeated, was a child of his time, but his theological "DNA" passed on fruits kept in secret from his own sight and that of many of his custodians. And what is kept secret must be accepted in faith; such is love of the enemy. This is love's labor's won.

THEOLOGY OF THE CROSS, LIBERATION AND DISCIPLESHIP

A Theology of the Cross and the Passion in Matthew: An Indian Dalit Perspective

Joseph Prabhakar Dayam

In this essay, I shall explore the understanding of the cross in texts used in Dalit Christian traditions—the Bible, lyrics and contemporary Dalit poetry—and relate these to the interpretation of the passion narrative in Matthew.

Indian theologians are constantly in search of their identity that can be singular, multiple, accidental or intentionally chosen. All identities are historical accidents, yet also agential. Such a claim has methodological consequences when doing theology. The "theology of the cross" suggests my confessional identity, "Dalit" my socio-cultural identity, and Bible carrying Indian Christian my religious identity. All of them are theological and therefore political and political therefore theological and suggestive of the wells that I drink from as I seek to quench my theological and political thirst.

Dalit Christians and their world of texts

My self-understanding as a Bible carrying Dalit Christian does not mean that I am a Biblicist. As a Dalit, I am part of a community that was historically excluded from reading and writing texts. Our memory includes the pain of our ancestors who had molten lead poured into their ears for hearing the sacred chant and their tongues pierced for reciting any sacred text. Today, Dalits have begun to wage war against the centuries-old oppression by entering into and claiming their space in the textual world. This was facilitated by two historical movements: the church's educational mission and the Ambedkarite movement that emphasizes education. Both movements gave the Dalits access to the written word and opened up a space to understand their world and to express their opposition to the oppression they have had to endure. Although the majority of Dalit communities remain illiterate, they have embraced written texts as the source of their liberation. For a Dalit Christian, the Bible is a liberative text, whose liberative potential is contained not only in its message but also in its magic. As its message mediates the spirit of liberation, its physical presence mediates healing from the forces that bind and wound. Many a Dalit Christian goes to bed with the Bible placed next to their head to prevent nightmares and to ward off "evil spirits."

Although it comes from outside their world (one might call it a colonial text thus needing to be decolonized!), the Dalit community embraces the Bible as its identity marker and source of liberation. It is unthinkable for a believer to go to worship without a Bible in their hand. Even if one is not literate, one will carry the Bible to worship services or prayer meetings. Since this can evoke scorn from the dominant caste communities, the carrying of the Bible becomes a political act. It is a claim to share in power and an act of defiance of a caste dictate that excludes Dalits from the act of reading. Holding the Bible is as much a political act as reading the Bible. It defies the centuries-old dictate of Manu, the law-giver, and reclaims the freedom to be informed, think and to act. This theological and political act of holding and reading the Bible is part of the road to freedom, to pursue the truth in order to be free. Any Dalit reading therefore is a political reading; it is both submission and liberation. We submit to the Bible, trusting that it anticipates the truth while, at the same time, freeing ourselves from the text, since we are aware of the texts and their interpretations that have rendered us untouchables.

The Dalit understanding of the biblical message is shaped by the sermons preached and the lyrics sung in the context of collective worship. The biblical witness to the person and work of Christ is handed over through the lyrics that shape their faith. Perhaps these Christian lyrics are the earliest Dalit literary works in the sense that they are written by Dalits and embraced by the community as their own. They are handed down to succeeding generations as repositories of faith and thus constitute the faith memory of the Dalit Christian community. The community's understanding of the divine and their aspiration for authentic humanity shapes the way in which they understand the text. The Christ who is experienced becomes normative as the text is engaged with. The Dalit use of the Bible therefore is one of critical adaptation with Christ (the freeing Spirit) being the norm.

In their iconography the Dalit community have embraced Ambedkar as their icon. Today, at the entrance or center of most Dalit communities one will find a statue of Ambedkar, who with one hand points toward the community while the other holds a book (understood either as the constitution of India or

Ambedkar's *Buddha and His Dhamma*). This iconography of Ambedkar holding a book that he wrote is to counter another dominant Indian icon, Gandhi with the *Bhagavat Gita* in his hand and a stick on which he leans in the other. The Dalits consider the latter a source of bondage, and the former a source of liberation. It is thanks to certain constitutional provisions and educational opportunities provided to the Dalits that the Dalit communities have gained access to the literary world. By converting to Buddhism, a Dalit could die in dignity. Contemporary Dalit literature in India stems from the empowerment facilitated by the church and expressed in the Ambedkarite movement.

Dalit theology considers, among others, these two textual traditions, the Bible and contemporary Dalit literature, as its sources. As it weaves its theological tapestry, it employs the Bible and Dalit literature as its threads.

DALITS AND A THEOLOGY OF THE CROSS

THE EMBARRASSMENT OF THE CROSS

Contemporary theologies have rightly claimed that all theologies are culturally conditioned and have emerged out of their own contextual needs. Theologies of the cross are no exception to this. The traditional theologies of the cross and contemporary rearticulations of the cross emerged in their own political, historical, philosophical and religio-cultural contexts, trying to make sense of the handed-down Christian tradition and at the same time attempting to be sensitive to their contemporary consciousness. In this process, some theologians embraced the message of the cross as having significant prophetic and redemptive relevance for our world, while others expressed their embarrassment and revolt against the traditional theologies of the cross. Rebecca Parker and Rita Nakashima Brock argue that the cross does not save but, instead, is life celebrated in the collective life of the community that saves.[1] They view crucifixion not as an inevitable outcome of God's will, but as an act of state-sponsored violence. Jesus accepted the cross [...] not because it was God's will, but because it was the necessary price for speaking the truth to a corrupted world.[2]

Marit A. Trelstad outlines four major issues that shape the contemporary critique of the cross:

---

[1] Rita Nakashima Brock and Rebecca Parker, *Proverbs of Ashes: Violence, Redemptive Suffering and the Search for What Saves Us* (Boston: Beacon, 2001).
[2] Ibid., 25.

First, glorifying the cross potentially treats suffering as though it is God-given and inevitable. This makes the loving character of God in relation to the world dubious and also models God-human relations on a patriarchal model of relationship that idealizes the roles of hero and helpless victim. Second, it valorizes passive suffering as redemptive. Third, the weight of "redemptive" suffering is borne primarily by the oppressed and disadvantaged, and it is promoted and preached most often by those who stand to benefit from the suffering of others. Finally, it may lead to a human neglect of our individual and collective responsibility to end suffering and hold perpetrators of violence accountable.[3]

These critiques raise questions at two levels: first, at the level of human understanding of the divine, traditional atonement theories are viewed as distorting the Christian vision of God. Second, such an understanding of God has significant negative consequences for the oppressed. Therefore, either Christian theology has to do away with the very idea of the cross or reimagine the meaning of the cross in such a way that it does not turn God into an arbitrary, violent feudal lord.

Within Indian Christian theology, the rebellion against the traditional view of the cross is expressed by Pandepeddi Chenchiah on the grounds that atonement theology that is articulated within the language of the sacrificial and judiciary systems is abhorrent and the idea of God that is suggested in such language is contrary to the Christian idea of God understood in Jesus Christ. He writes,

The juridical conception of Christianity is an attempt to reduce Jesus to the ideology of Judaism or the political ideology of the State of Rome: in other words, to interpret Jesus in terms of sacrifice and propitiation of the law, offence and punishment. The "sacrificial" system is a mystery core of religion. Dealing with sacrifices, we may talk with some appropriateness of sin as a stain and the sacrifice, an eraser of sin by the washing in blood. It should, however, be noted that the effect of sacrifice is mystical and unconscious. No devotee came out of the temple after a sacrifice with a light heart and a joyous sense of redemption. Sacrifice acts as a tragedy. It produces the eerie feeling of midnight and purifies us by terror. We do not feel saved, we come with a feeling of faith that we are saved. But this propitiation theology stands condemned as an inadequate distortion of truth when we set it side by side with the story in the Gospels. Jesus may have called himself a ransom. John the Baptist may have hailed Jesus as the lamb that taketh away the sin of the world. The Lord's Supper may evoke the mental picture of a lamb broken for the sinner. The cross may be soul shattering. Yet, as we accompany Jesus we never get 'the Kalighat' feeling. I do not know how Jesus felt when they witnessed sacrifices. I have been to kalighat.

---

[3] Marit A. Trelstad, "Introduction: The Cross in Context," in Marit Trelstad, *Cross Examinations: Readings on the Meaning of the Cross Today* (Minneapolis, MN: Fortress Press, 2006), 7.

Neither in my studies of the Gospel, nor even in my private devotion, can I capture the feeling that in Jesus I am in temple where he is sacrificed for me to satisfy a terror-inspiring deity. No Indian gets this feeling. Nor do I think any modern has it. This idea of sacrifice is diluted in Western theology with the idea of offence, offender, punishment, hostages. I am a judge and have seen men in the dock. I realize the solemnity of a court of law, of the majesty of law, of the value of punishment. Yet, once you step out of Church-theology into the atmosphere of the Gospels, we leave behind judges and arraignments, verdicts and punishments. I do not deny that man has a sense of sin and guilt- even a desire to atone for it by suffering punishment. Yet, the nearer I get to the historic Jesus, the farther I go away from the temple and the court-hall. The classical theology distorts Jesus; it invests him with too much terror [...] I want to emphasize that we can never get to the heart of Christianity by the way of juridical theology. It is the genetic or creative aspects of Jesus; it is the Holy Spirit as a creative energy that takes the Indian into the new "given"–in Jesus.[4]

What to Chenchiah was abhorrent in the atonement theologies is the violence involved in the sacrificial ritual and the idea of the divine that emerges from witnessing such ritual practice. It does not take into account the fact that ritual language and practice emerge from the world in which the community is placed. The subaltern religion takes its shape in its own world that is marked by violence.

THE CENTRALITY OF THE CROSS IN DALIT CHRISTIAN TRADITION

The cross is central to the Dalit Christian understanding of the divine and the consequent spiritual practice. The Christian God is the crucified God, and the call to Christian discipleship includes the carrying of the cross. In their liturgical and spiritual practice the cross takes a central place and it is during the Lenten season that a conscious effort is made to encounter and be encountered by God. Many Christians fast on Fridays—some even every night—and the congregation meets every night either in the homes of the believers or in the church for Lenten devotions. The Good Friday service is the longest of the year when, from 11 am to 3 pm, the congregation sings Lenten songs and listens to the passion narrative and devotions on the seven words Jesus spoke from the cross, which are considered the windows of the cross that give us access to the glimpses of the meaning of the cross. During the entire Lenten season the believers concentrate on singing the lyrics and listening to the preached word in the hope of getting

---

[4] D.A. Thangasamy (ed.), *The Theology of Chenchiah With Selections from His Writings* (Bangalore: The Christian Institute for the Study of Religion and Society, 1966), 91–92.

closer to God. This aim of this spiritual practice is *Upavasa* (living closer to God) which is believed to transform life.

Dalit Christian rituals too are centered on the symbol of the cross. Both on auspicious occasions and in difficult times the community is drawn near to the cross. Before a bride or a bridegroom is taken to the church for the wedding, the oldest person in the family places the mark of the cross on their forehead. When a new house is built the marks of the cross are painted in red on the walls. During the house warming ceremony the pastor raises the hand and places the mark of the cross in the air after a prayer in each room. When someone is sick, the mark of the cross is placed on the aching body part. Children are taught to say *Yesu Raktha Sthuthi* (praise to the blood of Jesus) when they are scared. In some parts of India, the mark of the cross is placed on the rice with a spoon before it is served.

Dalit Christian communities, whose world is characterized by the presence of many crosses, embrace the symbol of the cross as central to their religious and domestic life. This centrality of the cross was not imposed by the missionaries or the spiritual élite of the church, but evolved within the community as a way of making sense of their own identity as Christians. Any reimagination of the theology of the cross needs to take this Dalit agential phenomenon of embracing the cross into account.

The cross in the Dalit lyrical tradition

Since the majority of Dalit Christians in rural India are illiterate, their faith is nurtured primarily through collective worship and family prayers. Their devotion to and understanding of the cross is shaped by the Lenten lyrics. During the Lenten season, the Christian community meets daily at one of the believer's houses. The meetings are held until late at night, usually beginning at 8 pm and ending at 10 pm. The service is simple with several Lenten songs, Bible readings, a sermon and prayers. Since many Dalits work in the fields during the day they are tired by the time the pastor/catechist begins to preach and usually doze off. Whenever the preacher notices this happening, they simply start a song and the congregation joins in. What is striking about these meetings is the way in which, particularly the women, express their emotions while the Lenten hymns are being sung. Some of them even to weep as they sing.

Focus on the passion of Christ: Embracing the crucified and abandoning the cross

Most of the Lenten lyrics are poetic reconstructions of the passion narratives. Although they might contain certain element of their understanding of the cross, the writer essentially recounts the story of Jesus carrying the cross through the streets of Jerusalem and finally being crucified on Calvary. Some of these lyrics begin and end with what the writers believe to be the meaning of the cross. Between these faith statements is the passion narrative put together in lyrical form. The writer seeks to paint before the eyes, and sing in the ears of the listener the story of the crucified Jesus so as to invoke devotion to Christ. The following lyric written by an anonymous writer evidences this feature.

> How strange and how tragic is the death of Christ my savior!
> Killed him with grit, his own.
> They caught him, tied him, pushed him and abused my savior there.
> Though he suffered such cruelty, did not say a word, my savior, then.
> They laid on his back a log that he could not carry.
> Unable to carry that log, fainted he, Jesus my father.
> They laid Jesus on the log and nailed his hands and legs.
> All the cruel people got together and abused Christ Jesus mercilessly.
> Thirsty was he,
> the betrayers gave him the bitter liquid.
> Persevered did he, the one who came to this world
> the sufferings inflicted by the people of his land.
> They pierced him in the ribs,
> and from there flowed the stream of blood and water
> to give life to all.[5]

As the community sings this song, their attention is turned to Christ's passion and the violence of the crucifixion is exposed. The community embraces the crucified Christ and accuse those who perpetrate the violence. On the one hand, they acknowledge the meaning of the cross while, on the other, suggesting that the cross should not have happened. The meaning of the cross does not lie in the act of crucifixion but in Jesus, the one who is crucified. Therefore, in a way, they embrace the crucified and abandon the cross.

THE CROSS AS THE SITE OF GOD'S POURED OUT LOVE: DEVOTION TO THE CROSS

Many of the lyrics that are sung during the Lenten season imply that Christ redeems from sin and suffered for the sake of our sins; they do not suggest how this happens. Their concern is not to theorize on the "how" of atonement but to elicit a response to the cross. In so doing the focus is

---

[5] *Lutheran Sangārādhanalu, Andhra Christava Keerthanalu* (Rajahmundry: Edward Press, 1988), lyric no. 191, 165. Author's own translation.

placed on the outpoured love of Christ on the cross. The following lyric portrays the cross as the site of Christ's outpoured love.

Refrain: Oh the embodiment of purity, the redeemer of sin
my God, and the one who knows no sin
have you taken all these troubles for my sins?

1. Have they woven a crown with thorns and thrust on your head?
Having been shaken with pain in your head, have you fainted, my savior?

2. Unable to carry the cross unto Calvary, have you been troubled in your soul?
Have those thugs given you another one to carry the cross with you?

3. Unable to bear the insults and the pain inflicted by the cruel Jews, have you stumbled on the way?
Having reached Calvary at last, have you laid the cross on the ground?

4. Have those spiteful soldiers beaten you until you bleed and laid you on the cross? Nailed your feet and palms to that log?

5. As the pain became intense, have you cried unto the Father?
For the ever increasing pain have you thirsted?

6. Has the cruel soldier taken the spear and pierced you on your side and satisfied his anger as the water flowed from your side?

7. Have you persevered this pain, just to deal with my sin?
How wide is your love and how deep is your patience?
How could I explain such love?[6]

Here the community affirms the following:

- The cross has something to do with humankind's sin, although the "how" remains ambiguous

- Christ died as an innocent person and the community is angry with those who nailed Jesus to the cross

- Christ willfully walked the way of the cross and it was an excruciating experience for him

---

[6] Yermanashetty Daveedu, "Ye Paapamerugani Yo Pavanamoorthi," in ibid., 161–62.

- On the cross Christ manifested greater depths of his love.

As the community sings this song, they locate themselves on both sides. As they make the Jews and the Romans responsible for Christ's death, they too take their responsibility for the death of Christ. Simultaneously they see Jesus being on their side, bearing the cross for their sake.

Its impact is felt very clearly. As they cry, they repent of their sins and at the same time they cry for Christ. It is a way by which the community participates in the passion of Christ. As they observe Lent and sing these lyrics, they engage in a psychological pilgrimage, rather like visiting and revisiting Calvary so as to have a glimpse of the crucified Christ. This visitation to Calvary brings about faith, healing and wholeness. For instance, the following frequently sung lyric calls the soul to reach Calvary and take shelter in the cross.

> Refrain: Go on to the mount of Calvary Oh my soul,
> Nearer to the cross.
>
> 1. Look who is there on the cross, It is our Lord Jesus,
> look what is there on his head, the crown of thorns.
>
> 2. The feet that walked around doing good to the others!
> Why do they nail them so cruelly?
>
> 3. The hands that held the lowly and taken them to the safe shores,
> Why do they nail those merciful hands?
>
> 4. Why do the ignorant spit on his face
> that reflected love, grace and purity?
>
> 5. As one gazes at your excruciating pain and brutal death
> however cruel one is, his heart should melt.
>
> 6. Oh my God of heaven, you knew no sin.
> Yet, why have you suffered such pain?
>
> 7. It is your love, the reason for you to vouch for us.
> Let the world come to know it.
>
> 8. Draw me near to the cross, a terrible sinner,
> give me the power to abandon sin as I meditate upon your cross.[7]

---

[7] Panthagani Paradesi, "Kalvarygiri Cheru Manasa," in ibid., 172–73.

Here the cross is viewed as the site of God's out-poured love. In drawing near to it and meditating on the passion of Christ, one comes to know Christ and is thereby empowered to deal with one's own sin.

The cross in Dalit revolutionary literature

Dalit literature seeks to reflect the Dalits' growing identity, awareness and consciousness. It is one of the major sites of Dalit resistance and creativity. Dalit literature can be understood as that which is written by Dalits based on a Dalit consciousness seeking to reflect their pain, protest and vision.[8] In their article "Language and Literature of Dalits and Sants: Some Missed Opportunities," J. K. Lele and R. Singh trace the distinctiveness of Dalit literature to its unity of language and content.

> In it the disillusionment and disgust of young Dalits, often accompanied by a desire of revenge, come alive. It revives the memory of the pain and suffering of the past generations. It confronts centuries of hypocrisy, deceit and violence sustained in the name of tradition.[9]

Since it is closely linked to the hopes of the Dalit communities, Dalit literature is characterized by revolt, negativism[10] and expressions of hope. It directs its revolt against the caste system and its negative consequences on the Dalit communities and also against the norms that are set by "classical" literary endeavors in its form, language, style and thematic choices. Dalit literature seeks to provide a philosophical basis and inspiration for the Datlits' struggle and aims at exposing their pain and the systemic way in which they are subjugated. "In their writings the Dalit question is posed in terms of annihilation of the caste system and the building up of a casteless egalitarian society."[11]

As an expression of the pain, pathos and vision of the Dalits, Dalit literature becomes an important source when doing Dalit theology for the following reasons:

• Several of the Dalit writers either belong to the Dalit Christian tradition or have been raised in a Christian context. Consequently, they have extensively used Christian symbols in their literary expressions. As a reaction to the hegemony

---

[8] Challapalli Swaroopa Rani, "Dalit Women's wWritings in Telugu," in *Economic and Political Weekly*, 25 April 1998, 21.
[9] Quoted from A. Satyanarayana, "Dalit Protest Literature in Telugu: A Historical Perspective," in *Economic and Political Weekly*, 21 January 1995, 171.
[10] Arjun Dangle, "Introduction," in Arjun Dangle (ed.), *Poisoned Bread: Translations from Modern Marathi Dalit Literature* (Hyderabad: Orient Longman Limited, 1992), xi.
[11] Ibid.

of brahminical Hinduism, they have rejected traditional literary symbols and adopted alternatives from other religious traditions, often borrowed from the Christian religious tradition.[12] However, in this borrowing, Dalit writers have distinctively expressed their intellectual independence and representational freedom. It was a critical adaptation of themes and symbols.

• As an expression of contemporary Dalit consciousness, Dalit literature provides datum for Dalit theology. As a vehement protest against the historical and existing social inequalities, it envisions the transformation of the existing order into a new world order. Thus the vision of Dalit literature, though a secular one, has theological overtones that enrich the Christian theological exercise. Arvind Nirmal writes,

> Dalit literature serves as a mirror which reflects the past, the present and the future of Christian Dalits in India. It lays bare the Dalit consciousness and it is this Dalit consciousness which is our primary datum for Christian Dalit theology.[13]

• Dalit literature privileges freedom as the highest aesthetic value and justice, freedom, love and fraternity as basic human sentiments. Within Dalit literary theory these are considered more important than beauty and pleasure.[14] As theology has to do with these categories, an engagement with Dalit literature will enrich its task.

One of the prominent Telugu Dalit poets was the late Poet laureate Gurram Joshua, who is considered the father of Telugu Dalit poetry. He was a modern Telugu poet of rare distinction whose "literary compositions convey the sufferings and hopes and dreams of Dalits and their struggle for a new society."[15] Joshua was perhaps the first Dalit poet who rose above his situation by mastering Telugu to become a poet laureate. He was born in a Christian family. His mother was a Madiga[16] and

---

[12] They had used Christian symbols like Christ, cross, David, etc. to represent themselves and Satan, Serpent, Goliath to represent the caste systems.

[13] Arvind P. Nirmal, "A Dialogue with Dalit Literature," in M. E. Prabhakar (ed.), *Towards a Dalit Theology* (Delhi: ISPCK, 1988), 75.

[14] Arun Prabha Mukharji, "Introduction," in Valmiki, Omprakash, *Joothan* (New York: Columbia University Press, 2003), xxv.

[15] M. E. Prabhakar, "In Search of Roots—Dalit aspirations and the Christian Dalit Question: Perceptions of the Telugu Poet Laureate, Joshua," in *Religion and Society*, vol. XLI, no. 1, March 1994, 2.

[16] Madiga (also known as Maadiga, Maadigar, Maadar, Maatangi, Makkalu, Madigowd and Madigaru) is a scheduled caste that is found primarily in the southern Indian states of Telangana, Andhra Pradesh, Karnataka, Maharastra and Tamil Nadu.

his father belonged to the Yadava[17] (a Sudra) community. Although his father was a Yadava, he was considered an untouchable because he was born to a Madiga mother. Throughout his life he was discriminated against: by the dominant castes because of his birth and by the Christian community because of his radical views.

Joshua was attracted to the person of Christ because he understood Jesus as someone who has demonstrated in his life equality, fraternity and sorority and humility. He writes

> You have demonstrated to all equality.
> Eating with the poor, and the despised tax collectors,
> you have shown to the world, your humility.
> Washing and wiping your disciples feet,
> come to my house too, great teacher.
> You have displayed the essence of love
> by embracing the world,
> so let me embrace you too.[18]

Prabhakar suggests that Joshua's responses to the caste prejudices and untouchability stemmed from his faith in "Jesus Christ as the one who healed and reconciled people to each other."[19]

He portrays Christ's mission as that of bringing salvation from sin.

> The master who orders births and deaths
> bowed his head to births and deaths.
> How great was the love Lord Jesus has
> for the Human Beings, born in sin.
> On the mountain of Calvary
> was hanging the body of Christ on the cross.
> Showers his blood on the surface of earth
> from where sprouted pastures of salvation.
>
> Opened at the heaven
> the fastened golden gates.
> The world bitten by the venomous serpent
> was healed

---

[17] Yadava refers to a grouping of traditionally non-élite pastoral communities, or castes, in India that since the nineteenth and twentieth centuries has claimed descent from the mythological King Yadu as a part of a movement of social and political resurgence.

[18] Gurram Joshua, *Kanda Kavyam*, as cited by Prabhakar, op. cit. (note 13), 9.

[19] Prabhakar, ibid., 9.

as God's lamb died on Calvary.
Holding in his hand the gifts of grace
has God invited the saints.[20]

In this reflection on the cross, Joshua enumerates the accomplishments of the cross as the availability of salvation, healing and the gifts of grace. While narrating the healing effect of the cross, Joshua speaks of the world as being bitten by the venomous serpent. He begins his *Christhu Charithra* [the history of Christ] with the Genesis account of the creation of humankind and the "fall." It is interesting to note that elsewhere Joshua uses the serpent as the symbol for the caste system.[21] For instance, referring to the caste system, he talks of human beings being bitten by the venomous serpent. In such a context, Joshua says that through his death Jesus brought about healing. This healing effected by Jesus has to be actualized in the community.

The pace set by Joshua's articulations of and reflections on Dalit suffering was not followed up until the Karamchedu incident[22] after which the Dalit movement in Andhrapradesh gained traction resulting in the emergence of several Dalit organizations. Furthermore, it provided an occasion for the growth of Dalit literature.[23] Using their pens, several poets such as Endluri Sudhakar, Madduri Nagesh Babu, Sikhamani, Satish Chandur and Challapalli Swaruparani began to wage war against the caste system. The distinguishing feature of importance to Dalit theology is that they reject traditional literary symbols and employ symbols from the Christian tradition in order to describe their sufferings. They use imageries such as the crown of thorns and Christ and the cross in two contrasting ways. While some see the cross as a symbol of their own suffering and identify this with the suffering of Christ, others see it as a symbol of weakness and reject it as means of liberation.

Why stones to block the tombs?
Tell them to stack the mountains

---

[20] Gurram Joshua, *Christhu Charitra* (Delhi: ISPCK, 1963), 118–19.

[21] In his *Gabbilamu* (Bat), Joshua compares caste systems to a four hooded cobra. See Gurram Joshua, *Gabbilamu* (VijayaWada: Joshua Foundation, 1996), 10. For the English translation, see K. Madhava Rao (tr.), *Joshua's Gabbilamu (Bat)* (Hyderabad: Joshua Foundation, 1998).

[22] Karamchedu is a village in the Guntur district dominated by the Kammas, a dominant peasant caste. On 17 July 1985, unable to tolerate the assertion and self-respect of the Dalits, Kammas armed with spears and crowbars killed six persons, raped nine women and wounded as many

[23] A. Satyanarayana, "Dalit Protest Literature in Telugu: A Historical Perspective," in *Economic and Political Weekly*, 21 January 1995, 171.

all of a sudden like gleams
Jesus will rise in the end.

Tombs in the middle of the village?
As if the village is excommunicated.

Four directions to a village
four legs to living beings
four rows to sway
caste that crawls on four feet.

Somewhere in a fifth direction at a distance
birth of a two legged baby in a manger.

Whether a shooting star showed up or not
but a sound of cut tail in the village.

Soiled cattle angry for the touch of the child's feet
barked, snarled, howl of a sad cry.

This child is the
apple of the slaves' eye
a speck of a century's dream
first stanza of *Vandemataram*
according to the law of the animal the child's birth is a felony.

For the child
go have two legs is a crime.
Nailed them
to prevent from treading the rest of the land.

To have two hands is a crime.
drilled holes into them
to prevent from demanding work.

To have brain in the head is a crime.
Jabbed the crown of thorns
to prevent from writing the Constitution again and again.

To have radiance in the face is a crime.
Spat on it
to prevent from any mother kissing it.

Above all to have a heart in the chest is a crime.
Pierced with a spear
thinking that there is no need for love for a slave's son

Death of the child in the fields and meadows
darkness enveloped in the broad day light.
The sky split into five parts.
The sun fastened the four parts and covered his face.

The last word of the child on the cross:
"Father! They know what they are doing.
Let them be alive even till I rise."

The cattle in the village escape.
In the four roads junction
the mother land impregnated
all the tombs of the heroes are ready for delivery.

Cowards are the cattle keepers! Even before the child had risen
they banished the slaughter of animals.
"To seek and punish the animals
the child has come into this world."

O mothers, whose hearts have been grieved as for the offspring of their womb
wipe your eyes.
With radiant clothes greet welcome
"The Child has today risen, Halleluiah."[24]

Here one can observe a dialectical approach to the cross. On the one hand there is an acceptance of the cross as a symbol to denote their suffering while, on the other, there appears to be a rejection of the cross as a means of liberation. Christ is viewed as embodying Dalitness and, in the cross of Christ, the writer discerns the crosses that the Dalit community carries and Christ's participation in those cross bearing experiences.

The imagery of the cross in Dalit poetry suggests a dialectic tension. On the one hand Dalit poets employed this imagery to describe their own suffering and attempted to identify their suffering with that of Jesus on the cross. On the other, they seem to have rejected the cross as a means

---

[24] Satish Chandar, "Sisuvu Nedu Lechenu," in G. Laxmi Narayana and Tripuraneni Srinivas (eds), *Chikkanavuthunna Pata: Dalita Kavitvam* (Vijayawada: Kavitvam Prachuranalu, 1995), 144–45, transl. Chaitanya Motupalli.

of their liberation. While the former aspect becomes a useful pointer in the construction of the theology of the cross, the later calls for a critical review of the traditional theology that portrays the cross as a mere symbol of forgiveness.

The Dalit understanding of the cross and reading the passion in Matthew for a theology of the cross

As they articulate their understanding of the cross in their Christian piety, Dalit communities in India suggest a hermeneutical posture that is biblically founded. The gospel traditions with their distinctive theological commitments express their understanding of the cross with multiple voices. This polyvocality calls for a non-dogmatic but dialogical interpretation of the cross. They are dialogical in the sense, that the passion narratives (in this case Matthew) provides an elaborate description of the passion while refusing to theorize and allowing an interpretation to evolve as the communities engage with the text. The gospel describes the event so that the reader can engage with the text and appropriate it in their contexts. Dalit lyrical traditions of the cross invite the devotee to meditate on the cross during collective worship. These lyrics emphasize Jesus who was crucified as the one who manifested God's unconditional love. The crucifier is named and blamed and in naming and blaming they deeply regret the cross as the human refusal of God's love. Yet, by embracing the crucified they imagine their emancipation. The Passion in Matthew offers a similar perspective. On the one hand the passion narrative understands the death of Jesus as a necessity in the economy of God's self-disclosure while, on the other, making the accomplices responsible for their act. A further dialectic can be noted in Jesus' attitude to the cross: Jesus prays that it may be far from him, yet submits himself to the will of the Father.

What perhaps is certain for the gospel writer is the call to Christian discipleship that involves participation in the suffering of God in Christ (Mt 16:24–26). The passion narrative begins with a woman who anoints Jesus as a way of preparing him for his death and ends with a band of women disciples sitting at his tomb. Between these two events were numerous episodes of his male disciples deserting, betraying and denying him. The cross in Matthew is as much a story of the participation of the disciples in the passion of Christ as it is one of desertion. The participation comes from unexpected quarters.

One of the major themes in Matthew is the inclusion of the polluted into God's purposes. The inclusion and the lifting up of four women (all foreigners) in the genealogy account and the story of the Syro-phoenician woman suggest the privileging of "the polluted" alongside the "pure." The "polluted" ones are not the silenced. The ultimate speech of God's act comes from the tombs (polluted sites) that open up and let life spring forth. For Dalit and feminist theology in India, this detail is significant. The caste system and patriarchy rest on the idea of purity and pollution. While the twice borns (*dvija*—men) are ontologically pure, Dalits and women are ontologically impure. Dalits are impure since they come from body parts of the Brahman that are beneath the navel. Women are impure because of the menstrual fluids that flow from them. Dalit religious imagination counters the Hindu notion of purity and pollution by privileging pollution as a necessary condition for accepting a divine figure (Dalit Goddess).[25] The idea of incarnation (by including the idea of virgin birth Mathew possibly alludes to the idea that Jesus is the God incarnate) is central to New Testament Christianity. New Testament Christianity evolved within and over against Greek dualism which refuses to discern the divine in the flesh since divine embodiment is an idea that smacks of pollution. Within the Jewish tradition, contact with a dead body results in pollution. If Jesus is God incarnate and his death and burial are real, they turn God into a polluted one. The crucified God and the God interred is a polluted God. It is not merely redeeming the idea of pollution but privileging the idea of pollution as a necessary condition in God's self-disclosure. If God reveals Godself in the seeming sites of God's absence (a theology of the cross), it is precisely in the polluting sites and from the polluted people (the crucified people) that the crucified God speaks. The tombs open up and speak of God's act of salvation.

---

[25] I dealt with this idea elsewhere in "*Gonthemma Korika:* Reimagining the Divine Feminine in Dalit The/alogy," in Sathianathan Clarke, Deenabandhu Manchala and Philip Peacock (eds), *Dalit Theology in 21 Century: Discordant Voices, Discerning Pathways* (New Delhi: Oxford University Press, 2010).

The Flight to Egypt: A Migrant Reading—Implications for a Lutheran Understanding of Salvation

Monica Jyotsna Melanchthon

> Butterflies have always had wings; people have always had legs. While history is marked by the hybridity of human societies and the desire for movement, the reality of most of migration today reveals the unequal relations between rich and poor, between North and South, between whiteness and it's others.[1]

> I came to your country with pangs in my heart. I had left my own, partly because I wanted to, but mostly because I needed to. I came, we came, to earn a living, to provide for our deaths, to create a future for our children, somewhere to end our weary lives. To make provision for a posterity we need not be ashamed of.[2]

I write as an Indian woman and a recent migrant. As I did not have to flee from anything in particular, I am hindered from fully appreciating the trials and dangers of those coming by boat or walking for miles to what they hope will be places of refuge. My life has been shaped instead by marriage to a Tongan, who at the time of my meeting him was already a resident in Australia. Through our recent acts of relocation, we reside on an Other's land and are recipients and beneficiaries of all that this land has and offers. All migrants, regardless of where we come from, live on a land that was originally occupied by indigenous people. To the indigene, the question of dominant and minority cultures may not be as relevant as the denial of ancestral lands. One reaction to our story of migration is being seen as the "guilty other" for in our claim to a place in Australia, as immigrants, we are now settlers. We contribute to the diversity of our new

---

[1] Harsha Walia, *Undoing Border Imperialism* (Oakland, California: AK Press, 2013).
[2] Ben Jelloun Tahar, *La Réclusion Solitaire* (Paris: Seuil, 1981).

home. Along with other migrants we help give Australia its international and multicultural identity but we "settle with one of the burdens of migration"[3] and that is, we have become "occupier" and "displacer," and complicit in some ways in indigenous (aboriginal) experiences of colonization, displacement, discrimination and marginalization as we subscribe to boundaries and barriers, creations of the communities we belong to, and that of the dominant Anglo-Celtic community and neglect the first peoples of the land. I am conscious of this, while I also agree with Havea, that we are all, irrespective of who we are, "settlers" and we owe our "respect to the earth."[4] I come to this work as a student of the Bible rather than as a scholar of globalization, migration, or economics. My interests thus are in registering more specifically the insights that the Bible might provide in addressing the issues raised by a world and context in which millions are "on the move" in search of safety, refuge and the opportunity to live life.

Migration and asylum as context

Climbing over razor wire fences, drifting in the sea in leaking boats or stowing away in airless containers, refugees and migrants around the world risk their lives every day in the desperate attempt to find safety or a better life. More people were forced to flee their homes in the recent past than ever before in modern-day history.[5] Nearly 2 million people have fled the brutal conflict in the Syrian Arab Republic (Syria) and hundreds of thousands escaped war, violence and persecution in the Central African Republic, the eastern Democratic Republic of the Congo, Libya, Somalia, Myanmar, South Sudan and Sudan. In just five years, from being the second largest refugee-hosting country in the world, Syria has become the largest refugee-producing country, followed by Afghanistan.[6] It is estimated that 4.1 million individuals were newly displaced within the borders of their countries as a result of war and conflict during the first half of 2014.[7]

Factors that have contributed to the increase in the scale of international migration include globalization and growing disparities in living conditions, both within and between countries. Among the people on the move today, many

---

[3] Jione Havea, "Migration Bodies: A Musing around Gemma Tulud Cruz's 'Migration as *Locus Theologicus*'," in *Colloquim* 46/1 (2014), 107.

[4] Ibid., 108.

[5] "Between January and June 2014, UNHCR offices reported an estimated 5.5 million new forcibly displaced persons either within or outside their own country. As a result [...] the total number of persons of concern to UNHCR by mid- 2014 stood at 46.3 million, compared to 42.9 million at the end of 2013.*UNHCR Mid-Year Trends 2014*, 4. Available at **unhcr.org/54aa91d89.html**

[6] Ibid., 4.

[7] Ibid., 6.

are seeking employment or educational opportunities; others want to reunite with family members and still more are fleeing persecution, conflict or blind violence in their countries. While refugees and asylum seekers account for only a small proportion of the global movement of people, they frequently travel alongside migrants. Many of these movements are irregular, in the sense that they often take place without the requisite documentation, use unauthorized border crossing points or involve smugglers. The people who move in this manner place their lives at risk. They are often obliged to travel in inhumane conditions and may be exposed to exploitation and abuse. States regard such movements as a threat to their sovereignty and security. And, yet, this may be, in some cases, the only escape route open to those fleeing war or persecution.

MIGRATION AS THE "LOCUS" OF THEOLOGY

The complex issue of migration requires responses—social, political, economic, ethical and theological—that are as diverse as the problems themselves. As Peter C. Phan prompts us,

> [M]igration is a permanent feature of the church [...]. Like unity, catholicity, holiness, and apostolicity, "migrantness," to coin a new word, is a note of the true church because only a church that is conscious of being an institutional migrant and caring for all the migrants of the world can truly practice faith, hope, and love, in obedience to Jesus' command.[8]

Significant publications, particularly those by Roman Catholic scholars, have placed migration at the forefront of theological reflection Key concepts are the church's ministry of reconciliation and its nature as "provisional" and as "pilgrim."[9] The issues that migrants struggle with are economic, cultural, social and psychological—issues of identity and belonging,[10] of isolation and being out of place[11] and so

---

[8] Peter C. Phan, "Migration in the Patristic Era: History and Theology," in Daniel Groody and Gioacchino Campese (eds), *A Promised Land, a Perilous Journey: Theological Perspectives on Migration* (Notre Dame, IN: University of Notre Dame Press, 2008), 57–58.
[9] Daniel G. Groody, "Crossing the Divide: Foundations of a Theology of Migration and Refugees," in *Theological Studies 70* (2009), 638–67, here 642; Stephen Bevans, "Mission among Migrants, Mission of Migrants: Mission of the Church," in Groody and Campese, ibid., 100; Samuel Escobar, "Migration: Avenue and Challenge to Mission," in *Missiology: An International Review 31:1* (January 2003), 19.
[10] Lester Edwin J. Ruiz, "The Stranger in Our Midst: Diaspora, Ethics, Transformation," in Fumitaka Matsuoka and Eleazar S. Fernandez (eds), *Realizing the America of Our Hearts: Theological Voices of Asian Americans* (St Louis: Chalice Press, 2003), 226.
[11] Christine Lienemann-Perrin, "Theological Stimuli from the Migrant Churches," in *The Ecumenical Review, 61:4* (December, 2009), 383.

on. A theology of migration is urgently required to assist migrants and asylum seekers as they negotiate life in this process of settlement and integration.

The ingredients for articulating a theological response are, I believe, integral to our scriptural and theological traditions. Our conceptions and understanding of key theological concepts such as God, the human being, justice, creation, shalom, salvation, liberation, human rights, redemption, to name a few, could make a significant contribution to articulating a theology of migration. Hence, beginning with God's preferential option for the poor, Gutiérrez calls for the recognition of the humanity/human dignity of migrants and asylum seekers, and respect for their subjectivity and agency as shapers of their own history.[12]

Migrant readings

What does the Bible say about migration? How might we read the biblical text in order to highlight the issues that arise from migration? The dynamic nature of the biblical text allows for every succeeding generation that receives it to seize from it a message that can be used in a significant manner to address the issues, the needs and concerns of the time in which that generation is placed. The challenge before us then is to determine what the Bible says about migration. Any discerning reader will recognize that the Bible is replete with stories of journeying, alienation, strangeness and encounters with foreigners and outsiders. The thread of journeying into foreign lands on account of famine or experiencing exile in foreign lands is pervasive in the Hebrew Bible. The Bible therefore addresses the "central problem of homelessness"[13] and strangeness.

The exilic experience of the Israelites was both a symbolic and real catastrophe. It formed the predominant material, the theological, psychological and spiritual context for the writing, editing and compiling of the Hebrew Bible.[14] Jonathan Burnside, for example, has very convincingly argued that Moses was a refugee seeking asylum in Median (Ex 2:11-22) when he fled the Pharaoh. Through the Exodus from Egypt, "Israel saw itself, not simply as a

---

[12] Gustavo Gutiérrez, "Poverty, Migration and the Option of the Poor," in Groody and Campese, op. cit. (note 8), 84; cf. Escobar, op. cit. (note 9), 19; Gemma Tulud Cruz, *An Intercultural Theology of Migration* (Leiden: Brill, 2010); Gemma Tulud Cruz, *Toward a Theology of Migration: Social Justice and Religious Experience – Content and Context in Theological Ethics* (Palgrave Macmillan, 2014); Havea, op. cit. (note 3), 87-100.

[13] Walter Brueggemann, *The Land: Place as Gift, Promise and Challenge in Biblical Faith*, 2nd ed. (Minneapolis: Fortress, 2002), 200.

[14] Walter Brueggemann, *Cadences of Home: Preaching Among Exiles*, (Louisville: Westminster John Knox, 1997) 4-11, 115. Cf. also, R. P. Caroll, "Deportation and Diasporic Discourses in the Prophetic Literature," in J. M. Scott (ed.), *Exile: Old Testament, Jewish and Christian Conceptions* (Leiden/New York/Köln: Brill): 226-28.

nation of escaped slaves, but also as a nation of successful asylum-seekers."[15] It is this experience as narrated in Exodus, of seeking asylum, that helped shape biblical law (Ex 20:22–23; 33).

Dianne Bergant makes a case for a theology of migration based on her study of the book of Ruth.[16] She says that the story of Ruth,

> demonstrates that openness to and incorporation of the vulnerable migrant is the way to restoration or salvation [...]. That the vulnerable should be agents of salvation demonstrates that the glory of victory belongs to God alone [...]. The migrant Ruth is a metaphor of this theological tenet.[17]

In what follows I hope to identify some hermeneutical markers that would be applied to a migrant reading and follow that with a reading of the flight to Egypt.

Matthew 2:13–23: The flight to Egypt—A migrant reading

How might we read the biblical text in order to highlight the issues that arise from migration? I tentatively propose the following hermeneutical principles in this migrant reading of Matthew 2:13–23.

A migrant reading would:

- Give serious consideration to the experience of the migrant, including the personal and corporate trauma of the migration experience, the state of being in betwixt and between geographically, culturally, linguistically and socially, the sense of rootlessness and the desire to belong.[18]

- Expose and critique systemic and systematic ills both in the country from which the migrant/refugee/asylum seeker comes and also in the host country.

---

[15] Jonathan Burnside, "Exodus and Asylum: Uncovering the Relationship between Biblical Law and Narrative," in *JSOT*, 34.3 (2010), 243.

[16] Dianne Bergant, "Ruth: The Migrant Who Saved the People," in Gioacchino Campese and Pietro Ciallella (eds), *Migration, Religious Experience, and Globalization*, (Staten Island, NY: Center for Migration Studies, 2003), 49–61, at **onlinelibrary. wiley.com/doi/10.1111/j.2050-411X.2003.tb00316.x/abstract**

[17] Ibid., 60. Cf. Susanna Snyder, *Explorations in Practical, Pastoral and Empirical Theology: Asylum-Seeking, Migration and Church* (Farnham, UK: Ashgate Publishing Co., 2012), 178–86.

[18] Peter C. Phan, "The Dragon and the Eagle: Toward a Vietnamese American Theology," in Matsuoka and Fernandez, op. cit. (note 10), 165.

- Unsettle the dominant—people, readings and perspectives that might militate against the migrant and give space to voices and experiences that are unheard or suppressed.

- Be liberative in intent—it would maintain and reinforce the humanity, the dignity and the freedom of the migrant.

The text narrates the flight of the holy family to Egypt to escape the machinations of Herod seeking to destroy the life of the new born child. In a recent article, Elaine Wainwright calls attention to the word, *anachoresanton*, "to withdraw," "to retire," "to take refuge" or "depart from a location."[19] Matthew uses it consistently to indicate withdrawal from a hostile environment. This word links our passage to the previous narrative which speaks of the magi who journeyed from afar looking for the new child, "a new political era presaged by a star: they were 'people on the move' in search of new possibilities."[20] These wise men, "outsiders to the law and prophecies of Israel,"[21] arrive in Jerusalem asking about the one born "king of the Jews,"—one who symbolises, "the potential for political and socio-cultural change."[22] In response, Herod and "all of Jerusalem," responds to this search for the "king of the Jews." Matthew uses numerical hyperbole and this "all" according to Bradley,

> [...] suggests that for the dialectic frame of the moment, Jerusalem had become in effect the entire Jewish universe." Hence Matthew as religious historian: the quasi universal Jewish world should recognize Jesus as the truly universal king of the Jews.[23]

Herod is panic stricken. Inquiries into someone identified as the "king of the Jews" called into question his own standing and ability as the political, Roman authorized king of the Jews. He consults the experts over this potential rival, and he is told that according to prophecy this child is to be born in Bethlehem. Herod meets again with the magi, this time secretly and informs them of his wish also to worship this new child. But the magi realise that their coming to Jerusalem posed a threat to the new child.

---

[19] Elaine Wainwright, "Crossing Over; Taking Refuge: A Contrapuntal Reading," in *HTS Teologiese Studies/Theological Studies,* vol 70/1 (2014), Art #2720, at **dx.doi. org/10.4102/hts.v70i1.2720**

[20] Ibid.

[21] Thomas G. Long, *Matthew* (Louisville, Kentucky: Westminster John Knox Press, 1997), 18.

[22] Wainwright, op. cit. (note 19).

[23] Mathew Carl Bradley, *Matthew: Poet, Historian, Dialectician* (New York: Peter Lang, 2007), 9.

Alerted to this, they return to their home by another route and the "departure" is once again described with the use of the verb, *anachoreo* (v 12).

Herod, then, in an action strongly reminiscent of the Pharaoh's treatment of the male offspring of Hebrew slaves, dictates that all male children under the age of two were to be slain. Joseph is warned in a dream and instructed to "flee to Egypt" (v 13) and Joseph is forced to move his family to Egypt. Again the same verb is used to describe this departure to Egypt (v 14). Jesus had to be taken away from his homeland, from the place of his birth into Egypt—a place far removed from Herod's power, a place that held powerful imagery and memory—only to be brought out again from Egypt. The holy family therefore recapitulates the exodus, although unlike their ancestors who were environmental refugees, they enter Egypt as political refugees. The use of the verb *anachoreo* helps establish the text as a narrative of migration, of fleeing from situations of subjugation and violence. Matthew describes the insecurity that faces Joseph, Mary and the child as they set out to Egypt. The story teaches us that Jesus was a refugee (Mt 2:13-14).

In reading this narrative we often envision a lone family of three on the move on a donkey—influenced perhaps by the many artists who have depicted it in this way. One only needs to recall the images of those crossing the Mediterranean today from Africa to note that migrations are almost never only individual—they are always communal. Refugees come in bands or groups in contemporary migration. By portraying them as a lone family, the narrative removes them from the experience of migration.[24]

Herod becomes aware of this child via the actions of the magi. The magi and the star challenge the "political stability by witnessing to an alternative king."[25] He feels duped when the magi do not return to Jerusalem and his anger results in the decree to slay all male babies in the district of Bethlehem. The family is instructed "to flee" and flee it does from a tyrant who has issued his murderous command to kill all male children under two. The story reveals the heinousness of Herod's act vis-à-vis the powerlessness of the oppressed, his malice and his violence. The narrative exposes the severity of political conflict. Matthew locates Jesus' birth not within a utopian or idealistic world but a world of injustice[26] and the paranoid brutality of the dominant when their power is challenged, threatened or confronted. "All of Jerusalem"—namely, the powerful, dominant but now a disturbed center/élite, including the religious leadership—join Herod out

[24] Wainwright, op. cit. (note 19).
[25] Warren Carter, *Matthew and the Margins: A Socio-Political Reading* (London: T&T Clark, 2010), 76.
[26] Craig S. Keener, *The Gospel of Matthew: A Socio-Rhetorical Commentary* (Grand Rapids: Wm. B. Eerdmans Publishing Co., 2009), 110.

of fear.[27] The narrative also sheds light on the manner in which various sections of the élite colluded, perhaps for varied reasons and with differing agendas, but united in purpose to quash attempts by the marginalized to assert their rights or request affirmation of their identity. This scene however, has many modern day parallels—as we image the hundreds of children who are dying in the attempt to cross borders in the USA or those in Syria that are being murdered.

Jesus is taken to safety, and yet the narrative leaves one with a sense of unease and many unanswered questions. What became of the rest of the children and their parents in Bethlehem?[28] Was there nobody to save them? It is significant that very few commentators even ask these questions. Most only emphasize that God protects Jesus and his family! And yet, when the text is read with the eyes of a migrant these questions are raised and become pertinent.

The text says nothing about the fate of the other children in Bethlehem. As in the stories of migration today, not all are able to flee and when they do try, not all are successful. I ask again, Was there no one to save them? The singular focus of the text on Jesus, the rescue of the chosen child, "can mask exclusion and injustice in relation to those not chosen."[29] The narrative highlights the fact that even amongst those that are oppressed some are privileged with life and success. Some are rescued while others lose their lives. Some have the money to find quicker and more effective means to escape a traumatic situation but those mired in poverty are forced to stay behind and face the consequences and lose their lives.

The effect of the violent and unjust act on the part of Herod is reported with a reference to the wailing of Rachel in Jeremiah 31:15. Rachel is first introduced in Genesis 29 as a woman shepherdess whose life and future are determined by two men, namely, Jacob and Laban. She waits for seven years to become the wife of the patriarch Jacob and being barren she waits for another seven years to bear children. She pleads with God to give her children (Gen 30:1). Against all odds she bears children but, eventually, it is motherhood that finally robs her of life (Gen 35:16-20). Rachel is remembered through her children, her grandchildren and their descendants. Rachel is remembered by Jeremiah in the aftermath of the destruction of Jerusalem. The people and the land were in pain and all they could do was shed tears in lamentation to God. Rachel is uplifted by the prophet Jeremiah, himself a descendant of Rachel; a Benjaminite from the village of Anathoth. She is

---

[27] Carter, op. cit. (note 25), 77.
[28] On questions about the historicity of this incident, see Margaret Davies, *Matthew*, 2nd ed. (Sheffield: Sheffield Phoenix Press, 2009), 35–37.
[29] Wainwright, op. cit. (note 19).

introduced as the personification of all Israel's mothers, who weeps over the graves of her children.[30] Jeremiah immortalizes her as a mother who weeps for her children and pleading with God on their behalf. Bethlehem, personified as Rachel, weeps and refuses to be comforted on account of the children massacred by Herod. The weeping and wailing mothers/parents over the loss of their children in situations of war and conflict is haunting and the extinguishing of young and innocent lives evokes a type of unparalleled grief and one which is hard to describe.

The text showcases Rachel as the mother figure weeping and inconsolable; but in what follows, one is drawn to the image of God as parent. The metaphor of parenthood takes a distinctly maternal shape as God shows motherly compassion for the child (Jer 31:20–22). Rachel's tears and lament stir/move the inner parts (the womb) of the Divine which trembles (yearns) for the child Ephraim and results in the voice of Mother God who declares compassion and salvation for Israel.[31] In the Jeremiah passage,

> the human mother refuses consolation; the divine mother changes grief into consolation. As a result the poem has moved from the desolate lamentation of Rachel to the redemptive compassion of God.[32]

Does Mathew hope that his readers will recall this compassion of the mothering God that offers the promise of hope in this situation? Is Mathew encouraging his readers to look beyond the radically different situations, to hope beyond the tragedy? The mothering and hope-giving God accompanies the migrant in her struggle and pain. Perhaps hope also lies in the ones that were saved or rescued and, in this case, it lies in the child Jesus who will grow up hearing the stories of rescue, of resistance against Herod and the risks taken by his parents to keep him alive. Hope lies in the manner in which these experiences form the person and character of Jesus and become intrinsic to the shape and form of his ministry.

For a migrant, of whatever origin, the primary issue on arrival in a new country is battling the sense of "foreignness." One becomes "the other," an alien in a strange place that in a variety of ways, whether overtly or subliminally, seems to reject the very things that constitute your identity. Lienemann-Perrin observes that dislocated people could feel out of place

---

[30] Terence E. Fretheim, *Jeremiah: Smyth and Helwys Bible Commentary* (Macon, GA: Smyth & Helwys, 2002), 434.

[31] Monica J. Melanchthon, "Mothering Ways and Reconciliation," in Robert Schreiter and Knud Jørgensen (eds), *Mission as Ministry of Reconciliation* (UK: Regnum, 2013).

[32] Phyllis Trible, *God and the Rhetoric of Sexuality* (Philadelphia: Fortress Press, 1978), 45.

for a long time. There are many contributing factors to this feeling of isolation, such as language barriers, immigration policies and cultural values and practices. She observes, "[t]heir presence in their receiving country is constantly being contested. Often they remain involuntarily associated with their country of origin. They must constantly justify their presence and their apparently strange identity."[33] Jesus becomes a child refugee and thereby shares an experience only too common today. Most refugees would be able to identify with the uncertainty, the reduction to dependency, the alienation from homeland, relatives and friends. It is a terrible fate for the parents who feel responsible for their children's welfare yet are often unable to safeguard it.

In a dream, Joseph is once again informed of Herod's death and instructed to take the child back to the land of Israel. And he obeys but only to face a situation where Archelaus, the son of Herod, was no different from his father, in that he demonstrated equal cruelty. Joseph and his family are therefore unable to return to Bethlehem, their hometown, and instead withdraw (*anachoreo*) to the politically insignificant and small village of Nazareth in the region of Galilee—a village that existed in the shadow of the wealthy, Hellenised Jewish city of Sepphoris. The family thereby becomes an internally displaced family. But what life might have been like for this family in this location is unclear.

Galilee is important for Matthew, because it was a region mixed with indigenous Gentiles, a good seed ground for the more inclusive kind of religious attitude that Jesus would eventually become known for and condemned.[34]

Jesus begins his earthly journey as a migrant and a displaced person. In the final analysis, he is remembered as the "Nazarene," thereby erasing his origins in Bethlehem and Jerusalem, an erasure that once again resonates with many migrants.[35]

When looked at with some empire sensitivity, this narrative in Matthew showcases two competing systems that have been identified as the Roman Empire and God's Empire (*basileia*). The magi and Joseph are followers of the latter while King Herod as king is contrasted with Jesus, the king of the Jews. King Herod is the ruthless retaliative leader, who strikes when in fear of being usurped. He is surrounded by his soldiers and religious leadership, typical retainers of empire, whose position in the text is one of blind obedience that is sometimes projected as a virtue. These are willing to kill one of their own if they were ordered to do so. In Arendt's terminology they represent

[33] Lienemann-Perrin, op. cit. (note 11), 383.
[34] George T. Montague, *Companion God: A Cross-Cultural Commentary on the Gospel of Matthew* (New York: Paulist Press, 2010), 35.
[35] Wainwright, op. cit. (note 19).

the "banality of evil," those who act with thoughtlessness or without critical thinking and who perpetuate the systemic violence in the Roman Empire.

The God of Matthew beats Herod through God's faithful agents in God's politics—the infant Jesus, the magi and Joseph. Unlike the story of the exodus, it is men who work toward the saving of this child—the magi and Joseph. In the context of male tyranny and power politics, the person of Joseph, the husband of Mary, paves the way for a different or new understanding of masculinity, one that is kenotic, for he gives up his own power for a positive and mutually transformative masculinity.

This reminds us also of the many fathers who risk their lives for the sake of their children and die trying to protect them by taking them and their children on hazardous journeys in search of life and a future for their children. They denounce the empires in their countries and the terror that they exercise to control by fleeing and this flight is both an act of courage as much as it is a quest for life.

> God's initiative in the conception and birth of Jesus is met by two responses: resistance, violence, and rejection from the center elite of political and religious power in Jerusalem, and worship, trust and obedience from those who, in the perspective of the center, occupy the insignificant margins where God's purposes of liberation are being accomplished. The danger and evil of empire constantly threaten and oppose those purposes, places and people. But the empire does not have the final word.[36]

The text raises several issues for me when seen in light of the challenges posed by migration and migrants:

- Fear and insecurity vis-à-vis the powers that be and the dominant that are driven by greed and the need for control to subdue all that might endanger their sovereignty.

- The apathy and thoughtlessness of those who subscribe to policies that dehumanize and subvert the innocent from seeking refuge

- The violence and loss of life surrounding migration and the search for asylum.

- In Rachel's cry I hear the cry of many mothers and fathers but also the gendering within migration and asylum seeking, the challenges that face many women and girls, boys and babies, their increased

---

[36] Carter, op. cit. (note 25), 89.

vulnerability to violence, sexual abuse, hunger and discrimination, all of which needs to be addressed.

• At the heart of the story is the life of a child. This reminds me of the many children who are caught in this deplorable situation.

What might the implications of this text be for our Lutheran understanding of a theology of the cross, of citizenship, of salvation or other key doctrines of the Lutheran church? Unfortunately, Luther seems to have made no comment on the flight to Egypt. His treatment of the second chapter of Matthew only attends to the first twelve verses.[37]

MIGRATION, LUTHER AND SALVATION

The migration of this family locates the Jesus story within a movement that spans history, of people desiring a better life or escaping the threat of death.[38]

Viewed as a theological concept, migration offers a rich hermeneutic for some of the most foundational dimensions of human existence and offers a different vantage point for making moral choices; it illuminates the gift and demand of Christian faith in light of the pressing social problems of the modern world, and it opens up space to bring out what is most human in a debate that often diminishes and dehumanizes those forcibly displaced.[39]

Migration was perhaps not at the forefront of the issues that confronted Luther's community. But I take inspiration from the fact that the Reformation was part of real life, with its many complexities and this aspect of the Reformation cannot be ignored.

Where once Luther sought to flee the world for what he thought would have been the shelter of the cloister to find certainty of salvation, instead he returned to embrace life in this world, living as part of God's created order, mindful of the

---

[37] Martin Luther, "The Gospel for the Festival of the Epiphany, Matthew 2[:1–12]," in Helmut T. Lehmann (ed), *Luther's Works*, vol. 52 (Philadelphia: Fortress Press, 1974), 159–286.

[38] M. Daniel Caroll R, *Christians at the Border: Immigration, the Church and the Bible* (Grand Rapids, MI: Baker Academic, 2008), 116.

[39] Daniel G. Groody, CSC., "Dying to Live: Theology, Migration, and the Human Journey," in *CMSM Forum* (Fall 2009), 4.

sin that by nature still remained while filled with joy for the message of salvation by grace and faith alone for Christ's sake.[40]

Luther struggled to address the many social and political issues of his day and sought to respond to them primarily as a pastor and theologian. Our response to the phenomenon of migration should be supported by both material and theological reasons.

At the heart of the biblical story are stories of migration. The journey from Egypt to the Promised Land, when seen in an historical context, was a journey from servitude, denial of material goods and alienation into a situation of non-exploitation, freedom, holistic life and abundance. The migration of the holy family to Egypt was a flight from death and serves as an archetype for every migrant, alien, or refugee, no matter what the motive for leaving their country of origin. It has been suggested that these stories offer persistent images of salvation and they have been used to articulate a theology of salvation.[41]

> If we understand salvation as something with merely "religious" or "spiritual" value for my soul, then it would not have much to contribute to human life. But if salvation is understood as passing from less human to more human conditions, it means that messianism brings about freedom of the captives and the oppressed, and liberates human beings. [...] [A]nd if within the most human elements we include grace, faith, and divine filiation then we comprehend profoundly why it can be said that working for development is the summary of all our duties.[42]

Luther used his theology to serve the proclamation of the gospel—"that salvation is received and not achieved."[43] Salvation was not a movement or progress from iniquity to virtue—rather a premise of life. Salvation or justification was therefore God's gift to the faithful—a present, a living experience, and not something in the future. It comes about through faith in the risen Christ, present here and now, with whom one becomes conjoined through faith and saved through his Spirit. The priority of Christ in justification is at the core of Luther's understanding of Salvation. By faith

---

[40] R. Rosin, "Humanism, Luther and the Wittenberg Reformation," in Robert Kolb, Irene Dingel and L'ubomír Batka (eds), *The Oxford Handbook of Martin Luther's Theology* (Oxford: University Press, 2014), 101.

[41] Cf. Gemma Tulud Cruz, "When Death Meets Life: Exploring the Links between Migration and Salvation," in *Asian Horizons*, vol. 6, no. 4 (December 2012), 752–66.

[42] Gustavo Gutierrez, *Essential Writings* (Maryknoll, New York: Orbis, 2002), 26.

[43] Carter Lindberg, "Luther's Struggle with Social-Ethical Issues," in Donald K. McKim (ed.), *The Cambridge Companion to Martin Luther* (Cambridge: University Press, 2003), 165.

we are renewed and this faith has an ethical dimension and it produces good works.

We do not become righteous by doing righteous deeds but having been made righteous, we do righteous deeds.[44]

> As I have frequently stated, the suffering and work of Christ is to be viewed in two lights: First, as grace bestowed on us, as a blessing conferred, requiring the exercise of faith on our part and our acceptance of the salvation offered. Second, we are to regard it as an example for us to follow; we are to offer up ourselves for our neighbours' benefit and for the honour of God. This offering is the exercise of our love—distributing our works for the benefit of our neighbours. He who does so is a Christian. He becomes one with Christ, and the offering of his body is identical with the offering of Christ's body.[45]

Righteous deeds are those that serve the neighbor; they are this worldly "directed to the neighbor as a response to God's promise."[46] These righteous deeds are an indicator of the presence of grace within us. Anyone who has faith is willing to serve God, by engaging themselves in the fight against all that is unjust, ungodly and sinful. Injustice and oppression are social sins and void of any saving significance. Continuing to live in situations of pain, suffering and fear has no saving value and hence need to be contested and fought. In the context of the issue under discussion, the neighbor is the person encountered in the concrete and complex situation of migration. The neighbor/migrant is not to be the object of charity and sympathy, but one who is to be served with love, justice and equity.

Suffering is a very strong part of the refugee experience. Where suffering is present in the world, there Christ is present, resisting, empowering and upholding all those who suffer and those who suffer along with. In the suffering of the migrant, Christ is revealed. The stories of migrants and the risks they take are expressions of the resilience of the human spirit that is able to emerge from brutality and inhumanity with strength and joy and hope and this, to my mind, is tantamount to the experience of salvation. The combination of these—profound oppression and subjugation and in its midst, a glimpse of human liberation, of life overcoming death—makes the experience of migration a lens through which one can understand salvation.

---

[44] *LW* 31, 12.

[45] Martin Luther, "First Sunday after Epiphany—The Fruits of Faith. Our Spiritual Service, Romans 12, 1-6," in John Nicholas Lenker (ed.), *Sermons of Martin Luther. Volume VII, Sermons on Epistle Texts for Epiphany and Pentecost*, transl. John Nicholas Lenker and others (Grand Rapids, MI: Baker Book House, 1989), 9.

[46] Lindberg, op. cit. (note 43), 166.

Migration is graced even through difficult circumstances and points to the notion that the divine is both present and absent and that life is both love and horror[47] as exemplified in Christ's own life.

The life of baby Jesus was saved from the tyrannical Herod, by virtue of the actions of several individuals—the magi, Joseph and others who perhaps welcomed them in Egypt and gave them a home. This drives home the fact that salvation takes place in communion and not in isolation.[48] It takes place through dynamic relationships and movements and through the crossing of borders—be they geographical, ethnic, lingual or social—in the realization of dreams of a secure life. Borders are sites of presence, of bodies on the move, of relationships. They are also places of inclusion and exclusion, of life and death, a gateway between hope and despair, of freedom, of home and a better quality of life, of life itself. They are therefore sites of promise and possibilities and places of salvation.

Luther objected to the notion of salvation as attained only through ritual, knowledge and the sacraments. Mere intellectual belief in a metaphysical God and a religious system which turned the gospel into a philosophy did not appeal to Luther. He rejected the whole system of abstractions, and instead of beginning with the logical concepts of his contemporaries, he began with the living person of Jesus Christ, in all his tenderness and mystery, and through him turned his eyes to God revealed in Christ. In many ways this text reinforces Luther's stance. The striking issue for me in this text is that it was a flight, a migration, a withdrawal from domestic terror toward the maintenance of life and this cannot be explained in abstract terms.

I am not advocating a simple sociological reduction of liberation and salvation. All that I want to suggest is that the two dimensions—the material and the spiritual— should not be polarized in our definitions and our understandings of salvation. For deeply embedded in the material quest of the marginalized and the migrant there is the spiritual quest and the material conditions that make it possible.

> [E]veryone must benefit and serve every other by means of his (sic) own work or office so that in this way many kinds of work may be done for the *bodily and spiritual welfare of the community* [...].[49]

---

[47] Silvano Tomasani, "The Prophetic Mission of the Churches: Theological Perspectives," in *The Prophetic Mission of the Churches in Response to Forced Displacement of Peoples,* Report of a Global Ecumenical Consultation, Addis Ababa, 6–11 November 1995 (Geneva: World Council of Churches, 1996), 41.

[48] Gemma Tulud Cruz, Migration as *Locus Theologicus,* in *Colloquim* 46/1 (2014), 94.

[49] *LW* 44, 130, author's own emphasis.

It is in this context that we need to widen the terms of our discussion and ask, Is not the material well-being an indispensable part of life? The ultimate bliss according to Matthew 25:31–46 is connected with having given food, drink and clothing—all available only in situations of peace, justice and freedom (life). These are the material realities that matter to the poor, to the least ones, essential for their well-being. It is the reference to these very physical realities, which many migrants are deprived of in their original locations—that lead them on a journey in search for a place where these are available. Salvation then is not alienation from these material realities, but the transformation of these realities from means of selfishness, greed and death to become realities of life through sharing.

The act of sharing one's land, one's home, one's bread and one's water resources with a migrant is an act of salvation because in that act for the well-being of that other, one encounters God, works alongside God and becomes one with the suffering migrant and with God.

Matthew, Judaism and Lutheran Tradition

Matthew's Pharisees: Seven Woes and Seven Warnings

Laurence Edwards

In 1532, Martin Luther wrote a letter to a recent convert from Judaism to Christianity. He attributes the failure of more Jews to convert to the distortions of "our Sophists and Pharisees." As David Nirenberg points out in his recent book, Luther was not referring here to Pharisees as the first-century Jewish sect, but to "Popes, priests, monks, and theology students."[1] The Pharisees figured regularly in the polemics of the Reformation, often used by the Reformers to represent the Catholic Church, which was characterized, in their view, by the same negative qualities of hypocrisy, formalism, obsessive attention to ritual detail and lack of true spirit attributed in the New Testament to the Jewish Pharisees of Jesus' time. By way of contrast, the Reformers saw themselves as aligned with the spiritual protest of Jesus, and therefore representing a return to original Christianity. This is a trope that can be seen in Protestant scholarship into the twentieth century.

The Pharisees have become an enduring figure in religious discourse, most often a negative one. With a capital "P" the term identifies one of the sects or schools of thought in first-century Judaism. With a lower-case "p" the term has become synonymous with hypocrisy and narrow-minded legalism. This negative image is primarily due to their portrayal in the gospels as Jesus' opponents, representatives of the Jewish establishment, scholars focused on outward show and intellectual gymnastics to the exclusion of true piety, a "brood of vipers" (Mt 23:33).

---

[1] David Nirenberg, *Anti-Judaism: The Western Tradition* (New York: W.W. Norton, 2013), 261.

I, however, was taught to admire the Pharisees as the sages whose teaching of the "Oral Torah" set the groundwork for Rabbinic Judaism, of which I am an inheritor. Among the Pharisees, the greatest figure in the late Second Temple period is the brilliant, kind, patient sage, Hillel the Elder, who taught that the essential teaching of Torah is, "That which is hateful to you do not do to another."[2] He was an older contemporary of Jesus of Nazareth, who offered similar teachings.

"Woe unto You"

In our time, when—thankfully—many Christians and Jews are seeking a less polemical, more dialogical relationship, we come up against certain passages of Christian Scripture and later Jewish writings that cry out for reinterpretation and contextualization. Many of those problematic passages relate to Jesus' interactions with Pharisees. If these passages were understood as distant from us in time and cultural setting they might not be so problematic. But we seek to read Scripture as a collection of texts that continue to speak to us. The Jewish leaders portrayed (I might say caricatured) in the gospel narratives have been read by Christians over many centuries as representatives of Judaism then and now. So how shall we hear and teach these passages that have been a source of pain and distancing between our communities?

Of all the gospel treatments of the Pharisees, the harshest denunciation is found in chapter 23 of Matthew, a passage often referred to as "The Woes of the Pharisees."

> They do all their deeds to be seen by others; for they make their phylacteries broad and their fringes long. They love to have the place of honor at banquets and the best seats in the synagogues, and to be greeted with respect in the market-places, and to have people call them rabbi [...].
>
> Woe to you, scribes and Pharisees, hypocrites! For you are like whitewashed tombs, which on the outside look beautiful, but inside they are full of the bones of the dead and of all kinds of filth. So you also on the outside look righteous to others, but inside you are full of hypocrisy and lawlessness. (vv. 5-7; 37–28)

Catholic scholar Philip Cunningham summarizes the social and historical background thus:

> Matthew's Church is evidently a predominantly Jewish community in the mid-80s which understands itself as being authentically Jewish because it lives ac-

---

[2] Babylonian Talmud *Shabbat* 31a.

cording to Jesus' authoritative presentation of the Torah ... a minority subgroup among the various competing Jewish movements which are seeking to fill the vacuum created by the destruction of the Temple in 70 CE. Consequently, the scribes and Pharisees are especially criticized in Matthew's Gospel because they are emblematic of those with whom the evangelist is vying for the post-Temple leadership of the Jewish community. [...].

By associating the Pharisees with the Temple leadership, the implication is made that just as the leadership of the chief priests had been corrupt and had proven to be fruitless (Matt 21:19, 33–44), so too the emerging leaders of Matthew's day are inauthentic blind guides [...] who seem to be learned Jews but really are not.[3]

Cunningham's description goes some way toward contextualizing the vehemence of Matthew's denunciation. It is more than just a "family quarrel;" there is intense competition, in a situation of devastation and imperial occupation.

Aaron Gale, in a more recent study, makes a case for Matthew's community being affluent, educated in both Greek and Hebrew, mainly Jewish, and knowledgeable in Torah and rabbinic interpretation.[4] The community is located, according to Gale, in the Galilee and probably in Sepphoris rather than in Syria, as others have argued. If he is correct, then Matthew's community was living in close proximity to centers of rabbinic activity in the decades following the destruction of the Temple. Such a social setting adds another dimension to the diatribe. Gale notes that it is not directed against scribes in general, and Matthew himself likely comes from such a circle. Instead, it is directed against those who are in competition with Matthew's community.[5]

On the basis of these and other descriptions, I propose at least three layers that form the background to Matthew's arguments:

• They surely reflect an early tradition that Jesus was in conflict with at least some of the pharisaic leaders of his time. Why was he arguing with them? Because he was closer to them than to any of the other Jewish groups of his time.

• Matthew's community and its leaders might well have been in conflict with the rabbinic leadership of its time. The vehemence of the diatribe suggests an intense conflict, perhaps even including pressure put

---

[3] Philip A. Cunningham, "The Synoptic Gospels and Their Presentation of Judaism," in Mary C. Boys et al. (eds), *Within Context: Essays on Jews and Judaism in the New Testament* (Collegeville, MN: Liturgical Press, 1993), 55–56.
[4] Aaron M. Gale, *Redefining Ancient Borders: The Jewish Scribal Framework of Matthew's Gospel* (New York: T & T Clark, 2005).
[5] Ibid., 105.

on Matthew's community by the rabbinic leadership. (Keep in mind, though, that the rabbis too were struggling to consolidate and exercise authority, within the constraints of Roman rule.)

• The leaders of Matthew's community presumably included the scribes who were compiling, writing and editing what would become Matthew's Gospel. It could be that their critique of the Pharisees also functioned as a rebuke to members of their own community, who were wealthy, pious and a little too self-satisfied. This last suggestion reflects my own historical imagination at work, but it would be consistent with the prophetic mode of self-critique.

Who were the Pharisees?

The Pharisees themselves left us no documents describing their philosophy or their approach to Torah interpretation. Those who wish to develop a historical perspective on this group begin with the gospel accounts and a few descriptions offered by the Jewish historian Josephus. They work with the general understanding that the Pharisees were the main forerunners of the rabbis, the Jewish sages who took on the arduous task of reconstituting Judaism after the destruction of the Second Temple by the Romans in 70 CE. The problem for historians is that all of these sources are secondary at best. A fair and careful picture is offered by Jacob Neusner:

> The Pharisees formed a social entity, of indeterminate classification (sect? church? political party? philosophical order? cult?), in the Jewish nation in the Land of Israel in the century or so before A.D. 70. They are of special interest for two reasons. First, they are mentioned in the Synoptic Gospels [also in John] as contemporaries of Jesus, represented sometimes as hostile, sometimes as neutral, and sometimes as friendly to the early Christians represented by Jesus. Second, they are commonly supposed to stand behind the authorities who, in the second century, made up the materials that come to us in the Mishnah, the first important document, after Scripture, of Judaism in its classical or normative form. Hence the Mishnah and some related writings are alleged to rest upon traditions going back to the Pharisees before A.D. 70. These views impute to the Pharisees greater importance than, in their own day, they are likely to have enjoyed. [...] No writings survive that were produced by them; all we do know is what later writers said about them.[6]

---

[6] Jacob Neusner, "Mr. Sanders' Pharisees—and Mine," in *The Twentieth Century Construction of "Judaism": Essays on the Religion of Torah in the History of Religion* (Atlanta: Scholars Press, 1991), 277.

Scholars have no doubt that there were Pharisees, but since we possess no descriptions in their own words, it is difficult to know even how to classify them.

The absence of direct sources creates a central problem. The goal of positive-historical study was and is to establish as many facts as possible, in an effort to reconstruct who the Pharisees actually were in their time.[7] But the lack of first-hand evidence necessarily means that the historical works that claim to fill out the portrait of the Pharisees are themselves constructed narratives. Postmodern interpreters would insist that this is always the case. The Pharisees are thus positioned to invite a range of assertions reflecting the ideological tendencies of those constructing them.

Josephus claims to have spent time among the Pharisees, but he wrote mainly for his Roman patrons, and Paul also claims pharisaic affiliation. But the gospel and rabbinic materials were written after the Pharisees as a group had ceased to exist. What we think we know about the historical Pharisees is based on some imaginative filling-in of the sources, and often on a lot of polemical projection. A similar use of historical imagination is required to reconstruct the social setting of the communities that produced the gospels. We can posit certain things based on our source material, but we have no independent access to the context in which the gospels were written.

TWO WARNINGS

We have referred to Matthew's seven "woes" of the Pharisees. Now for some warnings. Warning number one concerning the Pharisees is that we really do not know very much about who they actually were, and have no idea whether they would recognize themselves in any of our reconstructions of them. So beware: whether you see them as pious hypocrites or—like I do—as creative and compassionate teachers of Torah, we are likely distorting the historical reality.

Indeed, not only the Pharisees, but first-century Judaism as a whole, too often receives distorted treatment as the background that Jesus' message is said to supersede. Faithful preachers of the gospel will be careful

---

[7] See, for example, Ellis Rivkin, *A Hidden Revolution: The Pharisees' Search for the Kingdom Within* (Nashville: Abingdon, 1978). A helpful review of some of the leading scholarly theories of Pharisaic origins is offered by Hugo D. Mantel, "The Sadducees and the Pharisees," in Michael Avi-Yonah and Zvi Baras (eds), *The World History of the Jewish People, First Series: Ancient Times,* vol. VIII: *Society and Religion in the Second Temple Period* (Jerusalem: Massada Publishing Ltd., 1977), 99–123.

not to deliver their message at the cost of misrepresenting the tradition out of which Jesus and his teachings were born. It is one thing to see Jesus the Jew engaged in impassioned dialogue with other Jewish teachers of his time, who were his peers, and to recognize that they debated the interpretation of the Torah, which they all revered in common. It is a very different dynamic to see Jesus as God incarnate, engaged in condemning the representatives of the tradition from which he comes.

If Jesus' dispute with the Pharisees is an internal, critical dialogue it would be consistent with a distinctive feature of the biblical tradition. Israel is criticized throughout the Torah for backsliding and rebellion. The prophets, while critical of many nations, aim their sharpest barbs at their own people. If Jesus places himself within that prophetic tradition, it would make sense to read his polemics as a similar kind of internal critique. In Matthew's version, his sharpest rebukes are aimed precisely at those closest to him.

Unfortunately, the weight of Christian reading of Scripture has tended not to think that these polemics were aimed at Jesus' closest interlocutors or at religious hypocrisy in general. Instead, they are taken as a critique of the Jewish leadership of his time and, by extension over the centuries, of Jews and Judaism in general. Amy-Jill Levine has catalogued the anti-Jewish stereotypes that still too often remain in Christian preaching.[8] So a second warning: Do not bear false witness against Judaism. This applies to the Judaism of Jesus' time, which was once called "Late Judaism," but now is called "Early Judaism;" it also applies to the Judaism of today.

At the same time, the Talmud, the great compendium of rabbinic teaching, contains its own warning against religious hypocrisy. Interestingly, it puts it in terms of certain types of Pharisees! In Tractate *Sotah* of the Babylonian Talmud (section 22b), it is striking that the number seven appears again. Just as Matthew's Jesus hurled seven "woes" at Pharisees, so Tractate *Sotah* mentions seven types of Pharisees, five of which are clearly considered negative.[9]

---

[8] See Ammy-Jill Levine, "Bearing False Witness: Common Errors Made about Early Judaism," in Amy-Jill Levine and Marc Zvi Brettler (eds), *The Jewish Annotated New Testament* (Oxford & New York: Oxford University Press, 2011), 501–504.

[9] Tractate *Sotah* 22b reads: "AND THE PLAGUE OF PHARISEES etc. Our Rabbis have taught: There are seven types of Pharisees: the *shikmi* Pharisee, the *nikpi* Pharisee, the *kizai* Pharisee, the 'pestle' Pharisee, the Pharisee [who constantly exclaims] 'What is my duty that I may perform it?', the Pharisee from love [of God] and the Pharisee from fear. The *shikmi* Pharisee—he is one who performs the action of Shechem [who carries his religious duties ostentatiously]. The *nikpi* Pharisee—he is one who knocks his feet together[walks with exaggerated humility]. The *kizai* Pharisee— R. Nahman b. Isaac said: He is one who makes his blood to flow against

Sotah's description of pharisaic perversity is actually striking in its similarity to the "woes" of Matthew 23, which are so obviously polemical in nature. The *Sotah* text was redacted several centuries after Matthew's Gospel. If the Talmudic descriptions sound familiar, it is because the rhetoric of Matthew's Jesus has so thoroughly penetrated the common usage of the term. Matthew's Jesus decries "you Pharisees" as hypocrites, but it is not clear whether he was referring to all Pharisees, or only to some Pharisees, or perhaps the Pharisees to whom he was speaking at that moment. But a similar judgment is rendered in the Talmud against those who show a pious face to the world, but are in fact mainly concerned with their own image.

Repairing the relationship

In more recent years, some past Christian polemics have been cause for regret and reevaluation. The Vatican document, "Notes on the Correct Way to Present the Jews and Judaism," is part of an ongoing effort to defang some of the harsher anti-Jewish polemics of the New Testament and the Christian tradition. Note that the Vatican includes a reference to Talmud Sotah 22b in its discussion.

> It is noteworthy too that the Pharisees are not mentioned in accounts of the Passion. Gamaliel (Acts 5:34-39) defends the apostles in a meeting of the Sanhedrin. An exclusively negative picture of the Pharisees is likely to be inaccurate and unjust (*Guidelines*, note 1; *AAS*[10], p. 76). If in the Gospel and elsewhere in the New Testament there are all sorts of unfavorable references to the Pharisees, they should be seen against the background of a complex and diversified movement.

---

walls [he performs a good deed and then a bad deed, setting one off against the other]. The 'pestle' Pharisee—Rabbah b. Shila said: [His head] is bowed like [a pestle in] a mortar. The Pharisee [who constantly exclaims] 'What is my duty that I may perform it?' — but that is a virtue! — Nay, what he says is, 'What further duty is for me that I may perform it?' [as though he had fulfilled every obligation]. The Pharisee from love and the Pharisee from fear — Abaye and Raba said to the tanna [who was reciting this passage], Do not mention 'the Pharisee from love and the Pharisee from fear' [love and fear of God]; for Rab Judah has said in the name of Rab: A man should always engage himself in Torah and the commandments even though it be not for their own sake [from pure and disinterested motives], because from [engaging in them] not for their own sake, he will come [to engage in them] for their own sake. [...]" The translation and bracketed comments are based on the translation by A. Cohen, Tractate *Sotah* 22a in *The Babylonian Talmud* part 3, vol. 6 (London: Soncino Press, 1936).
[10] *Acta Apostolicae Sedis* (Official organ of the Holy See).

> Criticisms of various types of Pharisees are moreover not lacking in rabbinical sources (the *Babylonian Talmud* and the *Sotah* treatise, 22b). "Phariseeism" in the pejorative sense can be rife in any religion. It may also be stressed that, if Jesus shows himself severe towards the Pharisees, it is because he is closer to them than to other contemporary Jewish groups.[11]

So too, the Evangelical Lutheran Church in America (ELCA) offers among its "Guidelines for Jewish-Lutheran Relations":

> 13. Lutheran pastors should make it clear in their preaching and teaching that although the New Testament reflects early conflicts, it must not be used as justification for hostility towards present-day Jews. Blame for the death of Jesus should not be attributed to Judaism or the Jewish people, and stereotypes of Judaism as a legalistic religion should be avoided.[12] Lutheran curricular materials should exercise the same care.[13]

Such statements are part of a significant turn in the consciousness of many contemporary Christians vis-à-vis Judaism. Esther Menn, for example, points out that, for Jews, Torah is a source of joy.[14] In this spirit, many contemporary Christian preachers will emphasize the idea that the "Pharisees" represent hypocrisy in general, not something specific to and characteristic of Judaism alone. As one Presbyterian friend of mine said, "We were taught in church that, whenever the text says 'Pharisee,' read 'Presbyterian.'" This helps defuse the anti-Jewish sting of the Gospels. However, it creates another problem, namely, that it tends to erase the Jewish background of Christianity, thereby severing Christianity from its roots.[15]

---

[11] Vatican Commission for Religious Relations with the Jews, "Notes on the Correct Way to Present the Jews and Judaism in Preaching and Catechesis in the Roman Catholic Church" (June 24, 1985) III, 19, at **www.vatican.va/roman_curia/pontifical_councils/chrstuni/relations-jews-docs/rc_pc_chrstuni_doc_19820306_jews-judaism_en.html**

[12] "Legalistic" is itself a fraught term, and part of a relatively modern polemic. It takes on a negative valence in Christian, and especially Protestant, tradition, where "Law" is often contrasted with "Gospel." See G. F. Moore, "Christian Writers on Judaism," in *Harvard Theological Review* 14 (1921), 197–254, esp. 237–40 on Emil Schürer, and 250–54.

[13] At **download.elca.org/ELCA%20Resource%20Repository/Guidelines_For_Lutheran_Jewish_Relations_1998.pdf**

[14] Esther Menn, "Law and Gospel," in Darrell Jodeck (ed), *Covenantal Conversations: Christians in Dialogue with Jews and Judaism* (Minneapolis: Fortress Press, 2008), 42–59, and see also the response by Krister Stendahl, 59–60.

[15] A discussion of the problem of "erasure" of Jews from the New Testament text is currently taking place in response to an article by Adele Reinhartz. See **marginalia.lareviewofbooks.org/jew-judean-forum/**.

HERMENEUTICAL REFLECTIONS AND TWO MORE WARNINGS

Our scriptural readings can be nuanced by retrieval of historical context: perhaps the invective did begin simply as an internal critique, an argument among closely related teachers of Torah. Of course, no matter how much a nuanced reading may seem to improve the overall picture, problems remain. It is difficult to include and explain the background each time a passage is read. The general picture is still one of opposition, with sometimes lethal impact. Lectionary readings alone do not point up fine distinctions; these depend upon preachers and teachers. So, a third warning, or at least a guideline: Do not teach Jesus as one who is in continual conflict with his people, but as a teacher of Torah whose message would be impossible without his upbringing in and concern for the tradition of the Torah and prophets of Israel.

Matthew's critique of "the Pharisees" may have originated in a "fraternal" argument between emerging Judaisms and Christianities. In its original context, it may have been no more dangerous than the Talmud's critique of certain Pharisees. Transformed into Scripture, however, the words are placed in the mouth of a Jewish teacher who has come to be seen in one community as God incarnate. In that context the condemnation of Pharisees as an entire group (and not just any group, but the group that came to be associated with the "normative" Judaism of later generations) takes on a very different resonance. Here too, some contemporary Christian scholars seek a more nuanced view, as in this passage by Donald Senior:

> The historical reality was such that not all the leaders were hypocritical or corrupt. In fact, other sources suggest that the Pharisees had many goals in common with Jesus. [...]
>
> All this said, the potential of these Matthean passages to be read and interpreted as an unqualified attack on Jews and Judaism remains, and Christian teachers bear the responsibility for preventing such a toxic reading of the gospel.[16]

Senior seeks both historical context and responsible teaching.

As a written text, especially one canonized as Scripture, what may have originated as a "family quarrel" becomes weighted with the claim of truth, of God's truth. Hans Georg Gadamer, for one, has argued that "It is not altogether easy to realize that what is written down can be untrue. The written word has the tangible quality of something that can be demonstrated and is like a proof."[17] How can such a text be "re-contextualized"

---

[16] Donald Senior, *The Gospel of Matthew* (Nashville: Abingdon Press, 1997), 159–60.
[17] Hans-Georg Gadamer, *Truth and Method* (New York: Crossroad, 1984), 241.

to drain some of the venom that it has carried? Gadamer's statement comes in the context of his insistence that "the critique of the enlightenment is directed primarily against the religious tradition of christianity, i.e., the bible."[18] Historical recontextualization has been one hermeneutical strategy that has sometimes helped, in Walter Benjamin's well-known phrase, "to brush history against the grain."[19] We must pay attention not only to what is revealed in our texts, but also to what has been suppressed and covered up. Which voices have been allowed to speak, and which voices have been silenced?

An awareness of the role of communities in the production and use of texts is also crucial. Especially in the case of a sacred text, attention must be paid to the fact that various communities have participated in the interpretive enterprise over many generations. Indeed, James A. Sanders has described the ways in which communities have not only produced readings of texts, but have produced the texts themselves.[20] That is, our texts are products of communal readings and rereadings through many generations and circumstances. The reading activities of these communities comprise part of the process through which the text gathers communities around it, and gains importance. Thus, a text like the Bible is studied repeatedly by communities that gather around it in ways that sustain those communities, activate them in certain concrete ways, and empower them to produce further readings and understandings. The communal aspect of interpretation cannot be left aside.

Early Jews and Christians were surely watching each other, often locked in polemical embrace, and often crossing still-to-be-drawn boundaries. To return briefly to the "plague of Pharisees" (Hebrew: *makkot perushim*) of the Talmud. It seems probable that the rabbis have an eye on Christian polemics as this category gets elaborated in the Talmud. There are at least some parallels to be noted. The Talmud names seven kinds of Pharisees. Matthew's Jesus delivers seven "woes" to "you Pharisees."[21] If the "plagues of Pharisees" are understood as an example of rabbinic self-critique, they would be one of many examples of internal criticism (even including ridi-

---

[18] Ibid., 241. The translator renders all the nouns with lower-case.

[19] Walter Benjamin, "Theses on the Philosophy of History," in *Illuminations*, transl. Harry Zohn (New York: Schocken, 1969), 257.

[20] See, for example, James A. Sanders, *Canon and Community: A Guide to Canonical Criticism* (Philadelphia: Fortress Press, 1984), esp. chap. 2.

[21] The number is more than an interesting coincidence, even if it can be easily explained as a scriptural convention. Some scriptural background may be noted in Proverbs 24: "Seven times the righteous man falls and gets up, While the wicked are tripped by one misfortune" (Prov 24:16 NJV). The Jerusalem Talmud (*Sanhedrin* XI.30a) also makes reference to seven *middot*, or qualities, of the righteous.

cule!), which is a constant element within Jewish tradition. Viewed in this way, the passage lends support to the arguments of those who suggest that Matthew, Luke, or other New Testament writers may understand themselves to be still within a more or less Jewish context. Later, as these texts came to be read in separated communities, Pharisees became for Christians a trope for the Jewish establishment of Jesus' time and, hence, for "late" and dying Judaism. For Jews, however, the Pharisees of *Sotah* 22b are not representatives of Judaism per se, but of certain kinds of pious distortions that can be found in Judaism or, for that matter, in any religious tradition. Which leads to a fourth warning: There is indeed such a thing as religious hypocrisy; we must all be on guard against it.

MEANT, MEANS AND IDEOLOGICAL READING: ONE MORE WARNING

The great Lutheran scholar Krister Stendahl has written of the dichotomy between what a text "meant" in its original setting, i.e., what did the author intend, and what it "means," i.e., how it is now generally understood.[22] For Stendahl, recovering what a text meant can be a useful corrective to the ways in which it has been read subsequently. Thus a kind of hermeneutical dialectic set in motion.[23]

My own approach builds on Stendahl's formulation to ask, "What has it meant/What might it mean?"[24] This would be a way of taking seriously not only the question of what a text meant to its original author(s) and original hearers, insofar as that can be determined with any certainty, but also the history of its interpretation. The question, What might it mean? points to a living community of readers who continue to grapple

---

[22] This formulation of meant/means is expounded in Stendahl's article on "Biblical Theology, Contemporary," in George Arthur Buttrick, John Knox, Herbert Gordon May, Samuel Terrien, Emory Stevens Bucke (eds), *The Interpreter's Dictionary of the Bible* (Nashville: Abingdon Press, 1962), vol. I, 418–32.

[23] See Krister Stendahl, "Paul and the Introspective Conscience of the West," in *Paul among Jews and Gentiles* (Philadelphia: Fortress Press, 1976), 78–96. In it Stendahl employs a "Lutheran" approach to Scripture against Luther's own reading of Paul, who is the most famous Pharisee of all.

[24] See Stendahl's own summary of his position, which informs my own, in ibid., 125: "The responsibility of interpretation is a grave one. [...] I believe that the *first* and indispensable step in any such enterprise is to insist on a clear distinction between what a text meant according to its original intention, and what it came to mean and/or might mean at any later point in history or the future. [...] Such a program requires us never to ask 'What does it mean?' without adding '[...] to whom?'"

with the text and seek new ways to connect it to their own lives. This way of extending Stendahl's formulation, first of all, allows for greater range of interpretation. A text may never have meant only one thing: even the original author may have intended multiple levels of meaning. Further, the earliest audiences of a text may well have understood it differently from the author and from each other. Second, I take seriously what Stendahl's formulation implies, namely, that there is a history of interpretation that is attached to the text, and that there is an ethical responsibility to choose carefully among competing understandings.

A history of interpretation includes many possible readings of the text, explications which have had meaning for various communities. A community gathered around and by a sacred text understands itself to maintain a connection to the text's "original" meaning. But once a text leaves the author's hand, the author relinquishes the right to exclusive interpretation. The author does not control the reception of her text, nor what uses are made of it by future generations, though the author may well bear some responsibility. Thirdly, "what a text could mean" refers to two other important aspects of interpretation. Within the category of "could mean" I would place, first, the notion of "plenitude" in interpretation, i.e., that a text "means" all that it can mean.[25] And second, the text carries potential meanings—both benign and dangerous—that extend not only to the present but into the future as well.

Hence, a fifth warning. It is necessary always to be aware of the ideological layers of our own readings. Ideology is at work in our texts from the beginning. While it is not possible to change our texts, it is crucial that we read and teach them responsibly. In order to "own" them, we must "own up to" them. And this applies not only to ancient documents, but to contemporary readings as well. We make choices in our reading, both in terms of which texts and verses we consider most important, as well as how we interpret and apply them. According to Louis Althusser, "As there is no such thing as an innocent reading, we must say what reading we are guilty of."[26]

I gratefully acknowledge the comments of Mark Powell who, following our discussion, quickly offered two more "warnings" about the reading of

---

[25] Paul Ricoeur adopts this principle from Monroe Beardsley: "all the connotations that can fit are to be attached; the poem means all it can mean." Paul Ricoeur, "Metaphor and the Main Problem of Hermeneutics," transl. David Pellauer, in Mario J. Valdés (ed.), *A Ricoeur Reader: Reflection and Imagination* (Toronto: University of Toronto Press, 1991), 313. There he cites Monroe C. Beardsley, *Aesthetics: Problems in the Philosophy of Criticism* (New York, Harcourt, Brace and World, 1958).

[26] Louis Althusser, cited in "The Bible and Culture Collective," in *The Postmodern Bible* (New Haven: Yale University Press, 1995), 5.

Scripture, which I am happy to add here in abbreviated form as warnings six and seven:

> Do not compromise Christian theology by assigning responsibility for Jesus' death to anyone other than sinners in need of redemption [...]. [I]f anyone is to be held responsible for the death of Jesus, according to Christian teaching, it is Christians who confess that their sins made the cross necessary.

> Do not historicize literary motifs or seek historical explanations for literary devices... [E]ven if the events reported in the Gospels are historical, their order of presentation has been arranged by each evangelist in a way that will serve literary purposes (not in a way that faithfully recalls actual historical sequence). [. . .] Matthew's Gospel may be understood as one of the most profound narrative meditations on the nature of evil and hypocrisy ever written – it is, to my mind, unfortunate that he chose a group of people who had actually existed in history as "the fall guys" for scoring his points, but there was little sensitivity to such matters at the time. [...] The overall point is that the Gospels (all four of them) use literary motifs to accomplish rhetorical ends—and historicizing literary devices is like trying to use a mirror as a window.[27]

I hope that all these warnings will be heeded by all of us in our preaching and teaching. And I am sure there are other warnings as well, that can and will be brought to light through honest dialogue. To be empowered by our respective communities as teachers of Scripture is a privilege and a profound responsibility. Scripture should never be wielded as a weapon with which to beat those who are not like us—gay or straight, believers or non-believers, dissenters or conformists. I am convinced that more light is brought forth from our texts when we read them in dialogue with others. When Scripture offers words of comfort, may we be channels that convey comfort to our communities. When Scripture offers rebuke, may we hear it first as directed to ourselves, and then convey it in ways that can be heard.

---

[27] Mark Alan Powell, email sent to this author on September 5, 2014.

Preaching Reconciliation: From "Law and Gospel" to "Justice and Mercy" in Matthew

Esther Menn

The context out of which I write is the twentieth anniversary year of the 1994 *Declaration of the Evangelical Lutheran Church in America (ELCA) to the Jewish Community*. Through this document the ELCA, in concert with the Lutheran World Federation (LWF), repented and repudiated Martin Luther's anti-Judaic writings, as well as the legacy of the Reformer's writings in the anti-Semitic ideology that led up to and made possible the Shoah. The ELCA *Declaration*, along with *Nostra Aetate* from Vatican II, which is now about to mark its fiftieth anniversary, are two milestone documents from the second part of the twentieth century. They signal a fundamental shift in Jewish–Christian relations after the Holocaust.

Jewish colleagues have expressed their appreciation for the directness of the ELCA *Declaration*, as well as for the fact that it is addressed to the Jewish community, as appropriate for a first step in a process of reconciliation, in which the party who has inflicted harm speaks the truth. Franklin E. Sherman, a lead author of the ELCA *Declaration*, was formerly a professor at the Lutheran School of Theology at Chicago (LSTC). The Institute for Jewish Christian Understanding at Muhlenberg College that he directed after leaving LSTC is celebrating its twenty-fifth anniversary this year. The ELCA *Declaration* is a short address, worthy of reading in its entirety:

> In the long history of Christianity there exists no more tragic development than the treatment accorded the Jewish people on the part of Christian believers. Very few Christian communities of faith were able to escape the contagion of anti-Judaism

and its modern successor, anti-Semitism. Lutherans belonging to the Lutheran World Federation and the Evangelical Lutheran Church in America feel a special burden in this regard because of certain elements in the legacy of the reformer Martin Luther and the catastrophes, including the Holocaust of the twentieth century, suffered by Jews in places where the Lutheran churches were strongly represented.

The Lutheran communion of faith is linked by name and heritage to the memory of Martin Luther, teacher and reformer. Honoring his name in our own, we recall his bold stand for truth, his earthy and sublime words of wisdom, and above all his witness to God's saving Word. Luther proclaimed a gospel for people as we really are, bidding us to trust a grace sufficient to reach our deepest shames and address the most tragic truths.

In the spirit of that truth-telling, we who bear his name and heritage must with pain acknowledge also Luther's anti-Judaic diatribes and the violent recommendations of his later writings against the Jews. As did many of Luther's own companions in the sixteenth century, we reject this violent invective, and yet more do we express our deep and abiding sorrow over its tragic effects on subsequent generations. In concert with the Lutheran World Federation, we particularly deplore the appropriation of Luther's words by modern anti-Semites for the teaching of hatred toward Judaism or toward the Jewish people in our day.

Grieving the complicity of our own tradition within this history of hatred, moreover, we express our urgent desire to live out our faith in Jesus Christ with love and respect for the Jewish people. We recognize in anti-Semitism a contradiction and an affront to the Gospel, a violation of our hope and calling, and we pledge this church to oppose the deadly working of such bigotry, both within our own circles and in the society around us. Finally, we pray for the continued blessing of the Blessed One upon the increasing cooperation and understanding between Lutheran Christians and the Jewish community.[1]

Within the Third International LWF Consultation on Hermeneutics focusing on the Gospel of Matthew, my reflections build appreciatively on the papers by the Jewish participants, Rabbi Dr Larry Edwards and Dr Sarah Tanzer. I have added the voice of a Lutheran to underline the urgency of refocusing our vision of New Testament texts. It is also imperative that we not confine this hermeneutical effort within the boundaries of Jewish–Christian dialogue. Rather, new articulations of our confessional faith should be seen as a public statement of Christian responsibility for the history of our biblical interpretations.

I speak not as a preacher, since I myself am not ordained and am still a practicing novice in that area, or as a scholar of Matthew, although Matthew is my favorite gospel. And I do not speak as a scholar of the New Testament, since my field is Hebrew Scriptures, also known as the Old

---

[1] The ELCA *Declaration* can be found at **www.elca.org/en/Faith/Ecumenical-and-Inter-Religious-Relations/Inter-Religious-Relations/Online-Resources**.

Testament, or the Church's First Bible. My modest contribution is as a lay member of the ELCA who has heard a lot of sermons, and who is involved in Jewish-Christian relations as a member of the Consultative Panel on Lutheran Jewish Relations and of the ecumenical Christian Scholars Group on Jewish Christian Relations. I trust that a non-specialist may offer a simple and perhaps obvious critique worth taking to heart.

My worry is that there is still subtle and not so subtle anti-Judaism in much Christian preaching. Even more fundamentally, my worry is that the Lutheran "law and gospel" dialectic itself is implicitly anti-Jewish, in that it associates the "law," a term that in the Christian West has become a shorthand for Judaism, with judgment, death, sin and everything else negative in human experience.

BEYOND DEICIDE

Thankfully, we are at a point in history when words from the passion narratives, such as those in Matthew 27:25, when the crowd as a whole shouts "His blood be on us and our children," no longer incense Christian congregations leaving Good Friday services to the point of physically harming and even killing Jews, as was the case in medieval Europe. Texts such as this one historically have had powerful effects on Christians, and the charge of deicide, that the Jews as a collective killed not only Jesus, but God, that they were "Christ killers," was for two thousand years commonly accepted by the church. *Nostra Aetate* and other documents including the ELCA *Guidelines for Lutheran Jewish Relations* adopted in 1998 refute the deicide charge. The thirteenth point in the *ELCA Guidelines* urges:

> 13. Lutheran pastors should make it clear in their preaching and teaching that though the New Testament reflects early conflicts, it must not be used for justification for hostility toward present day Jews. Blame for the death of Jesus should not be attributed to Judaism or the Jewish people and stereotypes of Judaism as a legalistic religion should be avoided [...].[2]

Note that this admonition is from 1998, showing how recently it was felt that this correction still needed to be asserted!

There is more general awareness today that crucifixion was a Roman form of execution, and that Pontius Pilate was recalled to Rome because of

---

[2] The ELCA *Guidelines for Lutheran Jewish Relations* can be found at **www.elca. org/en/Faith/Ecumenical-and-Inter-Religious-Relations/Inter-Religious-Relations/Online-Resources**.

his brutality, including crucifying hundreds of Jews as a form of political repression and terror. Nevertheless, such popular depictions as Mel Gibson's *The Passion* revive images of Jewish responsibility for Jesus' death in a way that shows how recent and how fragile the scholarly reconsideration of the passion narratives is. The current resurgence of anti-Semitism and attacks on Jews in Europe and the Middle East unfortunately make these discussions far more than theoretical.

Difficult texts such as Matthew 27:25 bear a heavy interpretive history. They need to be treated with what Dorothee Soelle calls a "hermeneutics of consequences," attentive to the effect produced by Scripture and its influence over time.[3] One way for Christians to proceed with consciousness of the consequences of scriptural interpretation is to work together with Jewish colleagues and friends, to hear their responses to Christian texts and interpretations.

Christian, feminist, post-Holocaust

Here in the United States, with our large Jewish population, I treasure what I have learned and continue to learn from studying with Jewish professors, fellow students and Bible colleagues over the years. This scholarly inter-religious dialogue, as well as interactions with other Christians involved in Jewish–Christian relations, has strengthened my commitment to practicing a Christian, feminist, post-Holocaust hermeneutics.

A definition of this approach was developed by Katharina von Kellenbach, who is a member of the ELCA, as am I. It is taped to the wall above my desk. I find myself consulting it frequently. It keeps me considering whether or not I am falling back into old, unconscious interpretive grooves that have fostered the anti-Judaic heritage of the West. According to von Kellenbach:

> A Christian feminist post-Holocaust hermeneutic is committed to respecting the validity, vitality, and autonomy of Jewish interpretations of the Hebrew Bible, and renounces supersessionist readings of biblical Israel that denigrate and vilify its religion, politics, culture, and law as precursor, source or example of contemporary evils.[4]

---

[3] Dorothee Soelle, cited in Ulrich Luz, *Matthew 1-7:* Hermeneia (Minneapolis: Fortress Press, 2007), 91.

[4] Katharina von Kellenbach, "Cultivating a Hermeneutic of Respect for Judaism: Feminist Interpretation of the Hebrew Bible after the Holocaust," in Susanne Scholz (ed.), *A Retrospective of Feminist Hebrew Bible Exegesis: Contexts & Ideologies*, vol. 2 (Sheffield: Sheffield Phoenix Press, 2014) 253-70.

Von Kellenbach refers to interpretations of the Hebrew Bible, and since that is my own field, this definition is usually sufficient. For the current discussion of Matthew, however, the definition can be extended to a hermeneutic that "renounces supersessionist readings of the Jewish communities depicted in the New Testament that denigrate and vilify their religion, politics, culture, and law as precursor, source, or example of contemporary evils."

This is a helpful standard by which to measure one's scholarship, biblical interpretation, preaching and attitudes. The question is, as we move forward to healthier relationships with the Jewish community in so many areas, especially here in the United States, Where are we in our biblical interpretation, especially as it contributes to Lutheran preaching? We have moved away from explicit anti-Judaic biases, comparisons and statements, but have we replaced largely unconscious patterns that undergird former patterns of relating? Have we disrupted certain deep semantic triggers that have been part of Christian attitudes towards Judaism for centuries, even millennia? Have we addressed the unconscious part of the "iceberg" submerged below the surface of the ocean? In particular, the use of the term "law" in "law and gospel" seems to be part of the deeper iceberg. It is cautionary that in von Kellenbach's definition "law" appears prominently as one of the triggers for anti-Jewish denigration.

MATTHEW AS A "JEWISH GOSPEL"

Matthew is an especially appropriate case study, since this gospel has been considered the most "Jewish" of the gospels. Of course, these days we are becoming more and more aware that the whole New Testament is a collection of first-century Jewish literature, as attested by the recent project, *The Jewish Annotated New Testament*, involving prominent Jewish New Testament scholars such as Amy Jill Levine.[5] How could we have missed the Jewish origins of New Testament texts, when even Paul identifies himself as a "Pharisee"! The separation of the church and the synagogue was much later, and perhaps less complete, than has been traditionally thought.[6]

But within the context of the New Testament, tradition and scholarship of the past two centuries have identified Matthew as distinctively Jewish. It is not only the citation of so much Jewish Scripture, the recapitulation of Jewish history in Jesus' life, the genealogies connecting Jesus to Israelite

---

[5] Amy-Jill Levine and Marc Z. Brettler (eds), *The Jewish Annotated New Testament* (Oxford University Press, 2011).
[6] Adam H. Becker and Annette Y. Reed (eds), *The Ways That Never Parted: Jews and Christians in Late Antiquity and the Early Middle Ages* (Tübingen: Mohr Siebeck, 2003).

history and Jewish practices and themes that give this gospel a Jewish character. The emphasis of the entire Gospel of Matthew is on the practices and patterns of life, shaped by Torah, the life-giving revelation of how to live in relationship with God and the other human members of the covenant community, in anticipation of God's kingdom of justice. Jesus recognizes the Pharisees as having teaching authority to interpret Moses for the community, they "sit on Moses' seat" (Mt 23:2), even if he critiques their behavior as not conforming to their own high standards.[7] A thoroughly Jewish Jesus is portrayed as a Mosaic teacher of Torah; he points to a way of extreme Torah obedience, which urges a perfection of righteousness that undergirds just social relations and exceeds even that of the scribes and Pharisees (Mt 5:20).

How we Christians view Matthew is related to how we Christians view Judaism, or at least how we view our origins and ongoing grounding within a Jewish matrix. In some quarters, Matthew has been marginalized or despised because of its reputation as the "most Jewish" of gospels. For example, some have stereotyped as "Jewish" its reference to violent punishments and gnashing of teeth, and its emphasis on strict attention to the performance of the law. Such strictness extends even to interior motivations, with the ideal of being "perfect" as our Father in heaven is perfect through the fulfillment of every jot and tittle of the law and prophets.

If Matthew is the "Jewish gospel," if Matthew's Jesus is the Jewish teacher and new Moses, then Matthew becomes an icon, a concrete artifact in the form of a text. It reflects Judaism's relationship to Christianity, including the Jewish origins of the early Jewish movement and Christianity, the ongoing side-by-side relationship of a Jewish minority within the Christian West, and the recovery and reconciliation of Jews and Christians. Matthew attests to the Jewish roots and the deep and enduring connection that Christianity has with Judaism, without which Christianity becomes demonic by denying its identity as a mixed multitude worshiping Israel's God.

Christian stereotyping of Judaism as "law"

Matthew's emphasis on the ethical dimensions of communal life and how to live out the divine gift of "Torah," or "law," often proves to be a stumbling block for Christians. Within the long, intertwined history of Jews and Christians in the West, the inferiority of Judaism is often expressed

---

[7] Jon D. Levenson, in a personal conversation, suggested that Jesus' positive valuation of the Pharisees as credible interpreters of Moses is a more substantial biblical basis for a reclamation of a positive value of Judaism by Christians than Romans 9–11, a passage more commonly cited, as in *Nostra Aetate*.

as a contrast between Jewish "law" and salvation by "works" in contrast to the Christian "gospel" and salvation by "faith" in Christ.

"Their covenant is broken in pieces," boasts the *Epistle of Barnabus* (4.8), as the Mosaic tablets of law are shattered and the covenant of Jesus is sealed in the hearts of the faithful. The outdated, inferior law associated with Judaism becomes an integral part of a persistent polemic against the Jews as a minority culture, which has existed for centuries in the Christian West. University of Chicago professor David Nirenberg, in his recent book, *Anti-Judaism: The Western Tradition*, describes the problem in chilling detail chapter after chapter. He shows how patterns of thinking and semantic associations—including that of Judaism with "law," "legalism," "dead works" and the like—have marginalized and demonized the Jews as the eternal other, against whom the Christian majority culture of the West has defined itself.[8]

The Lutheran law and gospel dialectic becomes problematic because its first term intersects with "law" as a trigger for a deep-seated negative Jewish stereotype. It is clear that Lutheran thinking in terms of law and gospel does not have the denigration of Judaism as its primary intention. In this publication exploring Lutheran hermeneutics, the preaching and exegetical framework of a traditional Lutheran "law and gospel" dialectic as internal to Christianity has been explored. Both Mark Allen Powell and Timothy Wengert have illuminated "law and gospel" by showing that it refers to the effect on the Christian hearer of God's Word, as the law, which condemns and kills and the gospel which forgives and brings life. Whether intentional or not, however, the term "law" picks up traditional anti-Jewish rhetoric endemic to Western civilization. The words that we use in our theology are not inconsequential. If they have a resonance like the word "law" has had in the long history of hatred and marginalization of Jews in the West, then there is a problem that needs to be addressed decisively. Today in the pulpit anti-Judaism may be largely unconscious, based on ancient patterns with enduring power that are never directly addressed.

MATTHEW AS AN OPENING FOR RECONCILIATION

Matthew is one of the iconic points of connection between Christianity and Judaism, without which Christianity is unrecognizable.[9] The Gospel

---

[8] David Nirenberg, *Anti-Judaism: The Western Tradition* (New York: W.W. Norton, 2013). See also Jules Isaac, *The Teaching of Contempt: The Christian Roots of Anti-Semitism* (New York: Rinehart and Winston, 1964).

[9] Christianity must be understood in relation to Judaism. John C. Merkle affirms that "The time has come for Christians to acknowledge the fact that Christianity

of Matthew brings our connections with Judaism to the fore and provides us with an opportunity to renew our minds, to begin anew and to preach reconciliation. Christians are not the new Israel that has replaced old Israel. Instead, we can confess something less linear and more layered. Taking a clue from Joshua Abraham Heschel, we in the church might consider ourselves "an extension of Judaism,"[10] or from Krister Stendahl, we might see ourselves as "a peculiar kind of Jews," who may or may not be recognized as such by the Jewish community.[11]

Reconciliation is a term we hear more and more in the news and in theology. The archetypal instance of political reconciliation is the Truth and Reconciliation Commission in South Africa, set up by Nelson Mandela and headed by Archbishop Desmond Tutu. Reconciliation in that context and in others involves bringing the two parties together after one party has inflicted injury on another. Truth and reconciliation must include acknowledgment by the party that has meted out violence, the one who has abused power, whether it is a matter of human rights, bodily injury or death, reputation, or any other harm. The perpetrator of wrong must admit wrong and be open and committed to moving toward fundamental change.

Since World War II Christians in the West have started to admit wrong and to amend their stance toward Jews and Judaism. Christian preaching can be part of this process of truth telling and self-examination, which begins the process toward reconciliation. If preaching is to bring about reconciliation, it will first of all have to stop lying, by bearing false witness about Judaism, vilifying it as a legalistic religion without spirit, as a dead letter rejected by God, to be replaced by Christianity. It will have to

---

is valid not because it supersedes or even surpasses Judaism, but on the contrary, to the extent that it extends covenantal life with Israel's God to the Gentile world. This is not to say that Judaism is closed to Gentiles. Anyone who desires to respond to God by way of Torah may convert to Judaism. The fact remains, however, that Christianity has made covenantal life accessible to more Gentiles than has Judaism. Moreover, it is our conviction as Christians that God wills a way of covenantal life for Gentiles that is distinct from Israel's way of living in covenant [...]. But we must also transform the church, purging it of its chronic anti-Judaism, and making it a more identifiable offspring of Jewish faith and a true ally of the Jewish people. In order to do this we must understand the Jewish way [...] ." John C. Merkle, in Fritz A. Rothchild (ed.), *Jewish Perspectives on Christianity: The Views of Leo Baeck, Franz Rosensweig, Martin Buber, Will Herberg, and Abraham J. Heschel* (Crossroad Publishing Company, 1990), 276.

[10] Abraham J. Heschel, *The Insecurity of Freedom* (New York: Schocken Books, 1972), 169–70.

[11] Krister Stendahl, "Judaism on Christianity: Christianity on Judaism," in Frank Talmage (ed.), *Disputation and Dialogue: Readings in the Jewish-Christian Encounter* (New York: KTAV Publishing House, 1975), 338.

acknowledge how biblical texts have been misused by Christians. It will have to tell the story of Christian repentance as part of the work toward a new relationship with Jews and Judaism.

As a next step, Christian preaching would need to go beyond past patterns and stereotypes to a new and compelling narrative that includes the historical and theological truth about the Jewish origins of Christianity and about our ongoing connection with Judaism. It would acknowledge how Judaism and Christianity have influenced each other and defined each other over the centuries, perhaps largely through polemics, but in other less combative ways as well.

Preaching in this way might be a challenge for Christians, especially Lutheran Christians. In general, preachers want to show Christianity as unique and superior, as something beyond what has gone before. Certain ways of reading our lectionary texts may fall into this kind of contrast. It is all too easy to pit Jesus against Judaism, or the early church against the Jews. A mature Christianity would be one in which Christians witness to their faith without denigrating their sister faith, Judaism.[12] Since the gospels are not always understood as depicting a fully Jewish Jesus in a fully Jewish context debating matters of Jewish Torah, or law, too often the whole concept of "law" continues to take on a negative association linked to the Jews.

Lutheran preaching in terms of "law and gospel" also has a special challenge because the term law in its condemning second usage is clearly not Torah. Jewish Torah is a divine gift that brings life, joy and guidance for a relationship that God desires, both between God and humans, and within the human community itself. This apparent denigration of law as death, condemnation, human failure, and so on is not only incomprehensible to Jews, but it is also dangerous for Lutherans. As noted previously, the usage of this term "law" hooks us into entrenched patterns of denigrating Jews.[13]

PREACHING "JUSTICE AND MERCY"

Within the context of Matthew, the early Jewish followers of Jesus are grappling with the gift of Torah, as a way of life within the covenant com-

---

[12] Norman A. Beck, *Mature Christianity in the 21st Century: The Recognition and Repudiation of the Anti-Jewish Polemic in the New Testament*, rev. ed. (New York: Crossroad, 1994). See also Roland J. Allen and Clark M. Williamson, *Preaching the Gospels without Blaming the Jews* (Louisville: Westminster John Knox Press, 2004).

[13] Esther Menn, in conversation with Krister Stendahl, "Law and Gospel," in Darrell Jodock (ed.), *Covenantal Conversations: Christians in Dialogue with Jews and Judaism* (Minneapolis: Fortress Press, 2004).

munity, in light of Jesus the Messiah and the in-breaking of the kingdom of heaven. Within this Jewish milieu of the Gospel of Matthew itself, two Greek words deeply rooted in the Jewish tradition, are especially useful for Lutherans who want to retain a dialectic, one that spans the whole scope of human experience and epitomizes how God acts in our lives and how we are affected by God's transforming Word through Christ.

The first word, one predominant in Matthew, is *dikaiosynē* (δικαιοσύνη). This word is often translated as "righteousness," but this translation is too individualistic and too pious to be accurate and helpful. A better translation that keeps in mind the whole community and the values of the kingdom of heaven is "justice," stemming from the Hebrew word *mishpat* (טפשמ). Justice can mean good news for those wronged, neglected and powerless within the context of oppressive misuse of power, with a restorative shift in power and resources. Justice can also mean judgment or condemnation for those who fail to measure up to God's call to life in community, so it has resonance with the second use of the law in "law and gospel." Almost all of Matthew is about how to live in community, presenting an ethics of God's kingdom, of how the followers of Jesus show love to God and neighbor.[14] "Justice" is a multivalent word referring to the radical reorientation of a transformed community life together in God's kingdom, with Jesus as Lord and Messiah.

The second term from Matthew that I would identify is "mercy" (*eleos*/ ἔλεος), which Jesus lifted up twice in quotations of Hosea 6:6, "I desire mercy and not sacrifice" (Mt 9:13 and 12:7). This term in Greek means mercy or compassion, but it is actually an even stronger word in that it is a translation of the Hebrew word *hesed* (דסח), which is God's steadfast covenant loyalty and love for Israel. The passion and ardor of God for Israel in Hosea contributes to the power of this word in the dialectic pair.

These terms, drawn from the Gospel of Matthew and even farther back from Israel's scriptural tradition, provide a parallel "Lutheran dialectic" drawn from our most "Jewish" gospel, for correcting, reorienting and reconciling our preaching framework. Referring to God's "justice and mercy" in our sermons might be one way toward "preaching reconciliation" for Lutherans.[15]

---

[14] I thank Ray Pickett for a clarifying conversation on this translation of the Greek word δικαιοσύνη as "justice" rather than "righteousness."

[15] Another fascinating example of Jesus' articulation of a hermeneutical principle appears in Mt 23:23, where he identifies the weighty matters of the "law" (νόμος) as "justice (κρίσις), mercy (ἔλεος), and faith (πίστις)."

QUESTIONS FOR FURTHER REFLECTION:

• How important is the law and gospel dialectic for Lutheran preaching? Is this framework conscious or unconscious in those who actually prepare sermons? What other frameworks are operative?

• Krister Stendahl once suggested preaching the "beloved community" from John as an alternative framework. What additional frameworks for Lutheran preaching do other books of the Bible present?

• Luther was a contextual pastoral theologian, biblical interpreter and preacher, and "law and gospel" spoke to the existential situation of his generation. What are the issues of our day that might evoke new engagement with biblical texts and with preaching in new and meaningful frameworks?

List of Contributors

Becker, Eve-Marie, Dr, Professor of New Testament Exegesis, Section for Biblical Studies, Aarhus University, Denmark

Dayam, Joseph Prabhakar, Rev. Dr, serves as pastor in the Andhra Evangelical Lutheran Church, India. He is the honorary convener of the Collective of Dalit Ecumenical Christian Scholars (CODECS)

Edwards, Laurence L., Rabbi Dr, teaches at DePaul University, University of Illinois, Chicago, Hebrew Seminary (Skokie, IL), USA

Grosshans, Hans-Peter, Dr, Professor of Systematic and Ecumenical Theology, Faculty of Protestant Theology, University of Muenster, Germany

Koester, Craig, Dr, is Asher O. and Carrie Nasby Professor of New Testament and Vice President for Academic Affairs and Academic Dean at Luther Seminary, Saint Paul, Minnesota, USA

Junge, Martin, Rev. Dr, General Secretary, The Lutheran World Federation, Geneva, Switzerland

Melanchthon, Monica Jyotsna, Dr, Associate Professor of Old Testament, Pilgrim Theological College, University of Divinity, Melbourne, Australia

Menn, Esther, Dr, Dean and Vice President for Academic Affairs, Ralph W. and Marilyn R. Klein Professor of Old Testament/Hebrew Bible, Lutheran School of Theology at Chicago, USA

Mtata, Kenneth, Rev. Dr, Secretary for Lutheran Theology, Practice and Formation, The Lutheran World Federation, Geneva, Switzerland

Oberdorfer, Bernd, Dr, Professor of Sytematic Theology, Augsburg University, Germany

Powell, Mark Allan, Rev. Dr, Professor of New Testament, Trinity Lutheran Seminary, Columbus, Ohio, USA

Wanke, Roger Marcel, Dr, Professor of Old Testament and Hebrew, Academic Dean, Faculdade Luterana de Teologia, São Bento do Sul, Brazil

Wengert, Timothy J., Dr, Emeritus Professor of Reformation History, The Lutheran Theological Seminary at Philadelphia, USA

Westhelle, Vítor, Dr, Professor of Systematic Theology, Lutheran School of Theology at Chicago, USA

Wischmeyer, Oda, Dr Dr h.c, Ermeritus Professor of New Testament Studies, Department of Theology, Friedrich-Alexander Universität Erlangen-Nürnberg, Germany

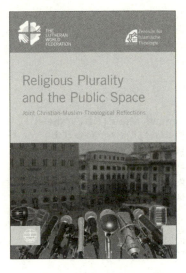

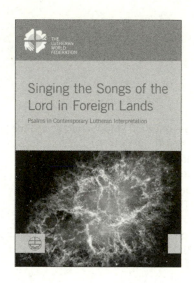